D1360759

jean-claude klotchkoff

tunisia
today

translation: melissa thackway

**82 pages of colour photos
by alain keler
unless specified otherwise
10 maps and plans**

LES EDITIONS DU
JAGUAR

summary

panorama

Cover and preceding pages:
*Hammamet, one of Tunisia's
most beautiful seaside
resorts, has grown
around the old fort
and charming medina.*

Overleaf:
*The north of Tunisia,
dubbed "Green Tunisia",
is characterised
by vast pasture lands
and cereal crops.*

site by site

the journey

panorama

tunisia today

■ Beautiful and welcoming Tunisia: this is the description that immediately springs to mind when visiting the country for the first time. It is worth travelling around the whole of Tunisia to appreciate its splendor as it unveils its incredible variety of sites and wonderful landscapes before the enchanted visitor's eyes.

Who could resist the charms of Gammarth, La Marsa or Sidi Bou Saïd's warm nights when the jasmine and blossoming mimosas perfume the air, and the magical panoramic view of Tunis Bay twinkles far away in the background?

Who could remain indifferent to Djérid's wild beauty? Under the torrid summer sun, the salt lakes sparkle like crystals and the reflections of the vast green palm groves form undulating, misty mirages as if ghosts of bygone caravans were passing one by one, Arabian cavaliers caracoling past in clouds of dust, or as if twinkling sugar-candy towns were piled high in the sky.

It is a sheer pleasure to listen, gathered like children around the village storyteller, to the legends of the innumerable peoples who have built Tunisia.

A stunning patrimony of countless vestiges

The remarkable intermingling of civilisations has left its mark everywhere! Since the beginning of time, the Berbers from the mountain regions and their indomitable chiefs – Masinissa, Jugurtha, Tacfarinas, Al Kahena –, Phoenician navigators and their beautiful queen Dido, Hamilcar and Hannibal's proud Carthaginians, educated Jews exiled from Babylon, Roman conquerors and empire-builders, have intermingled or succeeded one another, sometimes in battle. This astonishing historic procession continues with the refined and decadent Byzantines, the Genseric Vandal hoards, the dashing Arabian cavaliers who came to spread Islam, Saint Louis's crusaders, Charles Quint's Spanish hidalgos, and the terrible Turkish janissaries. In modern times came the French colonialists at the time of the Protectorate, and Rommel's armoured forces. Since independence, the young Tunisians of the "baby boom" generation, so impatient to build their new nation, are proud of their remarkable heritage.

To the great delight of the foreign visitor, it is possible to share this incredible patrimony by visiting the innumerable Roman or Carthaginian remains and the beautiful examples of Arabic architecture (mosques, palaces, monasteries, fortified towns, mausoleums, hammams, etc.).

Wonderful! From Gafsa to Djerba, from Tunis to Tabarka, tourists will hear the same thing said everywhere: "Feel free to do whatever you like, make yourself at home!" This spontaneous friendliness, this genuine warm welcome is astonishing in a country where the bulldozer of tourism has been been rolling for several decades.

Indeed, every year, this little Maghrebi country caters for over four million visitors. Tunisia has become the forerunner of African tourism, a long way ahead of Morocco, Egypt, Kenya or South Africa.

Nowhere else on the Mediterranean basin has tourism taken off so successfully without resulting in the unfortunate "concrete-frenzy" along the coasts and beaches which, elsewhere, has resulted in the anarchic construction of ugly buildings and cheap hotels. In Tunisia, the public authorities have almost systematically called upon talented architects. Inspired by the great traditions of Islamic architecture, they have built hotels that could easily be mistaken for palaces, especially in Djerba and Hammamet. Moreover, foreign visitors will be amazed not to be hassled by the usual cohort of beggars, pickpockets, drug dealers and prostitutes.

It can be concluded from this that tourism has not really had negative side-effects in Tunisia. Another surprise is that Tunisia, flanked by its two turbulent neighbours, Algeria and Libya, leads a peaceful existence. There are never any terrorist attacks, and all religions are accepted (Islam is predominant, but is not fundamentalist). Tunisia thus offers even the most nervous tourist the prospect of a charming, tranquil oasis. All over the country the incomparable perfume of democracy lingers as enticingly as the perfume of the tiny bouquets of jasmine the Tunisians sport every evening.

the land and landscapes

■ Along with Morocco and Algeria, Tunisia is part of a vast region of North Africa bordering on the Mediterranean basin called the *Maghreb*. Arabian geographers from the Orient were the first to use the name "Maghreb", or more precisely, "Djazirat el Maghreb", which means "island of the setting sun". Indeed, they considered that the western Maghrebi countries looked like islands surrounded by the Mediterranean sea to the north and the sandy seas of the Sahara in the south.

The horn
of North Africa

Tunisia lies in one of the most strategic positions. Situated on the easternmost point of the Maghreb, it controls the passage between the eastern and western Mediterranean basins along with Sicily opposite (less than 150 km away).

This explains why so many people have fiercely fought over the country for centuries, for thousands of years even. The Phoenicians, and later their descendants the Carthaginians, owe their prosperity to their occupation of this strategic position. The latter founded a Mediterranean empire that perturbed their rivals, the Romans. Having annihilated the Punic power, the Romans in turn settled the advanced bastion of Carthage, turning it into the "African Rome". Next came the Byzantines, the Vandals, the Arabs, the Spanish, and, more recently the French who had the intention of firmly settling in Tunisia, making Bizerte a look-out post equal to Gibraltar.

With a surface area of 164,150 km² (that is, a little over two thirds the size of Britain), Tunisia is a small country. When travelling throughout the country, however, it takes on a greater aspect due to the frequently grandiose nature of its landscapes.

A vast panoramic view of the Bay of Tunis can be discovered from the heights of Carthage or Sidi Bou Saïd. By crossing the rich Medjerda Valley and the Kairouan plains, one

FROM AFRICA
TO TUNISIA

■ *As early as the 2nd century B.C., the Romans called Tunisia – which had been a predominant country for thousands of years – Africa. They may have borrowed and deformed the term* faraqa *(colony) used by the Carthaginians at the time to describe any territory surrounding their metropolis. At this point of the Roman occupation (which began in 146 B.C.), Tunisia, or "Africa", was part of a greater ensemble called Barbary, or the land of the Berbers, which included the whole of North Africa (the Maghreb countries and Libya). The rest of modern day Africa south of the Sahara was known as Ethiopia.*

According to other historians, Africa may be derived from Afer *(*Ifri *in the plural), the name of a Berber tribe, or from the Arabic* afar *(the land), or from* Ifrikos *in Philistine (the son of the giant Goliath mentioned in the Bible).*

When the Arabs arrived in the 7th century, Tunisia became known as Ifriqyya. The name Tunis, then Tunisia began to appear on geographic maps from the Middle Ages and was applied to the whole area currently known as Tunisia, whilst Africa-Ifriqyya began to be applied to the whole of the African continent.

The innumerable marabouts,
zawiyyas, and little mosques
dotted all over Tunisia
like the one here in the Tozeur palm grove,
are a charming part of the landscape.

comes to the expansive, sun-burnt High Steppes where nomadic herders roam.

Further south, are the Djérid, Fedjaj and Gharsa salty chotts, which form vast sparkling patches, bordered by the green Tozeur and Nefta Corbeille palm groves.

Finally, in the southernmost region, come the sandy seas of the Grand Erg Oriental which announce the desolate expanses of the Sahara to come.

The Tunisian landscape is quite rugged on the whole, especially in the north where the last foothills of the huge Atlas mountain range across the whole of North Africa come to an end. Culminating at over 3,000 m in Morocco and Algeria, the Tunisian tail end of the range is not so high. Djebel Chambi near to Kasserine in the west of the country, which culminates at a mere 1,554 m, is the highest point in Tunisia. The whole of this northern region is dotted with small mountains which form ranges running parallel to the north coast. These long ridges trace a straightforward path running from the south-west to the north-east.

The first range in the very north of the country is made up of the Medjerda Mountains (1,150 m). Beginning in Algeria in the west, and terminating at Lake Bizerte in the east, it includes the Khroumirie Mountains (from 500 to 800 m), and the Mogods (500 m on average). Further to the south are the Téboursouk Mountains (600 to 900 m) and the High Tell (1,200 m).

The Tunisian Dorsale

The Tunisian Dorsale, which prolongs the Saharan Atlas mountains and the Algerian Aurès in the east, begins in western Tunisia with the Tébessa Mountains (Djebel Bireno, 1,419 m) and the little parallel Djebel Chambi range. Cutting across Tunisia from west to east, it terminates with Djebel Zaghouan (1,295 m) and the mountainous Cap Bon peninsula (Djebel Sidi Abderrahmane, 637 m).

Further southwards, between Kassérine and Gafsa, are the High Steppes, which is a region of high plateaus that rise up into the Orbata and el Asker Djebels overlooking the chott el Djérid. The High Steppes serve as a transition between the relatively high northern parts and southern Tunisia which becomes increasingly low-lying.

After the huge salty depressions formed by the chotts which cut Tunisia in two on a level with Gabès, the country tapers, cutting deeply into the Grand Erg, wedged between Algeria and Libya.

South of the el Gharsa, el Djérid and el Fedjaj chotts, the Dahar plateau and the Ksour mountains rise up to form a low altitude chain (500 to 700 m), running in a north-south direction. The range begins at Matmata and ends at the Libyan border (Dehiba). A great deal of oueds (rivers) have hollowed out canyons in these high plateaus before flowing away into the Grand Erg in the west.

Few plains

The Tunisian plains are hemmed in by the highland masses of this country's generally elevated land surface, and thus represent only a fraction of the land: along the Mediterranean coast in eastern Tunisia, around Kairouan in the Sahel region (the Sousse-Kairouan-Sfax triangle), and in the south (the Nefzaoua plain south of Djérid and the Jeffara region east of Tataouine).

Thanks to over 1,200 km of coastline along the two Mediterranean basins, Tunisia's maritime vocation has been guaranteed since ancient times. Numerous fishing and trading ports were created, the largest of which today are Bizerte, Tunis-La Goulette, Sousse, Sfax and Gabès. This coastline is not always hospitable. To the north, the Khroumirie mountains and the Mogods drop straight down into the sea providing very little shelter (except at Tabarka). There are several beaches here nonetheless (Tabarka, Sidi Mechrig and Cap Serrat), and a few small archipelagos like La Galite and Fratelli islands.

In the north-east, where the sea has invaded the low-lying regions of the coast, large lakes and gulfs have formed enclosed by long rocky peninsulas (Bizerte and Tunis). In these well-sheltered havens, where numerous beaches are tucked away (Raouad, Gammarth, Carthage, La

Goulette), the large Bizerte and Tunis-La Goulette ports have developed.

Cap Bon, which looks like an index finger pointing at Sicily, is the largest peninsula in Tunisia. Djebel Sidi Abderrahmane plunges down into the sea on the northern coast of this mountainous peninsula, where there are only several small beaches and few ports (apart from Sidi Daoud). The little islands of Zembra and Zembretta off the Cap Bon coast are a paradise for divers. The beaches along the south coast have enabled the Tunisians to develop large international beach resorts (Nabeul and Hammamet).

The east coast of Tunisia runs directly southwards from the Cap Bon peninsula to Djerba Island. Large gulfs with long sandy beaches (the Gulf of Hammamet and the Gulf of Gabès) alternate with more rugged coastlines where rocky headlands harbour little beaches tucked in small bays (the coast from Sousse to Sfax).

Small rivers

Like the other North African countries, Tunisia does not have a particularly expansive network of waterways. This is the result of a combination of low and irregular rainfall, the relief of the land which does not retain the water, and to the small number of springs.

The country's few permanent rivers flow in the north of the country where the climate is more humid than in the Saharan south. These rivers are small, the longest, the Medjerda, measuring only 416 km long. The source of the Medjerda rises up in the Algerian Tell Atlas in the west, then flows towards Tunis in the east via the Medjerda mountain range. After cutting through Jendouba, its waters are swollen by the Méllègue and Siliana rivers, and then it flows via Mejez el-Bab and Tébourba into the Gulf of Tunis, north of the capital.

The Zéroud river further to the south is more capricious due to the drier climate. Rising in the Tunisian Dorsale in the west, it crosses the Sahelian steppes and, when it is not dry, flows eastwards towards Kairouan and into the Sebkhet Kelbia.

In the south, the oueds only flow intermittently. The little rivers in the Ksour Mountains and the Dahar escarpment that flow away into the sands of the Sahara, usually dry up in the summer.

In Tunisia there are vast numbers of sebkhas and chotts, which are great depressions where layers of sand or gypsum are deposited as the water evaporates. The chott el Djérid, one such lake, forms a veritable interior salt sea measuring over 70 km wide and over 100 km long.

On the whole, Tunisia can be divided into two vast territories: the temperate, but very rugged North where the large farming lands are found; and the desert-like South, where the Sahara already begins, inhabited by nomadic herders and the small settled farmers in the oases.

The northern and central part of the country is "Green Tunisia". Thanks to its temperate Mediterranean climate resulting from its latitude and the proximity to the sea, northern Tunisia's mountains are covered in thick vegetation. The last vast forests of cork-oak and eucalyptus grow in the Khroumirie mountains near to Tabarka in the north-west of Tunisia. With several permanent rivers like the Medjerda, northern Tunisia has always been the most fertile and the richest part of the country in agricultural terms.

In Roman times, the Medjerda and Sahel's cereal crops and olive groves supplied the *Urbs* (the "City" of Rome), thereby serving as one of Rome's main "granaries".

Northern Tunisia is still a major agricultural region today. Along with the cereal crops, citrus fruit, fruit, and market garden produce are grown, and vineyards make reputed wine. The biggest coastal towns have also developed in the north and centre of the country, namely, Tunis, Sfax, Sousse and Bizerte.

To the south: "Dry Tunisia", or the Sahara

The large barrier of chotts marks the real beginning of Southern Tunisia. Unlike the north, the southern region does not benefit from the humid Mediterranean climate as it is situated on the same latitude as the northern part of the Grand Erg Oriental situated mainly in Algeria and covering the whole of southern Tunisia.

The landscape changes from the bountiful Medjerda valley with its abundant crops, to vast arid stretches covered in salt deposits – in the Djérid chotts and sebkahs – or the infinite rolling light yellow sand dunes. In this desert-like region, every drop of water is counted as the oueds are usually dry, or gushing violently and haphazardly for a few hours before completely disappearing into the sands. Through man's undeterred labour, springs have been miraculously harnessed, wells dug and irrigation systems developed from scratch, allowing life to flourish in several oases (Tozeur, Nefta, Kébili, Douz). The palm groves provide some relief in this desolate landscape, producing dates and providing the necessary shade to grow lettuce, tomatoes, onions, mint, etc.

The inhabitants of these desert-like regions are also different. Many of them are nomadic herders who set their tents up in the middle of the scanty pastures where their herds of goats and dromedaries graze.

Right in the south, the Sahara, "land of thirst", begins. Distances are no longer calculated in kilometres, but in days' walk, even if four-wheel drive jeeps have replaced the old dromedary caravans for getting to the far-off Libyan and southern Algerian oases of Ghadamès, Djanet or Tamanrasset.

After the caravans, the "meharis"

The face of southern Tunisia may be changing with the advent of tourism. For a long time now, holiday-makers have had their hearts set on the Mediterranean coast and especially Djerba Island. Nowadays, however, Sahara-lovers who can no longer visit the Tassili or the Hoggar because of the troubles in Algeria, are heading to South Tunisia. Comfortable hotels are rapidly being well built, respecting the local style, in the oases of Tamerza, Tataouine, Tozeur, Nefta, Douz or Kébili in order to meet this influx of new clientele. The Tunisian Bedouins are abandoning traditional caravan traffic in order to take the Italian, German or French hikers on excursions or camel rides on "meharis".

"The Café des Nattes" in Sidi Bou Saïd
– which became famous thanks to
the French writer André Gide –
affords a magnificent view over the Tunis region
and is a highly appreciated rendezvous spot for foreign visitors.

the people

■ With a population of 8.4 million inhabitants in a country about two thirds the size of Britain, and a population density of 51 inhabitants per square kilometre, Tunisia is one of the most densely populated countries in Africa along with Nigeria, Egypt, Malawi and Ghana.

Tunisia has a much larger population than its immediate neighbours Algeria (11 inhabitants/km^2) and Libya (2 inhab./km^2). It must be said, however, that a great part of their land surface is taken up by the Sahara. In Tunisia, this desert covers only the southern tip of the country which is part of the Grand Erg Oriental. The Saharan regions of Tunisia are not completely deserted, however, and there are large concentrations of people in the Djérid oases (Tozeur, Nefta, Kébili, Douz) and in the Médenine-Tataouine region.

The "baby boom" period

These high population figures are recent as Tunisia had barely over 2 million inhabitants at the beginning of the century. On the eve of the Second World War, there were about 2.7 million inhabitants as demographic growth was considerably held back by the high infant mortality rate.

In the 1960s, shortly after independence, the "baby boom" took off. Tunisia's population figures rose even more rapidly (over 3% a year) as hygiene and medical progress significantly reduced the infant mortality rate and increased life expectancy from an average of 52 years old in 1965, to 68 today.

The Tunisian population increased to 4.5 million inhabitants in 1966, overtook 5.5 million ten years later, and was bordering on 8 million inhabitants in 1988.

Since the 1980s, the population growth rate has tended to slow down, however, averaging at an annual increase of 2.5% between 1980 and 1994. Specialists expect the growth rate to increase by 2.2% per year until the year 2000, when the Tunisian population should pass the 10 million mark, reaching 14 million in the year 2025.

The particularly rapid growth rate of the last few years poses serious problems for Tunisian society.

Overpopulation in the countryside has led to an acute rural exodus to towns that are hardly equipped to cater for so many new inhabitants. It has also forced a lot of Tunisians to go abroad to look for work.

It also means that the Tunisian population is extremely young (68% of Tunisians are under 30 years old, 38% of whom are under 15). Not only is this young population unproductive, but also has to be fed and educated.

Finally, Tunisia has a serious unemployment problem. Fifteen percent of the population is out of work.

On the whole, population distribution in Tunisia remains unequal, and there is a clear imbalance between the North and the South.

Indeed, Tunisians tend to live in the northern part of the country – "Green Tunisia" – and particularly in the rich agricultural Medjerda valley and fertile Sahelian lands. There is also a high concentration of inhabitants in the port side towns (Tunis, Sfax, Sousse, Bizerte, and Gabès) along the Mediterranean coast, as well as in areas where tourism is thriving, like the south of Cap Bon (Hammamet and Nabeul) and Djerba Island. It must be pointed out that the latter has always been highly populated as it served as a refuge for populations victim to the successive invasions over the centuries.

Kairouan, which is not on the coast nor in a prosperous agricultural region, provides the exception to the rule (nearly 100,000 inhabitants). The town owes its demographic development to its century-old vocation as a major Islamic religious and intellectual centre. It is also a major crossroads and an important agricultural centre.

A highly urbanised country

Tunisia is no longer a predominantly rural country. Since Independence, the countryside has been emptying as people head for the towns. Whereas two thirds of the population lived in the country in the 1960s, nowadays this tendency has inverted, and there are now 54 town-dwellers for every 100 inhabitants.

Along with neighbouring Algeria and Libya, and with Egypt and South Africa, Tunisia is one of the most urbanised countries in Africa, and even exceeds the world average of 41.6%.

Modern-day Tunisia has a whole string of large towns along its coast: Tabarka in the north-west (fishing port and tourist resort), Bizerte (large commercial port, 85,000 inhabitants), Tunis (the capital, seat of the government, the banking, commercial and industrial centre, 620,000 inhabitants), Sousse (docks and industrial town, 101,000 inhabitants), Kairouan (the fourth Islamic holy town and important artisanal and agricultural centre, 93,000 inhabitants), Sfax (second town in Tunisia, major port, commercial, agricultural and industrial centre, 222,000 inhabitants), Gabès (trading and petrol port and industrial town, 83,000 inhabitants)...

Settled farmers and nomadic herders

Rural Tunisians tend to be either settled farmers or nomadic herders. The former work principally in the north and centre of the country, as well as in the oases of the deep south (the Nefta, Tozeur, Kébili and Médenine palm groves).

Nomadism developed from the 11th century onwards with the arrival of the Beni Hillal Bedouin tribes. The caravan era is over, however, and nomadism now only involves a fraction of the Tunisian population. The nomads are herders who live in the Saharan south and who travel up to the central steppes in the summer when the torrid heat dries up their southern pastures.

Population density varies from one region to the next. Population levels are very low in the desert south (less than 5 inhabitants per km^2), whereas there are over 50 inhabitants per km^2 in the fertile northern region, and over 100 inhabitants per km^2 along the highly urbanised coastal belt.

The *Berbers*, who were the first known inhabitants of the Maghreb, have lived here for several thousand years. Their origins are a mystery, but it is thought that they are in part the descendants of an extremely ancient and unidentified people who lived in the Maghreb in prehistoric times.

In addition to this original African people, the Berbers appear to have been influenced by many populations from the Mediterranean basin including the Libyans and the Egyptians, Persian nomads, Aegeans, Phoenicians, Italic and Iberian people, etc. The Berbers apparently evolved from this combination.

According to many specialists, notably Professor Jean Servier, the term itself is inappropriate: "The term Berber which we habitually use to designate the earliest inhabitants of North Africa, is in fact, an inadequate term as it is derived from the Greek *barabaroi* and later from Semitic, then from the Arabic *brabra*. It first and foremost describes a people whose language is unintelligible. It is a despising term applied to the vanquished by the vanquisher, or by a traveller who is certain that he comes from a superior civilisation. It is not the name that a people gives itself."

In fact the Berbers do not constitute a homogeneous people, but rather a wide palette of ethnic groups who have common dialects. These dialects must not be confused with Arabic, which was introduced much later. Berber is in fact similar to the northern Semitic languages like Canaanite and Syriac, whereas Arabic is similar to the southern languages like Ethiopic.

Garamantes, Gaetulians, Numidians and Mauri

In ancient times, historians and geographers, including Herodotus (484-420 B.C.) and, later, Ibn Khaldun (1332-1406), classed the Berbers as a large grouping of ethnicities: the Garamantes of the Sahara, the Gaetulians, the Luata and Nefusa of Libya, the Numidians, the Mauri from northern Africa, etc. They occupied the vast region of North Africa from the Mediterranean coast to Niger, from the Atlantic to the Nile.

This profoundly individualist and divided people – whose basic political unit was the family (the "tribe") – rarely succumbed to a greater authority throughout the course of history. Each time that their identity and traditions were threatened, they

Traditional clothing, which is otherwise abandoned for modern dress, is worn for important occasions like weddings, Friday prayers at the mosque and other festivities.

revolted. The entire history of the Maghreb is punctuated by Berber insurrections against the successive invaders: the Romans, the Byzantines, and the Arabs. The latter set out to conquer North Africa in waves from the 7th century onwards. In the 11th century in particular, the nomadic Beni Hillal Bedouins managed to completely dominate North Africa, converting everyone to Islam and imposing their language. As the Berber specialist Gabriel Camps stresses, "It is strange and, it must be said, quite remarkable, that several tens of thousand Bedouins converted a population of several million Berbers."

Slowly the Arabic invaders and most of the different Berber ethnic groups intermingled, thereby founding a sole people: the Maghrebi. A few indomitable groups fled to the Atlas mountains (the Chleuhs in southern Morocco, the Mozabites in southern Algeria, and the Kabyles in the east) or to the Sahara desert (the Tuaregs).

In Tunisia, a few Berber families fled from the different invaders and retreated to the mountains and Saharan region of the deep south, convinced that these desolate and arid lands would ward off any possible attackers. Others retreated to Djerba Island.

To assure maximum security, most of the villages were built high up in the rocks, (the "mountain oases" of Tamerza, Chebika and Midès), or were protected by great earthen walls like the *ksour* in the Médenine-Tataouine region.

The even more practical inhabitants of Matmata, wanting to protect themselves not only from enemies, but from the heat too, buried themselves down at the bottom of great craters in troglodytic villages.

The arrival of the Arabs

The Arabs, who came from the Arabian peninsula, began their expansion in the 7th century during the lifetime of the Prophet Mohammed (Mahomet to the Christians).

First of all they conquered the whole of Arabia, then, under the caliphates of Abou Bakr (632-633) and Omar (634-644) after the death of the Prophet (in 632), Syria, Mesopotamia, and Egypt.

Under the third caliph Othman, the Arabs made their first incursion into Tunisia (647), but it was not until Mu'Awiyyah, the fifth caliph (661-680), and founder of the Damascus Umayyad dynasty, that the Arabs really began to take root in the Maghreb. The emir Uqba ibn Nafi founded Kairouan both as a base for spreading Islam, and as a military base for future expeditions in North Africa. He confronted the Byzantines, who were firmly implanted on the Tunisian coast, and the Berbers inland. The latter put up the fiercest fight, during which the emir was defeated and killed.

In 698, the Arab emir Al Ghassani chased the Byzantines out of Tunisia and settled in Tunis. This marked the end of Christianity and the use of Latin in North Africa. The Arab conquerors set about converting the Tunisian Berbers to Islam and the Arabic language.

After a period of unrest, Arabic civilisation flourished in Tunisia in the 9th century under the Aghlabid dynasty, which depended on the Abbasid caliphate of Baghdad. It was a "golden century" during which Muslim arts were encouraged, and which gave a new lease of life to the major towns of Kairouan, Sousse, Sfax and Monastir.

In the 11th century, a new wave of Arabic invasions took place with the fearsome Beni Hillal nomads, which reinforced Arabic influence in the country.

A pluralistic democracy

Later on the Hafsids, the Turks, the Husseinite beys, and – after Independence – the leaders of the Republic have all contributed to shaping the face of the Tunisia we know today: a pluralistic democracy where Islam – which is fervently practised – has not become a battleground for extremists of all factions.

The Tunisians, who are a moderate people, maintain good relations with both the Arab countries and the Western powers. Their sense of moderation and tolerance, the beautiful landscapes, and the country's cultural wealth have all contributed to placing Tunisia high on the list of international tourist destinations.

flora and fauna

It is a pleasure to travel in northern Tunisia all year round. Instead of "Green Tunisia", this region could well be dubbed "The land of eternal springtime". Indeed, with the waters of the Mediterranean lapping its coasts, Tunisia does not have a winter. It is always mild, and can get quite hot in the daytime during the summer. But as soon as the first stars begin to twinkle in the sky, the temperature becomes mild again.

Tunisian flora is always in bloom. All year round, the gardens of Carthage and Sidi Bou Saïd are fragrant with the scent of jasmine and mimosa, and the violet flames of the bougainvillea blaze against the immaculate whitewashed walls.

Further to the north-west is Lake Ichkeul. Here in the spring, the blooming moors, marshes and reed beds are a symphony of greens speckled with little moving splashes of yellow, white or red as poppies, irises, gladioli and marigolds flutter in the slightest breeze. In the Mogods and Khroumirie mountains, the suave scent of eucalyptus pierces the last cork oak forests. Around Tabarka and Aïn Draham, woods of birch, aspen, alder and willow trees, shelter the rosebay bushes below.

The northern and central regions are dominated by vast plantations. Cereals grow in the Medjerda valley, market produce and vineyards in the region of Tunis, citrus fruit on Cap Bon, and olive groves interspersed with clumps of almond trees stretch as far as the eye can see in the Sahel.

In the vast southern steppes where esparto grass grows, nomads set their temporary camps up amidst their herds of goats and sheep.

Vast palm groves

After the great salty stretches of the chotts, which are usually dried up by the intense heat, the first dunes of the Sahara can be seen rising up behind the green belt of the palm groves. The date palms – the last sign of life before entering the mineral world of the Sahara desert – are a great source of wealth in the oases as they produce the succulent "finger of light" (*deglet nour*) dates enjoyed all round the world. In the oases, the miraculous presence of water means that cereals, tomatoes, carrots and lettuce can also be grown on these thankless lands.

Like animals, plants shy away from intense heat which dehydrates and kills them. Like the animals, all the Saharan flora has developed ingenious means of survival.

Most of the perennial plants – especially the acacia – have adapted to the arid land by burrowing their roots down over ten metres deep where the layers of soil become fresher and moister.

On the surface, the roots of these Saharan plants act as barometers. When it is very hot and dry, they retract; when a shower of rain is coming, they stretch out over a large area like tentacles.

Furthermore, the plants stop themselves from dehydrating in the blazing sun by reducing the number and the surface area of their leaves as much as possible. Their leaves are also hard and waterproof like insect carapaces, which stops their sap from evaporating, and are shiny and smooth to reflect the sunrays.

Whilst the plants themselves only flourish for few weeks each year, their seeds are very resistant and can survive for years. The seeds lie dormant, but are ready to germinate within a few hours when the first drops of rain fall.

Others, like cram-cram seeds, bristle with minuscule thorns, enabling them to stick to animal hides or human clothing and perhaps be carried to less hostile climes.

Some seeds are so light that they can be blown long distances by the desert winds.

Finally, the hollow, ball-shaped colocynth fruit explodes in the heat, dispersing its seeds which germinate when the first rains come.

The lions and panthers of the past

No one knows Tunisia's wild fauna better than the old Khroumirs from the northern mountains around Aïn Draham and Tabarka. They had been hunting wild boar and jackals in the forests for generations before serving as trackers and beaters for today's hunting heroes who come from Europe at great expense. Between two puffs on their briar pipes, they like to recall that they killed the last lion at Babouch near Aïn Dra-

Tunisia's particularly abundant landscape
of pastures and
olive tree plantations
is seen here from an airplane.

ham in the 1920s, and the last panthers a few years later.

Since all the big cats have disappeared from these northern mountains, wild boar (*sus scrofa*) have become the undisputed animal kings. These awesome animals weigh between 80 and 90 kg on average, and sometimes as much as 130 kg. Covered in a thick brown hide, they have long hairless snouts which are very mobile.

Some wild boar have impressive little croissant-shaped tusks over 10 cm long. They are in fact canines that have grown much longer than the other teeth. The lower tusks are longer than the upper ones. Mature male boars live alone, whilst the young boars live together in family groups of about 8 to 10 boars.

These reputedly shy animals come out mainly at night to feed on plants and small animals. In the daytime they hide away in in the shade of rocks and in the thickets of the most remote forests.

Hunters are not the only predators to track wild boar: jackals also hunt for their stray youngsters. Villagers are not at all fond of these dog-like animals, which they track down, as jackals are not afraid to enter their yards to steal the poultry. Jackals are nonetheless useful animals as they rapidly eliminate all the village rubbish, from rotten fruit and vegetables to carcasses.

Amongst other animals found in northern Tunisia are foxes and their prey, hares, wild cats, and genets, the small nocturnal carnivores that feed on birds, frogs and poultry.

Swarms of birds

Foreign visitors arriving in Tunis will be taken aback by the deafening welcome the swarms of sparrows and swifts nested in the ficus on Bourguiba Avenue have in store for them. The last colonies of flamingos on the "Little Sea" of Tunis, which can sometimes be seen from La Goulette dyke, are more reserved and fearful.

Visitors will be delighted to watch storks building their nest in the chimney stacks of the northern villages, and especially in Sejnane. These birds here may have come from Alsace via Italy.

The secret of the migrations that take place all over the world when autumn comes and the cold weather begins to set in on the northern hemisphere, lies in the fact that the birds, which cannot keep flying for indefinite periods, instinctively seek "fords" – islands and straits – to cross seas and oceans. When they fly from European continent to North Africa via the Mediterranean, therefore, the migrating birds head across the Gibraltar Straits in the west, or the Sicilian Straits in the east.

Tunisia, especially the Bizerte and Cap Bon regions situated at less than 150 km from Sardinia and Sicily, is one of the privileged passing places for the migrating birds – greylag geese, teals, ducks, coots – fleeing Europe and its winter for the African continent.

Many are wader birds, and therefore seek lakes and reed beds: large white and black storks, grey and white herons, little white egrets, and their little cousin, the little white cattle egret (always perched on the back of a ruminant), or the brownish hammerhead, the little bittern, or the ibis.

The fat blue and red sultan fowl, small aquatic birds, and the harrier bird of prey can be found hiding away in the reeds. Very small birds like swallows, swifts, larks, and thrushes live in the woods and fields. The coast, islets and islands are a refuge for sea birds like puffins, petrels, seagulls, terns, and sandpipers.

Stunning swoops and dives

All of these aquatic birds are fond of briny and swampy waters full of alevins, fish and frogs, which is what makes Tunisia's sebkhas so appealing. One of their favorite places is Lake Ichkeul, near to Bizerte, which has been designated a national park (*see later*).

The migratory birds of prey – sparrowhawks and falcons – that come to Tunisia in March, are eagerly awaited by the Haouaria falconers on Cap Bon. Trained to hunt by villagers using age-old methods, these birds are the stars of the festival dedicated to them in June. Set free afterwards, some find their way back to Haouaria the following year.

These birds of prey are remarkably good hunters thanks to their piercing eyesight which enables them "to read the newspaper" 200 metres away, and thanks to the speed at which they dive (the falcon is capable of reaching the stunning speed of over 300 km/h, which makes it one of the fastest birds). Compared with vultures and eagles (whose wing span may reach up to 2 m), the European pelegrin falcons (*falco peregrinus*) and sparrowhawks are small birds of prey with a wing span that varies between 0.80 m and 1.20 m and 0.60 m and 0.80 m respectively.

The European sparrowhawk which comes essentially from Germany and Switzerland (as opposed to the sparrowhawks living in France, Britain and Belgium, which are sedentary), is a "light weight" bird of prey. It lays four to six eggs that have an incubation period of one month. After the chicks are born, they stay in the nest for one month before flying away. Sparrowhawks live in caves and wooded clumps and feed mainly on small birds (passerines).

Falcons, which are a little larger, have much the same habits as sparrowhawks. They prey on small rodents and birds.

An extraordinary aquarium

Tunisia's warm waters full of fish are a paradise for the fishermen and scuba divers who frequent this gigantic aquarium along the 1,200 km of coastline (164,000 km^2 of territorial waters) bordering on the two Mediterranean basins. The richness of the sea's resources explains why there are so many fishing ports dotted all along the coast.

In the south-east of the country in particular (Gulf of Gabès), all the Mediterranean's unique conditions converge, producing luxuriant underwater flora and fauna.

Indeed the coastline of ancient Syrtis Minor is well sheltered by the Kerkennah Islands in the north, and by Djerba Island in the south. The shallow waters are warm due to their latitude. Moreover, there is very little tide (no more than 2 m difference between low and high tide). Underwater, the vast plancton-covered prairies function like immense underwater farms where innumerable fish and shellfish are incubated, born and multiply.

Over 80 species of fish ranging from the "blue fish" (tuna, mackerel, sardines, anchovies) to sole, mullet, bonito, gilthead, skate and shark, all find refuge in the Gulf of Gabès' protective waters. In addition to the fish are the sponges, octopi, squid, and shellfish (clams). Squillas, shrimps, spider crabs, and crawfish hide away in the rocks.

The northern coast between Tabarka and Bizerte, which is nicknamed the "Coral Coast", as there is a lot of coral here, is less abundant in fish than the east coast, however. This rocky area is an ideal shelter for shrimps and lobsters. Out at sea from Tabarka, La Galite islet has become one of the last Mediterranean sanctuaries for colonies of monk seals. This large aquatic mammal is now a protected species as it was in danger of becoming extinct after being decimated by fishermen fed up with them ruining their nets. These islets are also a sanctuary for sea birds like puffins, petrels, silver gulls, terns and other species of seagulls.

The Ichkeul, Bizerte and Ghar el Melh Lakes in the north are also vast aquariums for eel, sole, mullet, perch and bream.

Parks and nature reserves

Aware of both the richness and the fragility of their natural heritage, the Tunisian authorities have begun to delimit animal protection zones and to set up parks and reserves.

In the north, La Galite Island has been classed a "nature reserve" in order to assure the longevity of the monk seal and of the sea bird colonies. In November 1973, the Tunisian Minister for Agriculture designated Zembra Island north of the Cap Bon peninsula a marine reserve. The reserve includes the island and Zembretta Islet where the huge rocks plunging into the sea provide a haven for shrimps, crawfish and lobsters.

The shoals of tunny fish that pass by these islands are fished by fishermen from Sidi Daoud, who practise the bloody "Matanza" ritual (carried out throughout the whole of the Mediterranean, notably by Sicilian and Portuguese fishermen from the Algarve).

Lake Ichkeul, also in the north near to Bizerte, is rich in birdlife and has also been designated a nature park.

"Desert ships"

European visitors heading southwards are always intrigued when they see dromedaries (most people use the term "camel", even if it is in fact incorrect. Purist zoologists will point out that dromedaries, which live in Africa, only have one hump, whereas camels have two and live in Asia).

Known for their legendary abstinence, camels can in fact resist thirst for several weeks as long as they have access to fodder green enough to contain water. If the earth is completely dry and the temperature very high, however, they can only go without drinking for a week.

The camel's secret is its body's excellent thermal regulation and its efficient conservation of liquids. Its urine is highly concentrated and it only sweats when its body temperature exceeds 40 °C. The animal's thick hide serves as thermic insulation: if it were shorn, the camel would perish within a few days as it would dehydrate like a squeezed sponge. The camel's hump is not a hidden water tank: it is in fact a fat store that enables the camel to go without eating (rather than without drinking). A deflated hump will very quickly build up again as soon as the camel finds food.

During long desert journeys, camels may loose up to a quarter of their weight. Once they reach an oasis, they "remake" themselves, sometimes quite spectacularly as a camel can drink over 100 litres of water in a few minutes! When a sand storm breaks out, camels hermetically close their nostrils and their very long eyelashes and lids protect their eyes.

Nomads distinguish between two types of camel: packsaddle camels and bearing camels (meharis). The former are small, stocky and very robust, and can therefore transport the heavy loads. The meharis are chosen amongst animals with the longest legs, which means they can walk faster.

Even though climatic conditions are extreme in the Sahara, the desert is not lifeless, as many people think. On the contrary, it is absolutely thriving. All desert animals and plants have accomplished extraordinary feats of adaptation and survival, however. This has involved making significant physiological modifications and adopting a different daily time schedule. Indeed, all species have had to employ all possible means to avoid the torrid heat which can dehydrate and kill them.

As a result, all animals stay in the shade, in burrows, holes and caves during the daytime and only come out at night. Furthermore, nature has equipped them with insulating shields that are often water tight (to stop their bodies from loosing any water): both small and big mammals have thick hides, reptiles have thick skin and scales, and insects have hermetic carapaces.

Ants, beetles and scorpions

Amongst the various inhabitants of the Tunisian Sahara to the south of the chott el Djérid – the Grand Erg Oriental –, ants are found hidden away in the depths of their ant hills where the temperature is cooler than on the surface; scarabs bury themselves in the sand dunes making sure they choose the shady side of the slope; and white scorpions sleep hidden under stones (legend has it that they were banished from the Kairouan steppes by the Arab emir Uqba ibn Nafi in 670).

Many reptiles are also capable of surviving in these arid, white hot lands, for example the various kinds of lizards – which, unlike their reputation, do not laze around basking in the sun, but seek out any available shade. The dob lizard is very well adapted to the desert as its skin absorbs the slightest trace of humidity in the air like blotting paper. The skink or "sand fish" is even more ingenious, using its head to wriggle its way down into the sandy soil.

The highly poisonous desert horned viper and the cobra (which uses the thick scales on its head like a spade to dig into the ground) – are less appreciated by man.

Large addax and oryx desert antelopes were very common in the past, but have been so intensely hunted that they have taken refuge further southwards, especially in Niger, and are no longer found in the Maghreb. Small gazelles have also been so decimated by man, hyenas and jackals that it is now unusual to come across them in southern Tunisia.

Small mammals and birds

Tiny mammals like the lovely fennec which inspired Saint-Exupéry's fox in his famous novel "The Little Prince", are still common. The fennec has huge ears which it uses to keep cool, and to hear its pray moving at night at distances of over several hundred metres away. It is particularly fond of the little jerboa, otherwise known as the kangaroo rat as it uses its long hind legs to bound away when chased. Most of the Saharan mammals drink very rarely as they drink the water or blood of the flesh of their prey, which include insects, lizards, fruit and small rodents.

The Sahara is full of birds, most of which are in the process of migrating further southwards where its is wetter. These birds have to stop off in the oases if they are to complete the long journey across the desert. They too have adapted to the extremely dry regions – their feathers form excellent insulation and their high blood temperature makes them less vulnerable in the heat.

Furthermore, these birds eliminate excess heat by panting, and if it really gets too hot, they fly higher where the temperature is cooler.

The migratory birds are faced with the fatigue of the journey and the extreme conditions en route in the Sahara desert (lack of food and water, high temperatures, scarcity of stopping places and shelter); they also have to beware of their terrible predators who will give them no quarter. Indeed, predators of all types hide in the oases, spotting their prey when they are still high in the sky thanks to their sharp eyesight.

*Dromedaries, the faithful companions
of the Sahara desert nomads,
are less and less frequently used
on caravan trails, and more and more
frequently for tourist camel rides.*

religions and traditions

■ The majority of Tunisians are Muslim today (over 95% of the population). The remaining minority are Jewish or Christian. This was not always the case in the past, however, as other beliefs and religions dominated this eastern part of the Maghreb for a long time.

Berber beliefs

The Berbers, who settled in North Africa thousands of years ago, had their own beliefs long before the Carthaginian gods appeared several centuries B.C., and before they converted to Christianity and then to Islam in the first centuries A.D.

As the Berbers did not make written records of their life in the period preceding their successive conversions, ethnologists are having to carry out mammoth research in order to distinguish what belongs to Islam and what belongs to Berber beliefs of the past in today's practices. According to specialists, the implantation of Christianity and Islam in North Africa did not completely annihilate ancient Berber beliefs. Today's attachment to the dead and to funeral rites (the ancient ancestor cults) appears to be a remnant of these beliefs.

The Carthaginians believed themselves to be surrounded by demons or evil spirits from birth to the grave and held these forces responsible for illness, poor harvests, and even defeat in war. Hence the Punic people's essentially superstitious nature.

The Carthaginians were constantly making sacrifices (usually animals) and libations to the many gods in the Punic pantheon in order to ward off the evil spirits. In times of illness, they turned to the god of healing *Eshmoun* (Asclepios in Greek mythology, Aesculapius for the Romans). In very serious cases, when they believed that the gods were angry with the whole of the Punic community – notably after serious defeat or in times of famine – they sacrificed young children (usually the first born of the grand patrician families) to *Baal Hammon*, who was later wrongly called *Moloch* (deformation of the ritual name: the Molk). These sacrifices, which were meant to restore abundance, peace and prosperity, were held in public. The children were handed over to the priest by their families, who were forbidden to show the slightest emotion, and the children had their throats cut and their bodies thrown onto a brazier, or into the gaping mouth of a statue of Baal which worked like an oven.

These barbaric practices which shocked all ancient writers, are no longer considered to be plausible by several contemporary historians who claim that the young victims had already died from illness before being cremated. They think that such accounts were part of anti-Carthaginian propaganda fabricated by the Romans who felt it necessary to discredit Carthage in order to justify its annihilation.

Two supreme deities dominated the rest of the Carthaginian pantheon. The first was *Baal Hammon*, god of prosperity, whom the Romans continued to worship under the name of Saturne after the fall of Carthage in 146 B.C. Very few representations of Baal remain which can be clearly authenticated by the scientists (apart from the terracotta in the Bardo museum in Tunis), as the Romans most probably destroyed all the effigies when they razed Carthage. The second deity was *Tanit*, the "Lady of Carthage", goddess of the moon and fertility (Astarte of the Phoenicians, Ishtar of the Assyrians). She was represented on steles by the "sign of Tanit", a bottle and the solar disc surmounted by a crescent moon, or the stylised silhouette of a person with their arms raised up to the moon (a triangle for the body, bars for the raised arms, a circle for the head, and a crescent moon above the lot). At the beginning of the 4th century B.C., Tanit became the most important divinity in the Carthaginian pantheon. *Shadrapa*, the god of healing (identified with Horus and Dionysus) who cured snake bites, also featured amongst the Carthaginian gods.

The Carthaginians also accorded a lot of importance to divinities of Greek origin like *Demeter*, goddess of mother earth. She became highly popular with the Carthaginians at the beginning of the 4th century B.C. They also adopted *Hermes* (homologue of the semitic god Sakon), who was both a messenger and a protector of herds and travellers.

When the Romans came to North Africa in the 2nd century B.C., a Greco-Latin cult developed with many of its divinities, including Jupiter, Apollo, Mercury, Minerva, Neptune, Bacchus, Ceres, Juno, etc.

It was both a domestic and a State religion. Each family had an altar dedicated to the cult of the ancestors in their home, but also had to go to the capitol, the temple where the priests – or pontiffs – carried out rituals and sacrifices. Roman religion involved both the worship of supernatural powers present on the earth, and the celebration of deified emperors and dictators like Caesar, Augustus, Nero, etc. In Tunisia, and throughout the whole of the Roman Empire, temples and effigies of the deities sprang up in the main towns of *Provincia Africa*. Carthage, which was rebuilt by Caesar and Augustus, was the first, followed by the inland Roman towns of Dougga, Sufetula, Thuburbo Majus, etc. A capitoline temple devoted to the divine triad (Jupiter, Juno, Minerva) was built in each town along with other monuments.

The innumerable deities carved in marble, modelled in terracotta, cast in bronze, or depicted in mosaics firstly by Greek artists, then by locals, were taken off their pedestals when Christianity was decreed the official religion in 313 by the emperor Constantine.

Many of these have been now been dug up by archaeologists and are conserved in the Bardo museum in Tunis.

The rise and fall of Christianity

Christianity was the predominant religion in Tunisia throughout the Roman and Byzantine occupations (from the 3rd to the 7th centuries A.D). Born out of Judaism, Christianity evolved with the advent of Jesus Christ, who was crucified near to Jerusalem in the year 32 A.D.

After the death of Christ, Christianity began to spread throughout the whole of the Roman Empire – particularly in North Africa – during the 1st century A.D. thanks to the apostles and their followers. It very soon came into conflict with traditional Roman religion, hence the Romans' decision to violently repress the new religion. Right from the time of Tiberius's reign (14 to 37 A.D.) the first Christians were martyred in the amphitheatres. Massive persecutions punctuated the reigns of most of the Roman emperors from Nero, Domitian, Trajan, Marcus Aurelius, and Valerian to Diocletian. It was not until the emperor Constantine that the persecutions stopped in the 4th century A.D.

In 170 A.D., a Latin Church was set up in Carthage. The Holy Scriptures were taught in Latin, whereas Greek was used in Rome. (Carthage began this tendency, therefore, and Latin would later be imposed throughout the Christian world). For the five centuries up until the arrival of the Arabs in the 7th century, Carthage and the whole of Tunisia were to become major cultural and religious centres of the Christian West. Numerous writers, philosophers and highly-reputed Christian theologians lived here, including *Tertullian* (150/160 to 222), a Carthaginian priest and writer, *Saint Cyprian*, the first African bishop (from 248 to 258) who was martyred by the Romans, and above all, *Saint Augustine*, bishop of Hippone near to Annaba in Algeria, and Carthage, who was considered to be one of the greatest "doctors of the Catholic faith".

Christianity did not really take root in North Africa outside of the ruling elite and town-dwelling, educated, rich proprietors, however. In the countryside, it did not meet the aspirations of the great mass of Berber villagers and herders who lived in a state of poverty.

Convinced that they had been completely forgotten, they fostered a profound grudge against the city folk and their luxurious life-style and affluent religion. This explosive situation periodically erupted into violent revolts which were always bloodily repressed by the Carthaginian authorities supported by the Catholic clergy. Furthermore, when the few Christian priests did uphold the cause of the downtrodden masses, they ended up leaving the Roman Church to form dissident churches, break-away factions and heresies. In the 4th century A.D, Bishop *Donatus*, whose Donatist sect rivalled the official Church in North Africa up until the 6th century, was one such dissident.

Tunisia, which was occupied by the Romans
for several centuries,
has a multitude of antique art treasures,
in particular mosaics and
Hellenistic-style statues.

When the first Arab conquerors arrived in Tunisia in the 7th century, therefore, they found the Christian Church in a state of complete decline. Divided and undermined from within, it appeared to represent intolerance and corruption. The Prophet Mohammed's new religion had little trouble in taking root, even if Berber revolts did break out sporadically.

When the French forcefully took over Tunisia in the last century and set up the Protectorate, they tried to reinstate Christianity. This job was assigned to *Cardinal Lavigerie* who was placed in charge of the North African Christian community in Algiers, Carthage and Tunis. The "Pères Blancs" (Christian missionaries) created under him, set out to evangelize the whole of Africa. When independence was granted, however, the French colonialists, who represented the greatest part of the Tunisian Christian community, went home along with the clergy, and little by little churches were closed down. For the second time in the history of the country, Christianity gave way to Islam.

The Djerba Jews

Up until the 1950s, there was a large Jewish community in Tunisia, especially around Tunis and on the Isle of Djerba. With independence and the emergence of highly-Arabized Muslim political leaders, however, the Tunisian Jews – who are of a predominantly French-speaking culture – preferred to leave and go to France. A very small community has nonetheless remained on Djerba Island grouped around one of the oldest synagogues in the world.

The Jewish people's religion, one of the oldest in the world, is Judaism. The history of the Hebrew people is told in the *Old Testament*. It is a historic account, a poem, a moral code and a religious hymn all in one.

Several thousand years B.C., the ancient Jewish people were scattered tribes of herders who moved from pasture to pasture in Chaldea (Mesopotamia) near to the Euphrates River.

One of these tribes led by *Abraham*, the "patriarch" (the father, chief, judge, and priest), set out westwards and reached Canaan, near to Jordan, in about the 18th century B.C.

As they had come from the desert, the tribe found this land very fertile and therefore named it the "Promised Land". The indigenous Canaanites, on learning that these desert herders had come from far away, called them the "Hebrews" ("the people from far away").

Abraham is one of the first patriarchs to be designated by God to become the father of the Hebrew people. To prove his faith, however, God first asked him to sacrifice his son Isaac. As he was about to kill him, Abraham was stopped by an angel who gave him a ram to sacrifice in place of his child.

After Abraham, his grandson *Jacob* also had a vision from God who told him that his descendants would found a huge nation. Indeed, he had twelve sons who became the founders of the twelve main tribes of Israel.

Driven by famine, the Israelites emigrated to Egypt where Joseph, son of Jacob, became one of the Pharaoh's ministers. The Egyptians soon felt threatened by their numbers and persecuted them, killing their newborn children.

One woman managed to save her child by placing him in a floating crib on the Nile. He was miraculously found by the Pharaoh's daughter, who called him "*Moses*".

It was Moses who saved his people from the Egyptians in the 13th century B.C. during the *Exodus*, by leading them safely through the Red Sea to the Promised Land (Palestine, or the Land of Canaan).

God appeared to Moses on Mount Sinai and dictated the "Ten Commandments" to him which were then engraved on the Tables of the Law.

Along with the first five books of the Bible (the *Pentateuch*), in which the divine orders are recorded, the Ten Commandments constitute the foundation of the Jewish religion, which was the first religion in history to have been monotheist.

Islam, Tunisia's main religion, was introduced in the 7th century shortly after the death of the Prophet Mohammed. The Arab conqueror Uqba ibn Nafi was the first person to introduce it in 670 when he founded the town and the great mosque of Kairouan. At that time, Tunisia was occupied the Byzantines and the official religion Christianity was in complete decline.

Islam benefitted from the differences between North Africa's dissident Christian churches and firmly took root in the 7th and 8th centuries. Today, it is practically the sole religion in Tunisia. Practised by over a billion Muslims in the world today, Islam was revealed to the Prophet Mohammed who was born in Mecca in 570 and died in Medina in 632. The word of Allah was revealed to him during his retreat on Mount Hira in about 610.

Transmitted to Mohammed through the intermediary of the angel Djibril (Gabriel), Allah's word was recorded by his disciples in the numerous writings that constitute the Holy Book, *the Koran*. Written in Arabic, it contains 114 chapters, or *sura*, which lay the foundations of Muslim morals, religion and law. In addition to the Koran – which no Muslim can modify – there are other sacred texts like the *Sunna*, which is a collection of all the Prophet's traditions, including his sayings, silences, gestures, etc.

Only the *Sunnites* (the term is derived from Sunna) acknowledge this as the second source of Muslim law (*sharia*) after the Koran. *Shiite* Muslims, on the other hand, do not consider these texts worthy of the faith and contest their authenticity. It must be stressed that the Sunna traditions are not equal to the Koran and therefore cannot replace the Sacred Book: they are not the Law, only the first commentaries on Koranic Law.

Divisions in the Muslim world

Like all major religious movements, Islam was beset by divisions and internecine quarrels. After the death of the Prophet in 632, quarrels broke out over succession to the title of caliph (head of the world Muslim community). Most of the caliphs were assassinated, and a division

THE FIVE PILLARS OF ISLAM

■ *The five "pillars" of Islam are the obligatory dictates that all true Muslims faithfully carry out every day throughout their whole lives. These are:*
1 – the profession of faith (shahadah): *"There is no God but Allah. Mohammed is his prophet";*
2 – the five daily prayers (at dawn, in the early morning, at the end of the morning, in the afternoon and at dusk), which can only be pronounced once the worshipper has carried out the ritual ablutions, placed a prayer mat on the ground and turned to face Mecca in the east;
3 – the giving of alms (zakat);
4 – fasting during Ramadan, the period lasting one month and whose dates are fixed each year according to the phases of the moon (Muslim worshippers must fast completely during the day, but can eat and drink as soon as night falls. The end of Ramadan is marked by a series of celebrations during which families exchange gifts);
5 – the pilgrimage to Mecca (hadj) *which takes place every year in the Prophet Mohammed's birth town and which draws worshippers from all over the world (several pilgrimages to Kairouan may dispense Tunisian worshippers with the pilgrimage to Mecca, however).*

formed between the Sunnites (the majority) and the minority Shiite faction.

In the year 656, therefore, the Muslim world split into three factions: the *Sunnites* (the orthodox majority); the minority *Shiites* who did not accept the first three caliphs to succeed to the Prophet (Abou Bakr, Omar and Othman), but who did acknowledge the fourth caliph Ali (656-661), the Prophet's son-in-law, as the true successor; and finally the even fewer *Kharijites*, who were initially allies of the fourth caliph before they broke away (kharijite means "those who have left"), and apparently perpetrated Ali's assassination in 661.

The Kharijite theses advocating a radically egalitarian Islam, were popular amongst the North African Berbers and in Tunisia in particular, where the Berbers rose up against the representatives of the Damascus Umayyad dynasty at the end of this dynasty in the 8th century. Nowadays, there are still a few small groups of Ibadite Kharijites (disciples of Abd Alla ibn Ibad, 7th century) living on the Isle of Djerba in Tunisia.

Even though they have their differences, the international Muslim community is unanimous in its recognition of and obedience to the fundamental principals of Islamic faith: the "Five Pillars" (*see inset*).

Jurisprudence schools

Tunisian Islam is predominantly *Sunnite* and its rites belong to the *Malikite* school of jurisprudence (whereas in the coastal towns, a minority of Muslims of Turkish origin are *Hanifites*). As regards law, Sunnites belong to one of the following schools: the Malikite school (named after its founder Malik ibn Anas, who died in 795), the Hanifite school (after Abu Hanifah, died in 767), the *Hanbali* school (after Muhammad ibn Hanbal, died in 855), and finally the *Shafiite* school (after Shafi'i, who died in Cairo in 820). The Malikite are geographically situated principally in North and Sub-Saharan Africa, the Hanifites in Turkey, India and China, the Hanbali in Saudi Arabia, and the Shafiites in Egypt, India, the islands of South-East Asia, and in the Indian Ocean.

It must be stressed that these four schools have one thing in common: they are orthodox, i.e. they all fully acknowledge the tradition (they are by no means break-away factions). They tend to frequently diverge on the details of rituals and the practice of Islamic law, but do not question the religion's dogmas. When reciting the Koran, the Shafiites only allow Arabic, whereas the Hanifites consider it acceptable to translate into the language of the given country. Practising Muslims may change schools during their lifetime.

These schools came into existence during the second Hegira century when the foremost Muslim thinkers set up a law based on the interpretation of the Koran and the Sunna. Four of the schools laid down the laws drawn up into rules of conduct for all the Sunnite Muslims. This law provides the basis of the believer's family statute, public and penal rights and all that regulates religious life.

It must be firmly stressed that this law is an interpretation, albeit inspired by tradition, but an interpretation nonetheless. This law (*sharia*) has become the official law in certain countries (in Iran, for example).

Brotherhoods have developed here and there throughout the Muslim world, for example the *Qâdiryya* (founded by Abdal Qâdir Al-Jilani, who died in 1166), the *Tijâniyya* (set up in 1782 by Sid Ahmed Ben Mohamed Ben El Mokhtar), or the *Shâdilya* (founded by Ali al-Shâdhili, who died in 1256). These brotherhoods are mystical groups that meet in the *zawiyyas* to carry out group liturgical exercises: recital of the Muslim profession of faith (*chahâda*), prayers and mystical poems. Koranic universities (*medersas*) have also developed in these religious centres (zawiyyas), where the marabouts and their disciples teach Muslim theology as well as other scientific disciplines like mathematics, grammar, law, geography, history, medicine, etc. thereby giving the major Muslim towns (like Kairouan or Tunis) a considerable intellectual and spiritual influence.

Even though Islam is predominant,
all the major revealed religions –
Christianity and Judaism –
peacefully coexist in Tunisia
(above, for example, is the Djerba Jewish synagogue).

art and culture

■ The remarkable introduction and mixing of so many cultures in Tunisia (with the Berbers, Carthaginians, Romans, Byzantines, Vandals, Arabs, etc.) has given the country an exceptional artistic heritage.

Highly skilled
Berber craftsmen

For centuries, the Berbers have been skilfully weaving geometrically designed covers and rugs, especially the *kilims* and *mergoums* that were used as floor rugs in the nomads' tents. Decorated with abstract geometric designs, they were woven out of sheep, goat or dromedary wool and hair that was dyed using natural colours. Nowadays, synthetic dyes and industrial wool are increasingly common.

These rugs are made throughout the Berber regions in the north of the country (Tabarka, Bizerte and Sejnane), and particularly in the south (Gafsa, in the Djérid oases, in the Ksour mountains around Matmata, Médenine and Tataouine, the Isle of Djerba). Over the last few years, they have become so popular with the development of the tourist trade in Tunisia, that workshops have sprung up outside the original regions, for example in Matmata, where the troglodytic Berbers weave the same geometric patterns as those originally found in Gafsa, and in the far away Tunis Medina where weavers can be found making kilims.

Rug-making has become one of the most important activities in Kairouan where there are several hundred family workshops. The main types of Kairouan rugs are the *mergoum*, the *alloucha* and the *zerbia*. Amongst the most common Kairouan motifs are the highly-stylised Central Mosque chandelier, the "Kairouan Star", each branch of which symbolises a holy Islamic town (Mecca, Medina, Jerusalem, and Kairouan), the days of the week, the seasons, the jasmine flower, fish (against evil spells), etc.

In Gafsa, the brightly coloured *haoulis* and *ferrachias* rugs repre-

VILLAGES FOUNDED BY PATRON SAINTS

■ *Each Tunisian village has a founder who is usually a saint, i.e. a man who is said to be blessed with the grace of God, or* baraka.
This means he has the gift of helping others during his lifetime and after his death. He can only help those who come to visit the sanctuary in which he is buried, and who read him the first chapter of the Koran, bring him candles or incense, or a few lengths of beautiful cloth to hang above his tomb, or better still, perform all of these rituals.
The saint's descendants inherit a little of his baraka and can also intervene to help others. [...] They are the most respected people in the Tunisian village and form the highest social grouping. They receive the gifts brought by the visitors, but must also act as hosts to these guests. They make charms for the visitors and cure them thanks to the baraka they have inherited from their holy ancestor.
The villagers are strongly attached to their ancestors: they owe the village land to them, their names, their customs, and their specific conventions that form the basis of the "fundamental values of the community." [...]
Important religious ceremonies take place in the sanctuary under the saint's protection. Circumcisions take place whilst the parents sing and dance in the courtyard.

sent figures and animals.

Pottery is also an important Berber craft. According to archaeologists, this practice was passed down from neolithic artisans, as our distant ancestors' terracottas were already decorated with the same geometric motifs: triangles, diamonds, chevrons, checks, squares, etc. In Sejnane near to Bizerte, these products look like they have come straight out of prehistory. Here, plates and pots, little polychrome terracotta figures, and animals like camels, antelopes and cocks, are made using very ancient techniques.

In the *souks* (markets), modern jewellers make copies of Berber jewellery, the most beautiful original examples of which are exhibited in museums or sold in antique shops. Berber artisanal jewellers have always preferred silver to gold as a base for setting pieces of enamel, coloured glass, and amber, and for their innumerable pendants: Hands of Fatima, coins, amber or agate beads, and even bottle tops nowadays. A vast range of jewellery has been made out of these diverse materials over the centuries, including headbands, earrings, necklaces, chest plates, bracelets, rings, broaches, ankle bracelets, etc.

Berber music, dance and oral literature are still very much alive. These different artistic activities are deeply rooted in every day family life. Music and singing in particular accompany all domestic activities ranging from preparing various dishes to working in the fields. Traditional dances add liveliness and gusto too all celebrations, especially marriages.

Berber architecture: fortified villages

The Berbers built extensively using local materials: palm wood for the frames of buildings and earth (clay and daub bricks) for the walls which they modelled like potters and sculptors would, rather than architects. Village architecture has tended to be defensive as the Ber-

Young women generally go to visit the sanctuary with their friends before they get married and, later, with their husbands in order to receive the saint's blessing.

Each patron saint has his own particularities. Some may be known for their rigour, and the pilgrims will take great pains not to offend them. Others, on the contrary, will be known for their great patience with visitors. Certain saints will be famous for their love of riches, and others will be more concerned with reputation than anything else.

In addition to having personal characteristics, each saint excels in a precise field. They are generally thus endowed with the power to cure certain diseases. One saint may be a specialist in curing jaundice, whilst another will treat people suffering from skin diseases. Another will intervene during difficult births, another will exorcise djinn or evil spirits.

The patron saint's birthday is celebrated in every village. On that day, people come from all the surrounding towns and villages to benefit from the saint's baraka, divine grace, and to be cured if suffering from an illness that this saint can heal. The villagers make the most of the occasion to sell their local produce...

Dr Nadia Abu-Zahra
(Encyclopédie Alpha des Peuples du monde entier).

bers have continuously suffered the attacks of invaders over the centuries (from the Carthaginians to the Romans, Byzantines, Vandals, Arabs, etc.). As they did not have the force to fight them, many Berber tribes preferred to take refuge in Tunisia's most desolate regions, like the mountains in the north and south, or the oases of the Sahara desert.

In the country's southern mountain ranges near Tataouine and Médenine, they built innumerable *ksour*, or citadels perched up in eyries surrounded by solid walls and containing fortified granaries, or *ghorfas*.

The honeycomb houses and granaries in Ksar Hadada, Chenini or Ksar Ouled Soltane, built on top of each other like the layers of a beehive, are really quite remarkable. *Ksar Hadada*, which is now converted into a hotel, is one of the finest examples of the ksour and ghorfa architecture. This ochre roughcast and whitewashed tiered cake is riddled with a multitude of alleys, small courtyards and layers of interior terraces reached by tiny, steep staircases.

Berber refugees were also the ones to riddle the Matmata region with craters, creating what looks like a lunar landscape. The troglodytic dwellings built at the bottom of these craters had the double advantage of protecting inhabitants from both the heat and from their invading enemies. In the past, these pits were almost totally inaccessible to strangers as the only way in was via ropes or ladders. Today, however, underground exits have been tunnelled, so it is no longer necessary to perform such neck-breaking acrobatic feats.

It is well worth making the detour to see the Berber "architects" ingenious work. Caves have been hollowed out on several levels, each one with a specific function: the highest caves are granaries, and the lowest the sleeping quarters, kitchens, animal pens and workshops.

Their highly efficient thermal insulation is greatly appreciated by inhabitants – and now by tourists too as some of these troglodytic dwellings have been converted into most original hotels. When the temperature soars in the scorching sun outside, the pits stay invigoratingly cool like cellars, whereas during the coo-

*A magnificent example of traditional Berber architecture
in Ksar Haddada in southern Tunisia.
These fortified earthen granaries and houses
perched on the hilltops
were once almost impenetrable citadels.*

ler winter, the atmosphere stays nicely warm.

The Romans' determination to completely do away with their rival, Carthage, has deprived Tunisia and the rest of the world of extraordinary remains (palaces, temples, houses, sculptures, art works, etc.) of a highly-developed civilisation of fishermen and traders.

Anyone wishing to retrace the Punic past nowadays must be contented with the few vestiges excavated by archaeologists, and use as vivid an imagination as the wonderful French novelist Gustave Flaubert did in *Salammbô*. It is nonetheless certainly worth visiting Carthage to see the port basin and the Admiral's island ruins where the famous Punic ports were situated several centuries B.C. A map and model of these have been reconstituted in the Carthage Museum (just above on Byrsa hill).

The war port's remarkable layout is especially interesting for visitors: rings of buildings serving as sheds for the ships overlooked a circular basin in the middle of which the Admiral's island was entirely covered by a circular-shaped pavilion. This was built for the admiral, the supreme commander of the Carthaginian fleet. The admiral could survey the movements of the ships in the basin and out at sea, as these buildings had views over both the port and the channel leading to the sea.

The port, which was a key element in the Carthaginians' naval force, also contained dockyards where all the Punic war and merchant ships were built. According to the Greek historian Appian, the holds built on the ground floor of the Admiral's pavilion and the circular sheds could hold 220 ships.

Comfortable Carthaginian houses

The Carthaginians made very few domestic architectural innovations as, like the Romans, they based their models on the Greeks'.

The Carthage palaces and houses were thus built on several floors around an interior courtyard surrounded by columns (peristyles), just like the 3rd century B.C. Greek houses. The rooms inside usually had cement tiled floors incrusted with pieces of marble. The walls were covered in stucco with decors inspired by Egyptian Pharaonic art, notably *uraeus* friezes (erect cobras).

In terms of hygiene and comfort, the Carthaginians were ahead of their time – and ahead of the Romans in particular – as can be seen from the houses in Kerkouane, a little 5th century B.C Punic town set on the tip of the Cap Bon peninsula. Indeed, bathrooms with washbasins and hip-baths have been excavated here. The Carthaginians in fact copied the Greek models and adapted them to what at the time was a very new lifestyle.

Greek and Egyptian-style temples

The very few remaining vestiges of Punic temples, which were completely destroyed by the Romans, appear (although evidence is unconclusive) to indicate that the Carthaginians did not innovate in this domain either, instead borrowing their models from the Greeks and Egyptians. The 3rd century B.C. Dougga Punic mausoleum, an elegant monument in the form of a pointed tower, is also worth visiting.

Carthaginian artists excelled in sculpting funereal steles and masks. There are two types of mask: grimacing masks which were placed in tombs to ward off evil spirits, and tiny masks made out of coloured glass.

The Romans did not let their reputation down when they settled in Tunisia at the end of the Republic and at the beginning of the Empire. First of all they rebuilt Carthage according to their own style, i.e. with more temples and palaces, and also developed the major towns – particularly during the 2nd century A.D. –, building villas, forums, and vast public edifices (temples, baths, amphitheatres, triumphal arches, etc.). A 90 km aqueduct was also built linking Carthage to Mount Zaghouan.

Some of the marvels of Roman civil architecture can be discovered when travelling around Tunisia, for example the *Antonine Baths* in Carthage, in the suburbs of Tunis; the huge El Djem *Coliseum* between Sousse and Sfax; the *Diocletian*

Triumphal Arch in Sbeïtla-Sufetula; the beautiful underground villas in Bulla Regia with mosaics of the "Hunt" and "Aphrodite" (these houses built underground to escape the heat are unique in the history of Roman art); and the Dougga *Theatre* near to the Kef. Roman religious architecture is also well illustrated by the Sbeïtla-Sufetula and Dougga temples (capitols).

Mosaics, ceramics, stuccos

Tunisia is a heartland of mosaic art, an art which flourished in the towns built by the Romans in the first centuries A.D. Even though they did not actually invent mosaic making, the Romans – and then the Byzantines – gave an unprecedented boost to this art form. The invention of mosaics goes back far into ancient times. The first mosaics made in Uruk in Mesopotomania, date from the end of the 4th millennium B.C.

Later in the 4th century B.C., the Greeks were great mosaicists. It was not until the Roman Empire in the early centuries A.D, however, that the great vogue for these assemblies of tiny fragments of marble, glass or terracotta (*tesserae*) really took off. When rich Roman patricians had their imposing villas built, they usually commissioned artists to make sumptuous tiles and mosaics. Originally, Greek artists were the great masters of this art, but later mosaics were made in the innumerable schools that flourished all over the Empire from Gaul, Germany, and Syria to North Africa.

The Tunisian school's mosaics decorating the splendid villas of Bulla Regia, Sbeïtla, Carthage, and other towns, are remarkable for their beauty, variety and sheer numbers.

Today these mosaics have been taken out of their original settings in order to avoid possible damage, and are now exhibited in the Bardo Museum in Tunis, Gafsa and El Djem Museums.

Two epochs can be distinguished

TEMPLES AND GODS

The temples built in Barbary's Roman towns were occasionally dedicated to the local Moorish gods, but more often to Roman gods or to the emperors themselves. Some of these Roman gods are indeed quite simply the transposition of former Punic gods. The god of Tyre, Melqart, thus became Herakles then Hercules; Eschmoun became Aesculapius; Tanit, Caelestis and Baal Hammon, Saturn. The cult of Saturn, which was assimilated to that of Baal Hammon, remained particularly strong in the countryside at least up until the 5th century. This persistence is most likely an indication of the resistance of Berber specificity in the light of Roman foreign influence. This resistance was even greater and even more profoundly affirmed by the extraordinarily rapid spread of Christianity in the Berber regions.

R. AND M. CORNEVIN
Histoire de l'Afrique
(Petite Bibliothèque Payot).

*Archaeologists and tourists are increasingly passionate
about the numerous ancient towns
excavated throughout Tunisia
where treasures of mosaic art and statuary
have been found (above: the Dougga vestiges).*

in the mosaic styles: the primitive period during which the artist imitated the forms and motifs found on rugs; and a more evolved period in which mosaic art was inspired by painting and depicted figures and landscapes.

The most popular mosaic themes were often taken from Greek mythology (Bacchic scenes), but also included circus games or scenes of rural daily life (ploughing, harvesting, hunting) and seascapes (fishing).

When the Romans did not cover their walls in mosaics, they had frescoes painted on them (fishing scenes, the head of a woman with a crescent moon in the Sfax museum) or decorated them with ceramics.

Given the duration of Byzantine occupation in Tunisia, their artistic influence appears to have been limited. The only traces are the few churches, a few sections of walls, and a few forts. Many Byzantine buildings were later reoccupied by the Arabs. Certain Christian basilicas were transformed into mosques, and buildings like forts enlarged and remodelled from top to bottom.

Of the Byzantine forts whose style was kept intact, Kélibia fort perched on a hilltop at Cap Bon overlooking the town is quite remarkable. Amongst the Byzantine religious buildings intact are the palaeo-Christian Bellator and Vitalis churches in Sbeïtla-Sufetula with their magnificent baptism fonts decorated with mosaics.

Mosque architecture

Even though it is not explicitly stated in the Koran, the ban on representing living beings, whether human or animal, has become one of the dogmas of Muslim tradition over the centuries. Whilst this has deprived the Muslim world of sculpture and painting traditions, it has opened up a wide scope of activity for architects and decorative (or "minor") artists.

The *mosque* is the basic building for architects in Muslim countries (and not the palace, as in Western countries). Unlike other religions' sanctuaries, the mosque is not the "House of God" (as in Christian religion), nor a sacrificial temple (as it was for the Romans, Greeks and ancient Orientals). It is essentially a meeting place for collective prayer (indeed, the mosque is called *djami* or *jamaa* in Arabic, which means "meeting place"). Prayers are recited in the interior courtyard and in a covered room. The latter is a *hypostyle room* (the roof is supported by columns) with a flat roof, a *minbar* (pulpit), and a *mihrab* (a niche which indicates the direction of Mecca).

The original model was the Prophet Mohammed's house built in Medina in 622. This very simple house was built on one level, with a large interior courtyard and enclosed by high walls. The Prophet had an awning supported by palm trunks erected along one of these walls to protect the worshippers from the sun during prayers. Over the centuries this initial schema has been modified many times and become more complex with the addition of numerous clusters of buildings including lodgings for visitors or students, classrooms for the Koranic schools and universities, and even restaurants and *mida* washrooms (where worshippers perform the ritual ablutions).

In addition to mosques, architects designed a whole series of religious buildings: *medersas* (Koranic colleges), *zawiyyas* (headquarters of the Muslim brotherhoods), *marabouts* or *koubas* (tombs or mausoleums of saints). They also designed civil buildings – palaces (*dar*), patricians' homes (the *menzels* of Djerba), caravanserais (*fondouks*), public baths (*hammams*), etc. – and military buildings: monastery-fortresses (*ribat*), fortified villages (*ksour*), and citadels (*kasbah*).

All of these were based on the model of the mosque's high-ceiling rooms with colonnades, interior courtyards with galleries, and refined abstract decorations (stuccos, carved wood, polychrome ceramic tiling).

Byzantine and Persian touches

Right from the early centuries of the Hegira (the Islamic era, which begins in the year 622), the initial model was elaborated by outside influences as the Arab conquerors, who did not exercise building arts yet, employed local Greek, Coptic, Persian, Byzantine, and Spanish architects. Used to building the vast Byzantinium Christian basilicas, these architects introduced the imposing dimensions of certain mosques, and added the domes and the high towers (minarets) used to call worshippers to prayer, just like the bell towers and campaniles on Western churches.

Also inspired by the intrinsically oriental refinement of the Sassanid Persian empire buildings, they excelled in making luxurious decors, in particular the *muqarnas* (stuccos in the form of stalactites, honeycombs, or beehives which decorate the vaults of mosques and palaces).

The Kairouan model

The first Muslim building erected in Tunisia was the *Kairouan Central Mosque* which was built by the Arab emir Uqba ibn Nafi in 670. The original style is said to have resembled that of the buildings constructed in Damascus under the Umayyad caliphate (from 661 to 750), which was strongly influenced by Western Christian architecture. As the mosque was twice destroyed in the 8th century and entirely rebuilt during the Abbasid caliphate, however, it bears the mark of the Abbasid caliphs who were highly influenced by Sassanid Persian art and not by Hellenistic western art. It has nonetheless kept some of the characteristics of the *Umayyad* style, notably the vast dimensions of their religious buildings (like the Byzantine basilicas), the domes and minaret (that they were the first to build), the vast interior courtyard with arches, and the prayer room with several naves.

In the 9th century, the Kairouan Central Mosque was rebuilt according to the *Abbasids* of Baghdad's style (750-1258). Like the Persians, the Abbasids preferred brick to the freestone used by the *Umayyads*, and built square minarets with several floors which looked like the *ziggurat* towers of Babylon.

The prayer room was built on a T-shaped plan with a large central nave intersecting the transverse naves at right angles, leading to a large alley running alongside the wall of the *mihrab* (niche indicating the direction of Mecca). This T-shaped plan is characteristic of most of the mosques built afterwards throughout the Maghreb.

The Kairouan mosque prayer room is huge: there are 16 naves leading off the central nave which is delimited by a forest of columns.

Visitors cannot fail to notice the defensive aspect of the early mosques with their thick blind walls, powerful buttresses, crenels, and huge solid doors capable of resisting a siege. Indeed, these mosques were built by the armies fighting the "holy war" (*jihad*) during the long period of Islamic expansion.

Whilst the *Abbasids* were still reigning in Baghdad, the *Fatimids* (a dynasty created in Tunisia by Obeid Allah in 862 and which spread successively to Kairouan, Mahdia and finally to Cairo in Egypt in 970) instigated some architectural novelties. Mosques were built with several domes and groined vaults (a precursor to the Gothic intersecting ribs). Porches jutting out from the main body resembling triumphal arches were imported from Persia, like the one on the Mahdia Central Mosque, and stucco decorations – *muqarnas*, or "stalactites" – were added to the vaults.

As Turkish influence spread in Tunisia at the end of the 16th century, the Turks contributed to further architectural changes. Architecture became increasingly refined over the centuries, and the mosque's silhouette more and more elegant with its decorated domes and slender minarets which evolved from being square-shaped to octagonal to cylindrical. The minarets were built with several floors and balconies decorated with ceramics and stuccos, and supported by stalactite corbels (protruding consoles) with highly intricate designs.

A gem of a mosque

The decoration in the mosques became increasingly rich, with stucco strips covered in arabesque calligraphy, archivolts with stalactites and marble panelling.

The Sidi Mahrez mosque in Tunis

*Tunisia is home to a number of ancient mosques,
one of the most beautiful of which
is the Kairouan mosque.
Initially built in the 7th century,
it was then expanded in the 9th century.*

(1675) shows signs of Turkish influence. Apart from the minaret which is square, it has a series of domes and joining half domes.

A number of the little provincial mosques look like cubist sculptures, for example the gem of a mosque in the Kef (the Sidi Bou Makhlouf mosque), or those on Djerba Island, which quite ingeniously play on the cube shape, the half cylinder and the sphere (one of the best examples is the little Mahboubine mosque on the Isle of Djerba).

Medersas (Koranic universities), which were also built according to the standard original mosque plan, sprung up all over the Muslim world as of 1064 when the Nizzamiyya Koranic university was officially founded in Baghdad. Built round a central courtyard, the *medersa* has large open classrooms and numerous rooms for housing the students. If it is not next to a mosque (like the *medersas* of the Zitouna Central Mosque in Tunis), it also has prayer rooms. It is not unusual for the *medersa* to be associated with a *zawiyya* (a saint's mausoleum), like the "Barber's mosque" in Kairouan.

Towns and fortified buildings

The arrival of the Arabs in the 7th century did not bring peace to Tunisia, and the architecture of the time bears the mark of this troubled climate. The ancient towns (*medinas*) and villages were surrounded by high walls with towers and thick gates (*bab*). The beautiful Sfax, Sousse and Kairouan old medinas sheltered behind their high walls are especially stunning, and have been listed by UNESCO. The Medina in Tunis no longer has its surrounding walls, but the beautiful doors are still intact, for example the Bab el Bahar.

Forts and citadels (*kasbahs*) also sprung up and now adorn the landscape with their medieval silhouettes (for example the Kef kasbah perched on a hilltop).

Along with the other wonders of defensive architecture are the *ribats* (fortified monasteries) which make Sousse and Monastir so charming.

Houses and stores were also protected against possible attacks. The Djerba *menzels*, the master's house set in the middle of the farm land, look like little fortresses thanks to their blind walls and square turrets.

The roofs of these roughcast whitewashed buildings are a succession of barrel vaults and little domes, which fulfil the practical function of keeping the interior cool for the inhabitants (indeed, these vaults and domes provide a much larger radiating surface than flat roofs, and thus reflect many of the sunrays thereby providing excellent thermal insulation). Moreover, the *menzels* often have an impluvium in the interior courtyard for capturing rain water, a rare commodity in these regions. Given that they are also farms, they usually have granaries and are near to oil presses or an area for thrashing the grain.

Fondouks (or caravanserais), which were resting places for travellers and caravaneers, are also a part of this defensive architecture.

Built according to the layout of primitive mosques, they are vast buildings with a heavy door that leads into a square courtyard with a gallery. On the ground floor are stores for merchandise and stables for the animals (dromedaries, horses, donkeys and mules), whereas the men stayed in the rooms upstairs reached via the big staircase in the courtyard.

There is sometimes a well in the middle of the yard. Some fondouks have a mosque inside. Try to visit the "fondouk des Français" in the Tunis medina, and the Houmt Souk fondouks in Djerba.

Refined houses and palaces

Civil architecture is not always defensive, as can be seen from the innumerable houses and palaces dotted around the country. Each region has its own style.

The style found in the Tozeur medina is both remarkable and typical. The builders, who were not necessarily architects, but had inborn taste, built superb houses experimenting with decors of bricks laid in relief. Muslim oriental refinement is particularly well illustrated by the Tunisian palaces (*dar*). From Tunis to Sfax, Sousse, Hammamet and Sidi Bou Saïd, patios with their galleries and fountains, and the cool rooms surmounted by domes are hidden away in these houses far from the indiscreet eyes of the passersby.

Inside, all forms of decoration blend together harmoniously: the mosaics on the floor, the small ceramic tiles with floral motifs on the walls, and the columns supporting carved capitals and stuccoed arcatures which look just like plaster lace all around the courtyard.

The coffered ceilings of the rooms that open out onto the patio are nearly always painted and engraved, and the windows have stained glass or cast iron grills.

Each room has a specific function. There are the suites of the head of the family, and his wife. These include living and reception rooms with seats covered in rich materials and cushions, cabinets and desks made out of precious painted or carved wood and incrusted with mother-of-pearl or ivory.

In the bedrooms, an alcove is formed by a carved and painted wooden bed end which are increasingly found in the museums. More modest rooms are assigned to the kitchen and sometimes to the family hammam.

Some palaces have been converted into museums and thus are open to the public, for example the *dar* Abdallah in the Tunis medina, the *dar* Jallouli in the Sfax medina and the *dar* Chraiet in Tozeur.

Copied from the Romans, *hammams* – or "Turkish baths" – have spread throughout all the Muslim countries, perpetuating the ancient public baths. Islam brought these baths back into vogue as, given that prayers must be preceded by the ritual ablutions, mosques were often equipped with fountains, then washrooms, and eventually with the more sophisticated hammams.

Nowadays, a lot of hammams are essentially public baths and do not have a specifically religious function. People come here quite simply to wash, to keep fit (if there are saunas), and to meet their neighbours and friends of the same sex (mixed hammams are forbidden, except when adults are accompanied by young children). There are some fine examples of these Turkish baths in the Tunis medina (the hammam Kachachine and the hammam on Ed Deheb street).

The little ceramic tiles which form an integral part of the architecture decorating the walls of mosques, palaces and even the most humble homes, are still made by the Nabeul potters.

Amongst their finest inspirations are the shiny ceramic tiles with metallic glints that were the pride of the Syrian craftsmen.

Some tiles necessitate meticulous work, for example the *zelliges,* which are ceramic panels made out of several carved parts assembled to form geometric motifs. The "Barber's mosque" in Kairouan has some particularly beautiful ceramic wall decorations.

The potters' art also served in making widely varying types of decorated terracotta plates and dishes. The Bardo museum in Tunis has a beautiful collection of this Muslim pottery, notably plates from the Abbasid and Aghlabid period (9th-10th centuries).

The *muqarnas* (honeycomb or "beehive" stalactites) invented in Persia and Mesopotamia, are one kind of decoration typical in buildings all over the Muslim world. This veritable lacework carved in the stucco is found in mosques, palaces and any other type of Muslim buildings.

Some superb examples can be seen when travelling around Tunisia, for example in the Bey's Bardo Palace, which has been turned into a museum (the Virgil room), in the palaces of wealthy families (*dar* Abdallah in the medina and *dar* Jallouli in the Sfax medina), and in the little Sidi Bou Maklouf mosque in Kef.

Colonial architecture, modern architecture

The French, who flocked to Tunisia after the Protectorate treaty was signed in the last century, left several specimens of "colonial architecture" behind.

The most typical buildings of this period are the white municipal theatre on H. Bourguiba Avenue in Tunis, whose facade supports an immense group of sculpted Nereids; the hotel Majestic on Avenue de Paris; the Sfax Townhall, etc. Of the religious buildings, the Tunis Cathedral and the former Carthage Basilica on Byrsa hill (now converted into an exhibition centre) bear witness to this period.

In the 20th century, many Tunisian architects passionately drew on the great Islamic tradition for building modern mosques, palaces (in particular the presidential palace in Carthage), and many other diverse types of buildings ranging from villas, office blocks to large hotels.

Holiday resort architecture, which is respectful of the tradition, usually works very well: the half-cylindrical vaulted roofs of the Port El Kantaoui marina near to Sousse, inspired by the granary and menzel roofs in traditional south Tunisian villages, is a particularly good example.

The style of the hotels in Zarzis (the "Oamarit") and Djerba (the "Royal Garden Palace", the "Yadis", the "Djerba Plaza" and the "Menzel") with their bristling white domes, is in total harmony with the island's many little mosques (Houmt Souk, Mahboubine). Some look like real palaces, for example the "Yati Beach" hotel in Djerba, the "Dar Oasis" in Kébili and the "El Borj" and "El Mehdi" hotels in Mahdia, or the new "Dar Chraiet" hotel in Tozeur which is made out of pale coloured marble with a peristyle, Moorish cafe, etc.

The "Club Sangho" in Tataouine, which is built on one floor and in the colours of the surrounding earth and hills (pink ochre and pinkish beige), and the hotel-palace in Tamerza make use of both the Matmata trogloditic architecture, and the ksour architecture of the Tataouine-Médenine region.

A few hotels have nonetheless completely broken away from the traditional style and have a resolutely modern architectural style, for example the "Hotel du Lac" in Tunis which is shaped like an inverted pyramid or ship's hull.

Minor arts

Glass painting, which was introduced by the Turks during the last

THE MOSQUE

■ *Mosques are usually set out according to the following model: high walls surround a vast interior courtyard (sahn), in the centre of which is a fountain. A gallery with colonnades and one or more naves runs along three of the walls. The prayer room (haram), which is wider than it is deep, opens out along the fourth wall and is built facing the east. The numerous columns divide the prayer room into several naves parallel to the wall of the mirhab (the niche indicating the qibla, or direction of Mecca). A minbar (pulpit) is situated near to the mihrab.*

The mosque has one or more minarets, which are tall square or cylindrical towers where the muezzin calls the worshippers to prayer five times a day. Several clusters of buildings have been added to the mosque over the centuries: libraries, the medersa study rooms (Koranic university), rooms for pilgrims, and even a restaurant and a hammam which make some mosques into huge centres of diverse activity in the heart of the town.

*All the beauty of Islamic architecture is expressed
in these studded doors and windows
with their Moorish arches, and in these interior patios
where little fountains usually bubble away.*

century, developed particularly in Sfax around the artist *Fériani*, one of the best late-19th century glass painters. Several artists still carry on this trade today. Islamic themes constitute the bulk of subject matter, but more recently picturesque little day-to-day scenes have also emerged as a theme.

The Bardo museum's Islamic department (in Tunis) and the small museums around the country devoted to Tunisian traditions (Dar Abdallah in the Tunis medina, Dar Jallouli in the Sfax medina, and Dar Chraiet in Tozeur) exhibit a large selection of these objects. Exhibitions include furniture, jewellery, trinkets, and day-to-day utensils, all of which are classed as the so-called minor, or decorative arts. There are also displays of clothes exquisitely embroidered with silver and gold, marquetry and artistic woodwork (screens, mirrors, chests, desks inlaid with ivory or mother-of-pearl), ancient glasswork, brasswork (teapots, trays, ewers, "daghar" chased and embossed copper cauldrons and braziers), ceremonial crockery, weapons, musical instruments, jewellery and even coins.

Tunisian music

"*Malouf*", the Arabic music of the Andalousian Muslims chased out of Spain, was imported to North Africa, and Tunisia in particular, at the end of the 15th century. It grew so popular that it became *the* Tunisian music par excellence, supplanting all other forms, to the extent that it was named "malouf", which means "that which is normal".

The small orchestras who play this music uses violins (*rbab*), lutes, sitars and drums. The music is plaintiff, sometimes insistent, and has a hint of Berber influence notably in the rhythms and the forms. It is generally made up of several different pieces or "*nouba*" (equivalent of the "suites" in Western music), which alternate poems, songs, preludes and instrumental breaks.

GUIDE TO ARCHITECTURAL TERMS

■ jamma: *mosque*
dar: *palace*
kouttab: *dome*
tourbet: *mausoleum*
zawiyya: *headquarters of a religious brotherhood*
ghorfa: *traditional granary*
menzel: *Djerba house*
ksar (ksour): *citadel (s)*
kasbah: *fortified village*
ribat: *fortified monastery*
mihrab: *niche in a mosque indicating the direction of Mecca*
minbar: *pulpit in a mosque*
medersa: *Koranic university*
fondouk: *caravanserai*
medina: *the old town*
bab: *city gate*

The music-loving Baron Erlanger, who had a passion for "malouf" and who lived in the Sidi Bou Saïd palace now converted into the Music museum, compiled all the rules and history of this music in six volumes. In the 1930s he set up an association called the "Rachidia", which is a veritable conservatory of Arabic and Andalousian music, where most of today's great musicians studied. Among them were the fourteen musicians and singers from the Tunis *El Azifet* ensemble, one of the rare, exclusively female orchestras in the Arab world. Led by Amina Srarfi, the *El Azifet* ensemble is inspired by the traditional Tunisian *malouf* and oriental *mouachah*.

Anouar Brahem, a lute (*oud*) player from Tunis who perpetuates tradition whilst also remaining open to Mediterranean influences, is currently one of the established stars of Tunisian music (his main recordings include "Barzakh" and "Conte de l'incroyable amour").

Berber and Punic scholars

The Carthaginian slave *Terence* (190-159 B.C.) remains one of the first great dramatic authors of Antiquity. This young captive sold to a Roman senator after whom he was named, Terence was freed and received an education which introduced him to the arts and literature. From the age of 24 until his death seven years later, he made a brief but brilliant career as a writer, leaving behind six wonderful dramatic comedies: *Andria, Hecyra, Heauton Timoroumenos, Eunuchus, Phormio,* and *Adelphoe.* Less concerned with inventing effects than his illustrious predecessor Plautus was, Terence was a master of psychological satire and the themes of his works were to later inspire the great French dramatist Molière.

After the fall of Punic Carthage, Roman Carthage was restored in the early years A.D. and quickly became a brilliant cultural forum in the Mediterranean. It was here that the poet *Manilius* came to light (during Tiberius's reign) as did the stoic philosopher *Cornutus* (in Claude and Nero's time).

The numerous private residences and the number of baths in North Africa's Roman towns built during the Roman Empire in the 2nd and 3rd centuries A.D., show that a very rich bourgeoisie existed. A great majority of this class were Berber. These families learnt Latin, and their children learnt it in the highly-reputed schools, like those in Cirta (Constantine), and Madaure in Algeria. They were particularly good students, as some of the best Latin writers of the time were of Berber origin, like *Apuleius*, author of *The Golden Ass* (or *The Metamorphoses*) and who lived from 125 to 170.

The famous rhetorician *Cornelius Fronto* from Cirta was more or less his contemporary (100-175). He was consul in 143 and the emperor Marcus Aurelius' preceptor. His eloquence was considered equal to that of Cicero. The poet *Terentius the Moor* (193-235) and the grammarian *Porphyry* also shone under the Severus emperors.

When Christianity came to North Africa, several thinkers and theologians made Carthage, Tunisia's first major capital, an influential intellectual and spiritual centre in the Maghreb and the whole of the Mediterranean basin, notably *Tertullian* (150/160-222 A.D), author of numerous essays (including *Apologeticum* and *Concerning Spectacles*), and *Saint Cyprian* (beginning of the 3rd century-258). *Saint Augustine* the philosopher, moralist and theologian (354-430 A.D.) was to become one of the greatest doctors of the Christian Church. His principal works include *Confessions* and *De Civitate Dei.*

With the Arabic conquest in the 7th century, Tunisia (*Ifriqyya*) gained new religious thinkers, like *Sahnoun* (777-854) whose *Recueil Majeur* written in the new spiritual centre of Kairouan is a reflection on the precepts of Islam. *Al Qaysi* (966-1045) also studied the Holy Book and proposed diverse exegeses. *Ibn Jazzar*, the doctor and author of pediatric treaties (died in 1067), the critics *Ibn Rachik* and *Ibn Charaf,* and the poet *Al Husri* also lived in Kairouan at the same time.

In the Middle Ages, the Berber historian *Ibn Khaldun* born in Tunis became famous (1332-1406). Inventor of sociology, he wrote the highly significant *Kitab al Ihar.* In *Muqaddimah,* an introduction to history he elaborated a method giving a scientific foundation to history. His much later heir was *Hassan Husni Abd el Wahab*, the 20th century author of historical, sociological and linguistic works (i.e.: *The History of Civilisation in Tunisia*).

Contemporary writers

At the end of the 19th century and during the 20th century, Tunisian literature underwent a veritable renaissance. Amongst the pioneers were *Tahar Haddad* (1901-1935), who became a renowned social essayist, and *Ali Douagi* (1909-1949), the realist and comic writer who satirized Tunisian society in his tales, poems and plays (*Le Périple des bars de la Méditerranée, La Rue des pieds teintés au henné*). *Abdelaziz Al Arouô* (1898-1971) is another contemporary story-teller.

Other important writers in the realist vein include the talented *Mohamed Salah Jabri*, who sung the praises of the working class, and *Béchir Khraief* (born in 1917 in Nefta), author of *Régimes de dattes* and *Khlifa le teigneux* (made into a film by the director Hamouda Ben Halima). *Aboul Kacem Chabbi*, who died when he was 25 years old (1909-1934), was an innovator in Arabic poetry. Considered to be the "father of modern Tunisian poetry", he sadly left behind too few works. His *Chant de la vie* served as a model for many other writers including *Mohamed Laroussi Metoui* and *Oman As Sayyidi Al Qaribi*.

After the Second World War, poverty raged in this country devastated by the conflict. Moreover, Tunisia was still a French Protectorate. More and more Tunisian intellectuals began to denounce this poverty and started calling for independence. This realist, militant trend regrouped French language writers like *Albert Memmi* (born in 1920), author of the novel La *Statute de sel* and essayist (*The Colonizer and The Colonized*), *Hachémi Baccouche*, novelist, playwright and essayist (*Ma foi demeure, La Dame de Carthage, Baudruche, Décolonisation, grandeur et servitudes de l'anticolonialisme*) and *Mohamed Noômane*. As independence in 1956 did little to change the condition of the poorest, the realist literary trend became more critical in denouncing the bureaucracy's inequalities and oppression. This trend is represented by the writers *Mustapha Fersi, Rached Hamzaoui*, author of *L'Homme qui a bu la rivière*, and *Mohammed Salah Jabri*.

Poetry was still very much alive after the war. *Habib Zannad* (born in 1946) described his unease and the people's poverty in a straightforward language. *Tahar Hammani* (born in 1947) is influenced by the French poet Prévert.

Numerous writers began experimenting to renew language, for example *Ezzedine Madani* (born in 1938), author of *Mythes*. For his part, *Salah Garmadi* was attracted to surrealism (*Le Cireur*) and *Samir Al Ayyadi's* writing (born in 1947), took on a dreamlike quality (he wrote *Vacarme du silence*). The short story *Plat de kaftagi avec oeuf* by *Mahmoud Tounsi* (born in 1944) was close to the French "Nouveau Roman" tradition.

Other writers in the new generation include *Abdelwaheb Meddeb* (*Talismans, Phantasia*), *Mustapha Tlili* (*La Rage aux tripes, La Montagne du lion*), *Chems Nadir* (*Silence des sémaphores, Le Livre des Révélations*), *Héla Beji* (*L'Oeil du jour*), *Fawzi Mellah* (*Le Conclave des pleureuses, Elyssa, la reine vagabonde*), *Tahar Bekri* (*Le Chant du roi errant*), and *Marco Koskas* (*Balace Bouloun*).

Whereas *Mahmoud Messaâdi* gave Tunisian theatre its first tragedy, *Le Barrage*, the prolific novelist and storyteller *Ali Douagi* enriched the Tunisian dramatic repertory with about fifteen plays including *Au Pays de Tararani*, (adapted to the screen by *Férid Boughédir* in 1972). *Habib Boularès* developed a Shakespearian vein in *Mourad III* and *Le Temps du Bourak*. *Moncef Soumi* and *Ezzedine Madani* (the latter wrote *La Révolte des Zendji* and *Al Hallaj*) argued for plays that addressed a wider audience. Both were influenced by Brecht.

The New Tunisian Theatre Collective set up by *Mohamed Driss*, director of the TNT (Théâtre National de Tunis), put on productions of *L'Instruction et la pluie*, and *L'Averse des Greniers*. Another theatrical event was *Fadhel Jaibi* and the comic actor *Nahdi's* satirical play *Arab*.

From calligraphy to figurative art

As the depiction of living beings is prohibited in Islam, in the past Muslim artists took inspiration from writing and, as of the 9th century – during the reign of the Abbasids from Baghdad – invented sumptuous calligraphy based on arabesques composed of curves and interlacing forming stylized plant motifs.

Calligraphy is very frequently used to decorate sacred books and also the walls of religious buildings (mosques, medersas, zawiyyas, etc.). When this is the case, the abstract forms are carved in the stone and wood, or painted on the ceramic tiles.

Nowadays, Muslim calligraphy is as highly reputed as that of the traditional Japanese and Chinese artists. The calligraphy of the famous Kairouan Korans can be admired in the Bardo museum in Tunis, notably in the 11th century *"Blue Koran"* in which the suras are written in golden letters on blue parchment. A collection of *tiraz* can also be seen on display in the museum, i.e. material decorated with calligraphy that dates from the Fatimid epoch (10th-11th century) and which was bought in Egypt. The material bears Koranic inscriptions and also praises to the prince of the time. In the museum of popular traditions set up in the *dar* Jallouli, an ancient palace in the Sfax medina, there are also several specimens of this calligraphy in different writings (Thoulthi, Naskhi, Farsi, Reqa'a, Diwani and Kufic). The Turkish *firman* (edict written on parchment) with its particularly decorative arabesque letters is especially beautiful.

Under the French Protectorate at the end of the 19th century, the Tunisian painter *Ben Osman* and the portrait artist *Hedi Kayachi*, who was attached to the Bey court, turned to figurative painting. An art gallery was therefore set up in 1894 displaying academic style works exalting the Orient as imagined by European aesthetes, and picturesque scenes of Bedouin life. In about 1912, the Tunisian realist painter *Jilani Abdul Wahab*, student of the Pinchart atelier, came into vogue.

During the 1920s, the traditionalist trend was even stronger, and several painters called for a return to the ancient aesthetic of Persian miniatures and painting on glass. The majority of artists stifled under the canons of "orientalist" colonial art and tried to depict the day-to-day life of the Tunisian masses. They were influenced by the major international art movements like expressionism and fauvism which emphasized simple forms and the purity of colour. This movement is represented by painters like *Yahia Turki, Ali Ben Salem, Ammar Rarhat, Azouz Ben Raïs,* and *Hatem El Mekki*.

After the Second World War, Tunisian artists continued to exploit popular and social themes, as was the case with *Zoubeir Turki*, who was trained in European art ateliers. The taste for Persian miniatures persisted with *Gorgi* and *Ben Abdallah*, who developed a whole dreamlike realm. *Ali Bellagha* painted modern-style still lifes, *Hédi Turki* was drawn to abstract art, and *Amara Debèche* stood out for the quality of his sketches.

In the Sixties and Seventies, the plastic arts took off massively. Trained in the major European ateliers, the younger artists brought back a whole range of styles and showed great boldness in their expression. The most talented abstract artists included *Chebil, Chakroun, Rafik Kamel, Aloulou* and *Azzabi*. *Lakhdar* and *Ben Amor* distinguished themselves in the post-surrealist movement. The work of *Sehili, Soufi* and *Saïdi* stood out in the lyrical and colourist trends. *Gmach*, on the other hand, is better situated amongst the naturalists.

There is a more recent movement which has given a new lease of life to traditional Islamic art. *Nejib Belkhoha, Nja Mahdaoui* and particularly *Rachid Koraïchi* who is Algerian but lives and works in Sidi Bou Saïd have begun using calligraphy in their works again. Fauvist and expressionist influence are still most evident in the works of *Mensi, Zaouch* and *Jaber*.

The highly original painter *Gouider Triki* lives and works in Lesdine on Cap Bon. Once he had completed his studies at the Beaux-Arts school in Tunis, he went to study engraving in Paris. His work was recently exhibited during the "Rencontres africaines" show at the Institut du Monde Arabe in Paris in 1994. His brightly coloured, extremely turbulent paintings are full of strange figures and objects that look like they have been dreamed up by a modern-day Jérôme Bosch. Women with butterfly wings, men with bull or cock heads, and fish-snakes whirl in a wild dance.

Other talent painters include: *Hedi Labbane* (whose works are full of poetic melancholy), *Ahmed Hajeri* (naive style), *Mensiet Zaouch*, and the engravers *Brahim Dahak* (author of stunning bestiaries) and *Ben Meftah*.

The plastic artists *Selmi* and *Marzouk* are the foremost contemporary sculptors.

Thriving cinema

Tunisian cinema, which made its debut in the inter-war period, is increasingly recognised on the international front. The first pioneer filmmaker *Samama Chikly* made the short film *Zohra* in 1919, followed a few years later by the first Tunisian feature film *The Girl from Carthage* (*Aïn el-Ghezal*, 1924) a dramatic tale of a young girl's forced marriage. In 1927, *Slouma Abderrazak* founded the first Tunisian film distribution company *Tunis Films*.

During the same period, French colonial cinema dominated the Tunisian market, targeting the urban elites. These conditions made it hard for Tunisian cinema to find the necessary means to develop, and only a few amateurs – or a few geniuses – made the too rare films which only reached a very limited audience at the time, as was the case with *Abdelaziz Hassine*'s feature film *Tergui* shot in 1935.

In the 1930s, the Tunisian public developed a taste for going to the cinema and were avid fans of the first imported Egyptian films. The actors of these melodramas tended to sing more than act, like in *Widad*, with Oum Kalsoum. The popularity of this type of film encouraged Tunisian directors to use the same formula, and in 1937, the musical *The Madman of Kairouan* (*Majnun al-Kairouan*) was released. Otherwise, up until the end of the Second World War, little else changed in the world of Tunisian cinema.

It was not until 1964 that the first cinema club opened in Tunisia. In the same year the ephemeral *Centre du cinéma tunisien* was also created, which produced a few documentaries then disappeared. Four years later *Tahar Cheriaa*, an Arabic teacher mad on cinema, set up the Tunisian Federation of Ciné-Clubs, which was to remain the most important network in Africa. Most of the contemporary film directors' careers were born in these ciné-clubs.

In 1954, the creation of the Tunisian cinematheque helped increase the number of people interested in film, and thereby led to the setting up of the first film magazine "Nawadi-Cinéma" in 1958, whose editor was naturally Tahar Cheriaa. In the meantime, Tunisia gained independence and began to timidly take interest in developing its film industry. In 1958, the authorities chose the safe option of co-producing Jacques Baratier's film *Goha* which was shot in Tunisia and in which Claudia Cardinale and Omar Sharif made their debuts.

In 1961, *Omar Khlifi* made his first short films *A Page of Our History*, and *Uncle Mosbah Goes to Town*. At the same time a school of documentary film was born with the work of directors like *Ben Milad, Harzallah, Mechri, Ben Salem,* and *El Bahi*. The following year the Secretary of Cultural Affairs and Information helped the young Tunisian cinema by putting art centre screens at their disposal.

Tunisia became determined to gain full independence in the cinematic domain. It became a pioneer amongst the African countries when, in 1962, it organised a boycott of the major distributors of foreign films who monopolised the Tunisian movie theatres. For the Tunisian filmmakers, it was a matter of at last being able to show their work to mass audiences in their country. This firm stance was backed up by the Tunisian Ministry of Culture's decision to set up the SATPEC. This company, which became a model for a number of African companies, now controls film production and distribution in Tunisia.

In the years that followed, many events took place on the cinematographic front. "Le Globe", Tunis's first art house cinema, opened in 1965, and it was here that the first "Journées Cinématographiques de Carthage" film festival was held in 1966. At the same time the Tunisian television began its first broadcasts, and in 1967 the "Tunisian Cinecitta", an industrial film complex, was inaugurated at Gammarth in north-eastern Tunis.

Film production was also prolific at the end of the Sixties. In 1966, Omar Khlifi's film *Al Fajr* (*The Dawn*) opened a new chapter in Tunisian cinema. In 1968 he made *Al Moutammared* (*The Rebel*). In 1969, the following films were released: *Murky Death* (*La Mort trouble*) by *Férid Boughedir*, *Sous la pluie de l'autome* by *Hamed Khechine*, *Une si simple histoire* by *Férid Boughedir*, and *Fellagas* by *Omar Khlifi*. During the same period, the "Fédération panafricaine des cinéastes" (FEPACI) was created, regrouping both North and Black African directors.

By this time, Tunisian cinema was well established, and included a whole variety of genres ranging from comedy (*Ali Mansour's Two Thieves in Madness*) to the political (*Ridha Behi's Sun of the Hyenas*, which deals with colonisation by the tourists; *Mahmoud Ben Mahmoud's Crossings*, which deals with the East-West cultural clash), to poetic forms (*Naceur Khemir's The Drifters*) to sociological analyses (*Nacer Ktari's The Ambassadors,* and *Taïeb Louichi's The Shadow of the Earth*, a chronicle of a nomadic family's daily life) and finally to the psychological (*Nouri Bouzid's Man of Ashes*, which deals with sexuality, and notably homosexuality).

Very recently, Tunisian women have made a stunning entrance to the film world as directors. *Moufida Tlatli's* first feature film *The Silences of the Palace*, pulled off a great challenge, and the film won the "Quinzaine des Réalisateurs" special prize at the Cannes film festival in 1994.

A TRUE FILM ENTHUSIAST

■ *Tahar Cheriaa, born in Sayada near to Sousse in 1927, is a true film enthusiast, and could even be called "the father of Tunisian cinema". Originally a teacher, for decades he fought to develop the seventh Art in Tunisia with unerring energy.*
First of all organiser of the Sfax film clubs, he then ran the FTCC (Fédération Tunisienne des Ciné-Clubs) from 1960 to 1968.
In 1968 he set up the film magazine "Nawadi-Cinéma", which he ran until 1970, and was also editor of "Almasrah Wa Cinéma" (1965-1967).
In 1966 he founded the "Journées Cinématographiques de Carthage" film festival (J.C.C) which enables many African film directors to show their films to specialised audiences.
Tahar Cheriaa, who was also a film consultant at UNESCO and the ACCT (Agence de Coopération Culturelle et Technique), has recently taken his very well earned retirement.

*The Tourbet el Bey in the Tunis medina
is a superb mausoleum
where the tombs
of the royal families are located.*

prehistory and history

■ Africa is now considered to be the birthplace of humanity as it is in Eastern and Southern Africa that our very distant ancestors the *Australopithecus* or the "southern apes" appeared on earth 6.5 million years ago (becoming extinct over 5 million years later). Like apes, they wandered about the savannah in small groups and fed on plants. As they did not know how to build dwellings, they took shelter in trees and rocks. Although they were biped, they more often ran along on all fours.

We owe the invention of the first tools to them, however. These included splinters of quartz and roughly hewed pebbles out of which they made cutting tools (*pebble culture*).

Before the Australopithecus became extinct, *Homo habilis* appeared in Africa 4 million years ago. This species, which had great creative intelligence, may be our first real ancestor, as Homo habilis knew how to build huts and how to make a whole range of tools out of stone and bones (hence the name "habilis", which means skilled). This very first man, who disappeared 1.5 million years ago, was not a vegetarian like the Australopithecus, but omnivorous, hunting for fish and meat (eaten raw). In order to hunt, Homo habilis built weapons (carved stones) and scrapers for cutting up large game (elephants or hippopotami) into large chunks which could then be carried back to their camps.

Recent excavation works in the Sahara and North Africa have brought very ancient stone tools to light in Morocco, Algeria and Tunisia (Aïn Brimba, near to Kébili in the Djérid). These include hewed stones which date back to over 2 million years, and were probably made by the Homo habilis.

Fire helps
the upright man

About 1.9 million years ago, a new kind of hominid, the *Homo erectus* (upright man) began to move further afield from the initial homelands in Eastern and Southern Africa. Probably a descendant of the Homo habilis, the Homo erectus set out to conquer the whole world. At the same time, knowledge took a leap forwards as they learnt to make fire, which meant they could survive the cold, cook and conserve food, and frighten off fierce animals.

Like their predecessors, the Homo erectus were hunters, and excelled in carving and chipping stone, ivory and bone. They invented and improved tool forms, notably the *handaxe* – large stone blades that were either flat, olive shaped, heart shaped or pointed – *trihedrons* and *small axes*...

The Atlas man
in North Africa

In North Africa, traces of the Homo erectus have been found in Ternifine in Algeria (*Atlanthrope*, or the "Atlas man", about 600 to 700,000 years ago) and in Casablanca, Morocco (150,000 years ago).

No Homo erectus bones have been discovered in Tunisia, but many tools from this period have been found in the south (Gafsa, Metlaoui, Redeyef) and in the west (at Sidi Zine near to Kef, and in Koum el Majène near to Jendouba). At that time, Tunisia had a hot and humid tropical climate, and the country was covered in forests and swamps which served as sanctuaries for the large mammals like rhinoceri, elephants, zebras, and numerous antelopes. What is even more surprising is that the Mediterranean was much shallower during the Paleolithic era, and the site of towns like Sousse and Sfax were right inland, over 100 km away from the sea! Early man could walk across the Sicilian Straits, which explains many of the similarities between the people and cultures of northern Tunisia and the Italian islands during the prehistoric period.

Whereas the Homo erectus disappeared shortly after the Middle Paleolithic (about 100 to 200,000 years ago), *Neanderthal man* evolved. Not having mastered rearing or farming yet, the Neanderthals lived essentially from gathering, fishing and hunting, and used animal hides to make clothes and tents.

Another major innovation was that the Neanderthals carried out complex funeral rites. They placed corpses in their caves in the "foetus position", sometimes covered with ochre powder, and then covered them with flat stones and then soil. They also placed offerings of arms and food near to the tombs, which indicates that they believed in life after death.

In Tunisia, ten or so sites excavated in the south (in the Gabès and Gafsa regions) and in the west (Kef and Kassérine regions), have led to the discovery of *Mousterian* flint tools (little hand axes, scrapers, blades, etc.) and animal bones.

In El Guettar, about twenty kilometres south-east of Gafsa, the strange "monument to the spirit of the spring", or "*Hermaion*" was found *(see inset)*.

Flint blades and strips

At the end of the Middle Paleolithic (about 35,000 years B.C.), several specifically Maghrebi civilisations existed, namely the Aterian, the Ibero-Maurusian and the Capsian cultures.

The *Aterian civilisation*, which emerged between 35 and 25,000 years B.C, takes its name from the Bir el Ater site in Algeria. This civilisation, which is present in the coastal regions of Tunisia (Bizerte, Cap Bon, Monastir, Gabès) is characterised by the production of flint tools with a small stem (peduncle).

In about 20,000 B.C., a short "*strip civilisation*" (little 5 cm flint strips with a chipped edge) existed in southern Tunisia. This was the precursor of North Africa's wonderful Ibero-Maurusian civilisation (18,000 to 8,000 B.C.).

Contrary to what the name implies, the *Ibero-Maurusian civilisation* did not flourish on the Iberian Peninsula, but in the Maghreb, and was marked by a great abundance of flint blade tools with chipped edges and several bone tools.

The inhabitants of this civilisation were the *Homo sapiens*, whose anatomy was identical to that of modern man. They lived in a colder and more humid climate, lived in caves, and hunted for large game: antelopes, wild boar, wild cows. They used to chisel their upper incisors to beautify themselves.

The *Mechta el Arbi* type of Homo sapiens (named after the site near to Sétif in Algeria), buried their dead in the foetus position and covered their graves with large flat stones.

In Tunisia, traces of the Ibero-Maurusian civilisation have been found particularly on the north coast between Tabarka and Bizerte (the Ouchtata site), as other vestiges on the east coast have been submerged.

Thousands of tools, most of which are flint blades, have been dug up in the Nefza region and at Ouchtata.

The unusual *Capsian civilisation* developed in Tunisia from 7,000 to 4,500 B.C. It takes its name from Capsa (the former name for Gafsa), as a great deal of sites have been recorded here. Most of them are "*snaileries*" as the Capsian people ate snails, the shells of which have been found in great heaps near their dwellings.

The ashes of burnt stones and animal bones have also been found, along with thousands of tools (blades and strips, scrapers, burins) and jewellery (necklaces made out of rings of ostrich eggs). The Capsians were also artists as they used to carve highly stylised women's heads out of limestone, and carved pieces of ostrich eggs.

Only one skeleton of a Capsian man has been exhumed in the whole of Tunisia. It was found at Aïn Metherchem, near to Kassérine, surrounded by fineries (rings of ostrich eggs).

The Neolithic revolution

The *Neolithic* period (or *polished stone age*), which was the last period of prehistory, brought about a veritable revolution in our early ancestors' life styles, as they began to settle and form the first villages. The first domestic animals appeared, and man discovered farming (cereals), pottery, and metalwork, which enabled them to make metal tools, weapons and jewellery, in addition to more sophisticated stone tools (grindstones, arrow tips, axes and polished stones).

There are countless Neolithic sites scattered all over Tunisia. One of the most important sites is on the Zarzis peninsula, where another twenty or so sites have been recorded around the el Meleh sebkhet. The people here were fishermen. They may also have been navigators

– the first in their history – as tools made out of obsidian have been discovered in the region whereas this stone is only found in the southern islands of Italy.

Whilst the brilliant ancient Egyptian civilisation flourished for several thousands years B.C., little is known about the North African people as there are no, or few, traces of their lives. They were probably the descendants of the herders and farmers of the Neolithic period. Numerous invasions took place at this time, and the indigenous Maghrebi people intermixed with people from all of the Mediterranean basin (from Sicily, Sardinia, Italy, Spain, Libya, Egypt), forming a new people, the *Berbers* (see the chapter "the People" earlier).

It was still the proto-historic period (end of the Neolithic era) 2 to 3,000 years B.C. in Tunisia. In both the Maghreb and Europe, the *megalithic era* was beginning during which huge earth barrows served as tombs, lone stones were stood upright (*menhirs*), placed in circles (*cromlechs*) or laid flat as tables (*dolmens*).

In the Maghreb, troglodytic dwellings were also hollowed out in the cliffs (*haouanet*).

In the 12th century B.C., the Phoenicians from Tyre (in the south of modern day Lebanon) set up a whole series of trading posts in the Mediterranean, especially in Spain where they exported tin to the whole of the Orient. In Tunisia, they founded the port of Sousse (Hadrumete) in the 9th century B.C.

Legend has it that in 814 B.C., Elissa – or Dido – threatened by her brother Pygmalion, the king of Tyre, who had just killed her husband Sychaeus, went into exile in Tunisia. There she founded the "new capital" (Qart Hadasht), which later became Carthage. This trading post quickly gained dominance over the other older Tyrian posts like Utica and Thysdrus.

From the 8th to 3rd centuries B.C., Carthage became the first naval power of the Mediterranean basin. The Carthaginians settled in Sicily, Sardinia, Corsica, Spain and Africa.

Their principal enemies during this period were the Greeks whom they almost completely ousted from the western Mediterranean. When Tyre fell to Alexander the Great in 332, Carthage no longer owed anything to its former country.

In 311, the Carthaginians sieged the town of Syracuse ruled by the tyrant Agathocles. As they thought they had defeated him once and for all, they did not prevent Agathocles from escaping. Driven by his mad recklessness, Agathocles rose his army, took to the sea and landed on Cap Bon in Tunisia, where he burnt all his ships to prevent his troops from entertaining any idea of retreating. He then took his turn in sieging Carthage, ended up being defeated and returned to Sicily laden with war spoils.

This episode took on great significance in the Mediterranean world particularly for the Romans who took good note. They would soon conclude that Carthage's power was like that of an idol with feet of clay.

Rome against Carthage

Having completed its conquest of Italy in 272, Rome (founded in 753 B.C.), was ready for new battles to continue its expansion in the Mediterranean basin. It was therefore inevitable that it would soon come up against the Carthaginian empire.

The Romans needed a pretext for going to war, however. They found it in 264 B.C. with the Mamertini affair. The Mamertini, who were brigands from Italy, took over Messina in Sicily. As a result, Hieron, the tyrant of Syracuse, and the Carthaginians were hunting them down. The Mamertini turned to the Romans for help, which was a godsend for them. The Roman Senate immediately sent the legions. Led by Appius Claudius Caudex, they liberated Messina and forced Hieron to sign a peace treaty.

The Roman army stayed in Sicily to face the Carthaginians. This was the beginning of the first Punic war (264-146 B.C.).

In 262, the Romans conquered almost all of Sicily. The Carthaginians therefore began a sea offensive by organising a blockade in the Messina Straits to cut the Roman army in Sicily off from the rest of Italy.

The Roman land army was thus forced to turn itself into a navy. The Senate quickly took the decision to

*The immense columns surmounting the Antonine baths
built near to Carthage in the 2nd century A.D.
give an indication of this monument's majestic nature.
The baths were amongst the largest
in the Roman world at the time.*

build a fleet and recruited crews. They were in such a hurry that the future sailors practised rowing on dry land! Rome benefitted from the experience of its Etruscan, Volsci, Southern Greek, and Syracusian allies, all of whom were hardy sailors.

From 260 to 257, the Romans went from strength to strength, winning battles at Myles, Sulci and Tyndaris. They took over the whole of Sicily, and invaded Sardinia and Corsica which were occupied by the Carthaginians. In 256 they invaded Africa after having defeated the Carthaginian fleet at Ecnome in Sicily. Once they had landed in Clupea (now Kélibia on Cap Bon), the Roman army headed by Atilius Regulus and Manlius Vulso, reached Carthage and proposed unacceptable surrender conditions. The Carthaginians therefore decided to continue fighting, and recruited a highly experienced military chief, Xanthippe.

From 255 to 253, the Romans' fortune changed, as their armies were defeated near to Tunis, and their fleet was annihilated shortly afterwards. The Roman general Regulus was captured by the Carthaginians in Tunisia, and released on the understanding that he went to Rome to negotiate for peace. Once there he encouraged the Roman Senate not to negotiate, however, and, in a display of heroic courage, went to Carthage where he died under torture in 255.

Hamilcar
in Sicily

The Carthaginian general Hamilcar Barca was sent to Sicily to deal a final blow to the Romans. The war dragged on, however (247-242). Rome took advantage of this opportunity to reform its fleet and defeated the Carthaginians on the Egates Islands. Sicily was won back, and the Punic armies driven back into Africa in 241. Rome had definitively won control of the western Mediterranean sea, thus ending the first Punic war.

A 23 year long period of peace reigned between Rome and Carthage (241-218). In 241, a revolt broke out amongst the mercenaries in Carthage. It was led by their chiefs Matho and Spendius, who had not been paid by their Punic masters, and lasted until 237 when it was violently repressed by Hamilcar (this is the theme of the French novel *Salammbô*, by Gustave Flaubert).

Whilst its rival was otherwise occupied, Rome took advantage of the occasion to take over Sardinia and Corsica which were Carthaginian property. Carthage, exhausted by its own domestic strife, preferred to capitulate and abandon its islands to the Romans (237).

Up until 227, Rome increased its military expeditions to appease Sardinia and Corsica, which had become Roman provinces.

Carthage, for its part, set out to conquer Spain in 237 in the hope of finding new prosperity by exploiting the Iberian Peninsula's silver mines. Once he had founded Alicante, Hamilcar Barca founded Barcino, "town of the Barca family" which would later become Barcelona, but died shortly afterwards. His son-in-law Hasdrubal took over from him and founded the "New Carthage" (Carthagene) before he was assassinated in 226.

Worried by the Carthaginians' latest expansion, the Romans insisted that they did not adventure beyond the Ebro in a treaty signed in 226. The new Carthaginian general, Hannibal, Hamilcar's son, continued the conquests in Spain, taking over Sagonte in 219. Although this Carthaginian advance was within the limits of the treaty, it exasperated Rome who decided to break the peace and take up arms. In 218 B.C., the second Punic war broke out.

The second Punic war
(218 to 201 B.C.)

As they no longer had a powerful fleet with which to fight the Romans, Hannibal decided to move the battle onto land. In an incredible feat of boldness, he left Spain during the spring of 218, crossed France and the Alps with an army of Spanish soldiers, Numidian cavalry men, and a large troop of elephants.

The Carthaginian general received unhoped for support from the Gauls who came to strengthen his army, thereby enabling him to go from victory to victory. In 217, he thus managed to defeat the Romans near to lake Trasimene, then in Cannae in 216.

Rome seemed to be at his mercy and yet, for some paradoxical reason which modern historians still have not managed to explain, Hannibal avoided the Roman metropolis and turned his attention to the south of Italy where he allied himself with the local population. This diversion was a tactical error, however, as Hannibal soon found himself trapped in southern Italy whilst his Spanish reinforcements did not turn up.

The Romans regained momentum and won back Capoue (211), then Syracuse in Sicily. In Spain, the young Scipio captured Carthagene in 209. At this time Hannibal's fortunes changed. Sicily and Spain fell into the hands of the Romans, and his brother Hasdrubal was captured with part of his Spanish army when he began to penetrate northern Italy (207). His head was cut off and sent to Hannibal.

The war moved onto the African continent where Scipio landed in 204 after having made allies with the Numidian king Masinissa. Hannibal and his brother Magon were called back to Carthage and beaten by Scipio at Zama in 202. This was the end of the second Punic war (201).

Defeated, Carthage was forced to pay a heavy war indemnity to the Romans, to give up its fleet, to renounce fighting any wars, and finally, to exile Hannibal (in 195).

The third Punic war (149-146)

The Carthaginians' dynamism enabled them to become prosperous again and even to pay off their war debt to the Romans in advance (in ten years instead of in fifty!).

In 150 B.C., Carthage's new lease of power began to worry the Romans again, who already began to envisage the total and definitive destruction of the Carthaginian empire. During this period, Cato the Elder repeated his leitmotif incessantly: "Delenda est Carthago" ("Carthage must be destroyed"). The

MASINISSA OR THE UNION OF THE BERBERS

■ *The Numidian prince Masinissa, son of Gaia, king of the Massyli, was born in 238 B.C. Originally allied with the Carthaginians, he later sided with the Romans during the second Punic War (218-201), which enabled him to reconquer his kingdom usurped by Syphax. Having married the latter's wife – Sophonisbe – he was forced to turn her over to the Roman general Scipio Africanus, who made her poison herself as he was afraid that she would encourage Masinissa's return to the Carthaginian camp.*

Recognised as king of Numidia by the Romans, Masinissa successfully devoted himself to unifying the troubled Berber lands by turning the nomadic herders into sedentary farmers, most of whom lived in the towns.

He ruled over his kingdom from his capital Cirta (Constantine) by creating a permanent army and maintaining a merchant fleet that traded throughout the whole Mediterranean basin.

In order to guarantee his power further, he tried to impose a personality cult.

His territorial ambitions led him to grab more Punic land every day, leading to a confrontation with the Carthaginians, in which the Romans immediately became involved. Concerned by the Numidian expansion, Rome – after having destroyed Carthage and created the Province of Africa – constantly pushed back the borders of the Berber kingdom once Masinissa died in 148 B.C.

Numidian prince Masinissa was initially a Carthaginian ally in the first Punic war, but broke the alliance during the second war. By becoming a Roman ally, he was able to establish a powerful kingdom in North Africa (Algeria) at Carthage's expense, as he nibbled away at its territory. This was too much for Carthage, who decided to ignore the treaty signed with Rome (which forbade it to wage war), and went to war with Masinissa.

Rome used this as a pretext to wage the third and last Punic war (149-146).

Scipio's arrival

Elected consul in 147, Scipio Africanus Minor (Scipio Africanus Major's grandson), became commander of the Roman army in Africa and sieged Carthage.

In the spring of 146, after eight days' fierce fighting and massacres, Carthage fell as the last Carthaginians succumbed amidst the ruins of the Eschmoun temple on Byrsa hill. The town was burnt and razed to the ground. The site was then covered in salt and the Romans officially forbade that the town be rebuilt, as was the custom for cursed towns. Carthage was definitively erased from the map of the world, and the rare survivors were deported to Rome where they became slaves.

The Punic territory was annexed by the Romans who declared it a *Province of Africa* the same year. The province was governed by a praetor who was in charge of keeping law and order. A certain number of cities in Tunisia which had been loyal to Rome stayed relatively autonomous, for example Utica and Hadrumete (now Sousse) in Tunisia.

The Gracchi, grandsons of Scipio Africanus Major (Tiberius and his brother Caius Gracchus), were in turn elected tribunes of the plebians in Rome in 134 and 123 B.C. They promulgated social laws, notably an agricultural law in which part of the Republic's lands – in particular land

PORTRAITS OF HANNIBAL

Hannibal, son of the Carthaginian general Hamilcar Barca, was only twenty-six years old when the Punic Senate nominated him general-in-chief in 220 B.C.

This is the portrait the Roman historian Livy (64 B.C – 17 A.D) drew of him: "Never has a soul swayed more supplely between two more opposing qualities: subordination and command. It is difficult to decide if this made him dearer to the generals or to the army. Hasdrubal would not have chosen any other officer if vigour and boldness were needed. No other chief could inspire his soldiers with more confidence, more daring. Whilst full of courage when affronting perilous situations, he proved to be most prudent when in the midst of danger. No fatigue could wear out his body, nor break his spirit. He could bear both the heat and the cold. His meals were regulated by nature's needs and not sensuality. He made no difference between day and night whether keeping watch or sleeping. He devoted the moments his business left free to rest and did not need a soft sleeping place nor silence in order to sleep. He could often be seen lying on the ground amongst the sentinels and guards covered with a soldier's tabard. His clothes did not mark him out from others. He was both the best horse rider and the best infantryman. He was the first to throw himself into combat and the last to leave the melee. Some major vices accompanied such shining virtues: excessive cruelty, a more than Punic perfidy, nothing was true, in the African Province of Carthage – were redistributed to poor Roman citizens.

These reforms came up against the opposition of rich patrician and plebian landlords who did not want to go to Africa.

Whilst the civil war was raging in Rome shortly afterwards, king Jugurtha of Numidia, Masinissa's grandson, revolted in Tunisia. Rome sent legions commanded by the consul Cecilius Metellus and assisted by Caius Marius, to fight him.

During this campaign in 109-108, the Romans were beaten near to Zama. In a second campaign launched in 107 and led by Marius, seconded by Sylla, Jugurtha was completely defeated when his ally Bocchus, the king of Mauritania, abandoned him.

Jugurtha was taken to Rome where he was paraded tied to Marius's chariot like a trophy during the Roman general's triumphal celebration. He was then thrown in prison and strangled.

The Numidian kingdom, which was initially divided up between the Berber princes loyal to Rome, was declared a Roman province.

In the first century B.C., Rome was split by the rivalry between Julius Caesar and Pompey which ended with the latter's death in 48.

Caesar, who became a dictator in 49, went to North Africa where in 47, he crushed the Numidian army under King Jubaler, Pompey's last ally, at Thapsus (Moknine). He took the opportunity to annex a new part of the Maghreb which became the province *Africa Nova*.

Up until his assassination in Rome in 44, Caesar was working on the reform of the Roman institutions and the reorganisation of the conquered lands. It was thus that he decided to rebuild Rome's two former rivals – Carthage and Corinth from their ruins. He made them into colonies and encouraged Roman plebians and veterans of the legions to settle there.

The province of Africa (Eastern Maghreb) was then administered from Carthage by the historian Sal-

nothing was sacred for him, he did not fear the gods, did not respect the sermons, had no religion..."
Like Livy, the Greek historian Polybius (200-125 B.C.) – who lived in Rome – also admired Hannibal greatly, writing the following description of him: "How could anyone fail to admire Hannibal's science, his courage, his prowess on the battle field, when one considers the time his expedition lasted, the number of major combats or small battles he fought, the sieges he led, the defections and other difficulties with which he was faced, the grandeur of his projects and the war he fought non-stop for sixteen years in Italy. He never let his troops rest. He kept them under his reign like a good pilot and managed to avoid both dissension in their midsts, or revolt against him. And this in spite of the fact that he was dealing with a large army made up of men not only from different nations but of different races. There were Africans, Spanish, Ligurians, Gauls, Phoenicians, Italians, Greeks who did not abide by the same laws or customs, who did not speak the same language, and who had no natural affinity between them. All their chief's intelligence was needed to bring so many diverse peoples together under his sole authority in the most complicated circumstances during which fortune sometimes blew hot, sometimes cold. One therefore has to admire the ability Hannibal displayed in this field."

lust, a friend of Caesar, who was its first governor.

Caesar then developed other Roman colonies in the province of Africa, which were usually based around the former Carthaginian trading posts, for example Thabraca (Tabarka), Hippo Diarrhytus (Bizerte), Corpis, Clupea (Kélibia), Curubis (Korba), Neapolis (Nabeul), Hadrumetum (Sousse), and Thysdrus (El Djem).

In accordance with Caesar's will, his heir Octavianus Augustus (30 B.C.-14 A.D.), continued to rebuild Carthage. He named it after the deceased dictator and at the same placed it under the sign of the Concord: the new Roman city was now called the "Colonia Julia Concordia".

During Augustus' reign, the Latin poet Virgil wrote the *Aeneid*, the legendary tale of Aeneas, the Trojan war hero and ancestor hailed by Julius Caesar. After voyaging throughout the Mediterranean like Odysseus, and before reaching Italy where he founded the city of Rome, Aeneas stopped in Carthage where the queen Dido fell in love with him, and killed herself when he left.

During the first three centuries A.D., peace reigned almost continuously throughout the Roman Empire, apart from in North Africa which was frequently troubled by Berber revolts. The Romans had created well administrated Romanised provinces throughout the empire which reached a very high level of prosperity. In North Africa, where they tried to integrate the Berber elites by romanising them, they revealed stunning talent as builders. They built major towns, roads, and aqueducts protected by a huge fortified system called the "*limes*". This stretched from Libya to Morocco via southern Tunisia along the southern edge of the chott el Djérid.

Inside this area, the Roman army – notably the Third Augusta Legion based in Numidia – kept the peace and, in its free time, worked at developing agriculture in the provinces.

The Proconsular province, which included modern day Tunisia, and part of Libya and Algeria, was governed by a proconsul subordinate to the Roman Senate. The province's capital was Carthage, which thanks to Caesar and Augustus, became a major metropolis once

again. Its political, cultural and economic importance made it the third most important city in the Roman Empire after Rome and Alexandria.

The advent of Christianity

In the first century A.D., the first imperial Roman dynasty of the Julio-Caesareans (descendants of Julius Caesar and Augustus) began. During Tiberius's reign (14-37 A.D.) the Roman procurator Pontius Pilate allowed Jesus Christ to be put to death on Mount Golgotha near to Jerusalem. Christ's disciples set out to spread Christianity throughout the Mediterranean basin, nearly all of which was part of the Roman Empire.

The followers of the new religion arrived in Africa from the sea and spread Christianity in North Africa from their bases in the major ports where they landed. Small Christian communities emerged and took root particularly in Carthage, which was a major forum of cultural and spiritual influence.

Still during Tiberius's reign, several major Berber revolts broke out led by the Numidian chief Tacfarinas, a former Roman soldier who had become the general of the Musalams. The mad emperor Caligula (37-41) had King Juba II assassinated, thereby enabling him to annex Mauretania, which became a Roman province under the emperor Claudius (41-54).

When the emperor Nero died in 68, and during the emperor Domitian's reign (81-96), new Berber revolts broke out.

During this period, wheat, olive, and vine growing took off massively in North Africa.

Large Tunisian towns

During the 2nd century, North Africa, which was administered by the Romans, underwent a period of major building works. Towns like Bulla Regia, Utica, Maktar, Dougga, Thelepte and Sbeïtla (Sufetula) were founded and developed.

During the emperor Hadrian's reign (117-138), Berber revolts broke out again. They became so violent by Antonine's time (138-161) and under Marcus Aurelius (161-180), that the Romans sent troops from Syria and Spain to repress them back into the Algerian Aurès.

Furthermore, during Antonine's reign, Christian missionaries set up churches in most towns of the Proconsulate. They notably converted the educated Berber elites who were capable of reading the Bible in Latin. At the end of the day, however, Christianity did not reach the disinherited masses in the rural areas.

Like his predecessors, the Roman emperor Commodus (180-192) persecuted Christians throughout the Empire, North Africa included. The region experienced its first martyrdoms when twelve villagers were beheaded in 180 in Scilli near to Carthage under the proconsul's orders.

Born in Tripolitaine (modern day Libya), Septimius Severus was the first Roman emperor of Berber origin. In 193, he founded a dynasty that bore his name. North Africa entered into a new period of troubles.

In 196, the Christian priest and theologian Tertullian returned to Rome from Carthage, where he set up his apostolate and continued to develop Christianity. This religion was not always tolerated by Rome, however, and under the dynasties of the Severus emperors (Caracalla, 211-217; Macrinus, 217-218; Elagabalus, 218-222; and Severus Alexander, 222-235), the persecution of Christians took off with a vengeance throughout the Empire. In Carthage, for example, Saint Perpetue and five other Christians were martyred in the year 203.

Christians enjoyed a period of respite from the Romans for a short while, which enabled their religion to take off again in 230. Bishop Agrippina even managed to form a synod of 70 bishops in Carthage.

From 235 to 268, the Roman Empire went through a dark period of *military anarchy*. Maximinus, former head of the Rhine army, ruled from Rome. As he was too harsh with his subjects, revolts broke out, particularly in Thysdrus (El Djem) in Tunisia. The Roman settlers elected Gordian I, an 80-year old procurator as emperor. He committed suicide shortly after his son Gordian II was killed fighting loyalist troops.

Saint Cyprian, bishop of Carthage

During Philip the Arabian's reign, Cyprian, who was a Carthaginian noble, converted to Christianity and became a bishop in 249. From then on, he was responsible for organising the Christian faith in his diocese, but soon became the target of the persecutions launched by the Roman emperor Decius (249-252) and had to go into exile. Cyprian excommunicated all the Christians who renounced their faith during the Roman persecutions. He also opposed the bishop Novatianus, whose rupture he condemned in his little tract – *Unity of the Church*.

Cyprian was soon to be martyred, however, as the Roman emperor Valerian (253-260) ordered the proconsul Galerius Maximus to execute the bishop of Carthage in 258. After his death, Saint Cyprian was worshipped by the whole Christian community in Tunisia, and the posthumous influence of his teachings was so great that a widespread intellectual and spiritual movement called the Cyprianic school took root in Carthage. Two years later, emperor Gallius (260-268) put an end to the persecutions against the Christians.

At the end of the 3rd century, the Roman Empire which was in a state of complete decline, was taken in hand by Diocletian. In Tunisia, he divided the Proconsulate into three provinces: *Zeugitane* (Carthage), *Byzacene* (Sousse) and *Tripolitaine*. In 303, he started persecuting the Christians again. These persecutions were the most violent and the most widespread of the whole Roman Empire.

When Constantine I became emperor in 306 (until 337), the Roman Empire reached a turning point with the foundation of Constantinople in 330, which marked the beginning of the Byzantine era and the Eastern Roman Empire.

In North Africa, the church entered a long period of unrest and division. Two factions formed: one regrouping those who had renounced their faith during the Roman persecutions (partisans of Caecilianus, the bishop of Carthage), and the other which regrouped those who called for unconditional martyrdom (the partisans of Donatus, the bishop of Numidia). Donatus chased out Caecilianus and appointed a new clergy.

Emperor Constantine, who had officially recognised the Catholic religion, backed Caecilianus in 313. The Donatists (who were mainly poor North African Berbers) were deemed to be heretics and were subsequently persecuted up until 321, when Constantine finally called for an end to the repression. The Donatists were then able to organise a synod in Carthage which regrouped up to 270 bishops.

Constant, who was emperor from 340-350 after Constantine II, wanted to force the Donatists to reintegrate the official Church, and tracked down recalcitrant followers mercilessly (347). The Donatists therefore became the allies of peasant groups (the "Circoncellions") in revolt against the imperial power. Both were massacred by the imperial troops, who nonetheless did not succeed in subordinating them completely. When Donatus died in 355, he was succeeded in the struggle by Parmenianus.

Constance II (351-361), Constantine II's brother, favoured Christianity in Byzantium. During his reign, Saint Augustine (354-430) was born in Algeria. A few years later during the reigns of Valentinian, Gratian and Valentinian II, Berber revolts broke out again led by Firmus then Gidon.

In 380, the Spanish-born Roman emperor Theodosius (379-395), published the Thessalonian edict which made Christianity the official religion of the Roman Empire. This put an end to the long period of persecutions thereby allowing the religion to spread.

In 395, the Roman Empire was divided between Theodosius's two sons. Arcadius became the head of the Eastern Empire, and Honorius (408-423) the head of the Western Empire (including North Africa).

Defeated by the Visigoths in Spain in 415, Genseric, the king of the Vandals left Andalousia ("Vandalousia"). With his hoard of 80,000 Vandals, Goths and Alains (15,000 of whom were armed), Genseric landed in North Africa where the Berber people, fed up with the Romans,

welcomed him as a liberator.

Having reached *Africa Proconsularis* (Algeria and Tunisia), his troops captured Hippone (Bone) which they sieged for over a year (during the siege, Augustine died on 11 August 430). They then entered Carthage, the last point of resistance in Barbary. Carthage became their capital, and Genseric ruled over a maritime empire comprising of North Africa, Sicily, Sardinia, Corsica and the Balearic Islands. The empire was so powerful by 468 that the Byzantines sent a fleet to fight Genseric, but it was completely annihilated off Cap Bon in Tunisia.

In Rome, events turned when the Barbarians invaded. In 476 the last Roman emperor Romulus Augustulus was executed by the barbarian chief Odoacre, bringing an end to the Western Roman Empire.

Huneric, successor to Genseric in Tunisia, (477-485) was a follower of the Aryan religion. Intolerant of Christians, he persecuted them. At the end of the 6th century and beginning of the 7th century, several Vandal sovereigns succeeded each other in North Africa: Gunthamund (484-496), Thrasamund (496-523), and Hilderic (523-530). All of them had to deal with many a Berber revolt.

After Anastase I and Justin, Justinian (527-565) became one of the greatest Byzantine emperors, and for a short while, reestablished the Romans' power. He sent his armies to Tunisia under the command of Belisarius. They defeated the Vandal king Gelimer, definitively ridding Africa of the Barbarians in 534.

Justinian reorganises North Africa

The emperor Justinian took the opportunity to reorganise North Africa. He regrouped the seven provinces into one prefecture subordinate to Constantinople and administered by a praetorian prefect. Once Belisarius had returned to Byzantium, North Africa was shaken by its characteristic series of Berber revolts which the Byzantine occupation armies had difficulty in suppressing.

Under the emperor Justin II's reign (565-578), the prefect Thomas was defeated by the Berber prince Garmul. Garmul was soon killed,

*These two mosaics from Bulla Regia
indicate the very high level
of mosaic art in the workshops
of Roman and Byzantine Barbary.*

but a climate of insecurity reigned in North Africa. In an attempt to restore peace in North Africa, the Byzantium emperor Maurice (582-602) nominated an exarch-military governor to second the praetorian prefect. In 609, Phocas, who had succeeded to the emperor Maurice by assassinating him, was in turn assassinated.

Heraclius, the exarch of Carthage (610-641) who overturned Phocas, was crowned emperor of Byzantium.

The first Arab invasions

Arabic expansion, which began during the Prophet's time with the subduing of the whole Arabian peninsula, entered into its second phase after Mohammed's death in 632. Under his successors, the caliphs Abou Bakr (632-633), and Omar (634-644), the Arabs set out to conquer the world, successfully confronting the Persian and Byzantine Empires. Under the third caliph Othman (644-656), the first Arab conquerors were sent to the Maghreb. Abdallah ibn Saïd set out from Egypt in 647, entered into Ifriqyya and defeated the Byzantine armies led by Gregory, governor of Africa, posted near to Sbeïtla. He left with a wealth in war spoils, determined to come back now he knew the weakness of the Byzantine forces.

Ali, the Prophet's cousin who was married to his daughter Fatima, succeeded to Othman in 656 thus becoming the fourth caliph. His succession was disputed by Mu'awiyyah, the Syrian governor and grandson of Umayya (head of one of the principal quraichite clans of Mecca), and the Prophet's former secretary.

During the arbitration process between the two pretenders, Ali was deposed in 659 but held on to power until he was assassinated in 661 by his former partisans, the Kharijites (the "breakaways" of Ali's camp).

The way was now open for Mu'awiyyah, who succeeded Ali as the fifth caliph. During his reign, (661-680), he introduced some fundamental changes in the Muslim world. The foundation of the Umayyad dynasty (the descendants of Umayya, who reigned until 750) transformed the caliphate into a hereditary monarchy and its base was transferred to Damascus in Syria.

During the fifth caliphate, the third wave of Arab invasions took place in Persia and the Maghreb (which was still under the Byzantines), but failed to take Constantinople (Mu'awiyyah was forced to sign a peace treaty with the Byzantines).

The Arab emir Uqba ibn Nafi was sent by Mu'awiyyah to invade the Maghreb where he met little resistance from the Byzantines. In 670 he founded Kairouan in the heart of Tunisia, which was to serve as the base for future expeditions in the Maghreb. He too was confronted with the Berber revolts led by Kocaïla, and later died in one of their ambushes in the Aurès in 683. The way was now open for Kocaïla who took over Kairouan and ruled over Ifriqyya until troops sent by the Umayyad caliph Abd el Malik (685-705) arrived in 686. They defeated the Berber chief and took back control of Kairouan.

The "Berber Joan of Arc"

The Berber spirit was not quelled by this, however, and the Maghreb rose up again in response to the rallying cry of the Berber queen Kahena ("the prophetess"), whom Western historians have called the "Berber Joan of Arc". A powerful Arab army led by Hassan ibn al Nooman al Ghassani waged war against Kahena, but was defeated near to Tébessa in eastern Algeria and driven out of the Maghreb in 695.

Three years later Hassan al Ghassani seized Carthage and settled in Tunis, which became the new capital of Ifriqyya. Having defeated the Byzantines (who were definitively driven out of North Africa), the Arab conqueror became determined to subdue the Berber revolt.

According to some historical sources, Kahena was defeated and killed at the border between Tunisia and Algeria (near to Tabarka) in 702. Legend has it, however, that the Berber queen took refuge in the El Djem coliseum which was sieged by the Arabs. Betrayed and stabbed by her lover Khaled ben Yazid, her head was then apparently sent to her enemy. Leaderless and overrun by the Arabs, the Berbers submitted for a while, and some of them even enrolled in the Arab army.

In a new sign of resistance to the Arab invader, who advocated orthodox Islam, the Berbers converted to Kharijism, which was considered heretical within the Muslim religion.

Having become firmly settled in North Africa for some time, the Arabs were free to continue their expansion again, which took off in particular under the Umayyad caliph Walid I (705-715). The Tarik Arab armies based in North Africa crossed the Gibraltar Straits and conquered Spain. Under Umar II (717-720), the Umayyads launched some fierce assaults against Byzantium. Later, under Hicham (724-743), the Arab armies reached Poitiers in France, where they were driven back by Charles Martel in 732.

Shortly afterwards, a new series of Berber revolts broke out throughout the whole of the Maghreb (740-761) in the name of Kharijite Islam. The revolts were suppressed by Arab armies from Egypt in 742, however.

During this period, Abd er Rahman ibn Habib, who was a descendant of Uqba, occupied Tunis (in 744) and proclaimed its independence from the Damascus caliphate. He was soon assassinated, however. Diverse Kharijite factions disputed the control of Kairouan, which they ruled over in turn.

This lack of order was encouraged by the decline of the Damascus Umayyad dynasty which crumbled in 750 after revolts in Persia. This enabled Abu al Abbas (descendant of Abbas, the Prophet's uncle) to take over the caliphate, which he moved to Baghdad, thus founding the Abbasid dynasty (which reigned from Baghdad until 1258).

Aghlabid splendor

Until the end of the 8th century, the Abbasids of Baghdad – the most eminent of whom was the caliph Haroun al Rachid (786-809), the sultan made famous by *The Arabian Nights* – had to fight to reconquer the Maghreb and to repress the Kharijite heresy. On two occasions, the Arab armies from Egypt came to take Kairouan back from the Kharijite Berbers and finally reestablish order in Ifriqyya at the end of the 8th century.

In the 9th century, which was much less turbulent than the 8th, Arabic civilisation flourished under the Aghlabids. Some historians have even compared this "golden era" to the Italian Renaissance, only five hundred years earlier. The Aghlabids were the descendants of Ibn el Aghlab, who was made emir of Ifriqyya by the Baghdad caliphate in the year 800 (at the same time as Charlemagne became emperor in the West). This dynasty, which lasted for over a century, managed to obtain a certain degree of autonomy from the Baghdad caliphate and to really reign in Tunisia.

Under the Aghlabids, Kairouan, where they were based, became a major forum of cultural and religious influence. During the 9th century, the Kairouan Central Mosque built by Uqba ibn Nafi in the 7th century, was expanded and embellished, and Sousse, Sfax, and Monastir became major centres.

Abdallah I succeeded to Ibrahim ibn Aghlab I (812-817), followed by Zidayat Allah I (817-838). The latter was confronted with a revolt within the ranks of his army, which he managed to quell completely before setting out to conquer Sicily in 827. These campaigns were continued by his successors, giving the Arabs the control of the Mediterranean.

At the beginning of the 10th century, however, Ifriqyya underwent a new series of popular uprisings – caused by the over-taxation of the poorest part of the population – which brought an end to the Aghlabid reign.

The Fatimids come to power

Order reigned in Tunisia when suddenly Obeid Allah (862-934) appeared and declared himself Mahdi ("messenger from God, savior of the world"). This Shiite Muslim had fled from Syria to escape the oppression of the Abbasid Sunnite caliphs. A descendant of Fatima, daughter of the Prophet Mohammed – via the imam Ismail –, Obeid Allah created the Fatimid dynasty in the Maghreb. Initially settled in Morocco, he reached Ifriqyya (Tunisia) in 909, where he had himself nominated caliph of Kairouan in 910, thus renouncing the authority of the Baghdad caliphate.

In 926, Obeid Allah left Kairouan and founded his own capital on the Tunisian coast at Mahdia ("the town of Mahdi"). In order to impose Shiite Islam on the Kharijist Berbers, Obeid Allah and his Fatimid successors turned to the Zirid Berber tribes (Sanhadjas) who embraced their cause and their faith. The Zirids therefore fiercely repressed the Zenet nomadic Berber revolt and the latter's chief Abu Yazid was killed in combat in 947.

In order to show their gratitude, the Fatimids gave the Zirids and their leader Yusuf Bulukkin ibn Ziri power in Tunisia. The Fatimids, led by El Moezz (953-973), left for Egypt where they founded the town of Cairo in 969 and established the Fatimid caliphate (which lasted until 1171).

For decades, Tunisia underwent a new period of prosperity under the Zirid dynasty.

Good relationships between the Tunisian Zirids and the Egyptian Fatimids soon disintegrated, however, as the former committed a double fault. On the one hand they proclaimed their independence in 1047, and on the other hand, they abandoned Shiism for Sunnite Islam.

The punishment inflicted on the rebellious Maghreb was particularly severe. In retaliation, the Fatimid caliph al Mostansir (1036-1094) sent the Beni Hillal nomadic hoards in 1052. According to the historian Ibn Khaldun, these Bedouin tribes, who until then had lived in Upper Egypt, "swooped down on Ifriqyya like locusts" ravaging, pillaging and destroying everything on their path. Kairouan was not spared and the Tunisians who managed to escape being massacred were forced to take refuge in the Sahara desert or the Atlas mountains.

As for the Zirids, they continued to live in Mahdia, which became a pirates' hideout until 1148 when

DARGOUTH, THE PIRATE

■ *The Turkish pirate Dargouth, began to get a name for himself in 1533 when he attacked ships from Venice in the Mediterranean. He was taken prisoner by the Genoese in 1540 and freed in return for a ransom paid by the Barbary pirate Kheireddine (nicknamed "Barbarossa" by the Europeans), master of Algeria where his fleet was based.*

Having become one of Barbarossa's lieutenants, Dargouth set up his hideaway in Mahdia, the little port and former capital of the Fatimids' Tunisian dynasty on the east coast of Tunisia. He did not stay in Mahdia long as Charles Quint's Spanish forces drove him out when they captured back the town in 1550.

The following year, he managed to escape from Djerba which was encircled by the Genoese admiral Andrea Doria who was in the service of the emperor Charles Quint. Even though he was given the governorship of Tripoli by the Turkish sovereign Suleiman the Magnificent in 1556, Dargouth continued his piracy in the Mediterranean sea, ravaging the Italian coast, and fighting with the Spanish fleet (which he defeated in Djerba in 1560). On land, he took Kairouan in 1558. He died during the siege of Malta in 1565 when he was hit by a cannon ball.

King Roger II of Sicily occupied most of the towns on the Tunisian coast for a decade.

The Almohads and the Hafsids

The Almohad Berber princes from Marrakech succeeded to the Almoravids – Berber soldier monks – in Morocco and Spain, and built up a huge empire which included Tunisia, thereby bringing the whole of the Maghreb under the same authority.

In 1159, they delegated their power in Tunisia to Abou Hafs Umar, one of their lieutenants, who became governor of Ifriqyya and settled in Tunis. He created the Hafsid dynasty (the third Tunisian dynasty after the Aghlabids and the Zirids) which reigned until the beginning of the 16th century.

During the reign of the Hafsid sovereign Abou Abd-Allah (1249-1277), Tunis supplanted Kairouan as capital.

At the same time, the Mongols destroyed the Abbasid caliphate in Baghdad, forcing the Abbasids to go into exile in Cairo – which was ruled by the Mamelukes – until 1261 (the Mamelukes stayed in power until 1517, until supplanted by the Ottoman caliphate).

In 1270, the soldiers of the eighth crusade, which had set out from Aigues-Mortes in France, landed in Tunisia led by King Louis IX ("Saint Louis"). They captured Carthage, which became their base camp, and fought the Hafsids. The plague broke out in the crusaders' camp, however, and on 25 August, the King of France died along with a great number of his companions.

After the fall of the Almohads, the Merinids from Morocco ruled over the Maghreb. In 1347, the Merinid sultan Abou Al Hassan, claimed Tunisia, which remained under Hafsid rule. The country gradually deteriorated into economic depression and in the 15th century, under the last Hafsid rulers, it became the object of fighting between the Spanish and the Turks.

When the Turks captured Constantinople in 1453, the Byzantine empire collapsed and the Ottoman empire became all-powerful in the Mediterranean. During the follo-

wing century, it also became a major spiritual centre of the Muslim world with the creation of the Ottoman caliphate in 1517, which lasted until 1924.

Tunisia, the Turkish vassal

In 1534, the pirate Barbarossa (Kheireddine) captured Bizerte, Tunis and Kairouan under orders from the Turkish sultan of Constantinople. A year later, however, the German Emperor Charles Quint's fleet recaptured Tunis and La Goulette where a Spanish garrison was based.

Pirates sent by the Turks definitively reconquered Tunisia in 1574, making it a vassal of the Ottoman Empire and enabling them to make great gains from piracy in the Mediterranean.

A new administration was set up by the Turks in Tunisia, which from then on was governed by a "pasha", seconded by a military governor (the "dey") and a head administrator (the "bey").

The Husseinite dynasty

The early years of the 18th century marked the beginning of the long Husseinite dynasty which was to stay in power in Tunisia until independence and the creation of the Republic in 1957.

The dynasty was founded by Hussein ibn Ali who took over power in Tunisia in 1705 after having fought off an Algerian invasion with his army of janissaries.

Once he had become a bey under the name of Hussein I, he abolished the posts of dey and pasha, making the remaining bey position a hereditary title. Furthermore, he almost completely freed the country from Turkish domination and began a policy of cooperation with the West which led to the conclusion of a number of treaties with the great European powers. His favorite advisor was even a Frenchman called Raynaud.

At the end of his reign, Hussein I was confronted by his nephew Ali Pacha who deposed him in 1735. He tried to take back power, but was defeated by Younous, Ali Pacha's son, and was beheaded in Kairouan in 1740.

Invasions from Algeria

During the reigns of Ali Pacha's (1740-1754) successors, Mohamed Bey (1756-1758) and Ali Pacha II (1758-1781), domestic anarchy intensified. On several occasions, they had to fight off invasions from Algeria.

When he took over from his father Ali Bey in 1781, Hamouda Pacha developed a complex foreign policy. On the one hand he waged a long conflict against Venice (from 1784 to 1786), and on the other he maintained good relations with France of the Ancien Régime, the Convention and finally the Empire. In 1781, a French trading post was set up on Cape Nègre in northern Tunisia.

In 1811, Hamouda Pacha freed himself of the janissaries by having them assassinated. He died two years later, poisoned by his secretary.

The French Protectorate

After the reigns of beys Othman Ali II and Mahmoud (1813-1823), France became more and more interested in North Africa and, on 15 December 1824, she signed a treaty with bey Hussein II (1823-1835) giving France special privileges which were in fact the first steps towards the Protectorate. Moreover, the bey guaranteed his neutrality, which enabled the French to begin conquering Algeria in 1830 without fear of attack from the rear by Tunisian forces.

The 19th century bankrupted Tunisia, however. Heavily in debt, the Tunis sovereigns were forced to accept the harsh conditions imposed upon them by the European powers. In 1869, therefore, bey Mohamed Ag Sadok (1859-1882) was submitted to the intervention and control of

TUNISIA IN FEW DATES

■ *814 B.C.: Foundation of Carthage.*
■ *146 B.C.: Destruction of Carthage by the Romans.*
430 A.D: Genseric and the Vandals in Tunisia.
534: The Byzantine general Belisarius reconquers Tunisia from the Vandals.
671: The Arab emir Uqba ibn Nafi founds Kairouan.
800: The emir Ibrahim al Aghlab founds the Aghlabid dynasty.
909: Obeid Allah el Mahdi founds the Fatimid dynasty in Mahdia.
1057: The Beni Hillal nomads ravage Tunisia.
1159: The Hafsids reign in Tunisia.
1270: Eighth crusade in Tunisia. Death of Saint Louis.
1347: The Merinids reign in Morocco.
1535: The emperor Charles Quint forces the pirate Barbarossa out of Tunisia.
1574: Tunisia becomes part of the Ottoman empire.
1612: Bey Mourad founds the first beylik dynasty.
1705: Hussein ben Ali founds the Husseinite dynasty.
1881: Tunisia becomes a French Protectorate.
1934: Habib Bourguiba founds the Neo-Destour party.
1956: Tunisian independence.
1957: Tunisia becomes a republic presided over by Habib Bourguiba.
1987: Zine El Abidine Ben Ali, 2nd President of the Republic.

an Anglo-Franco-Italian commission in charge of overseeing their debt repayment. In fact once placed under supervision, the Tunis regency lost all its power. Once France had managed to distance its rivals England and Italy, all that remained was to find a pretext for completely taking over Tunisia.

By blowing a revolt in Khroumirie out of proportion into a border incident, the French army in Algeria invaded Tunisia and, in his Bardo palace, forced bey Sadok to sign the treaty making Tunisia a French Protectorate on 12 May 1881.

From now on the Tunisian sovereigns were nominal rulers only the real ruler of Tunisia being the French resident general. The history of Tunisia was now to follow the same path as that of Algeria.

French and Italian colonists arrived en masse at the end of the 19th century. Thanks to preferential land laws, they were able to dispossess the Tunisians of the best land in order to "valorize" the country, initially taking over 70,000 hectares of good arable land, that is one fifth of the farming land.

Whilst it is true that the country developed economically, this development hardly benefitted the Tunisian masses whose conditions stayed close to the poverty level (low salaries and acute unemployment). As a result, fierce discontentment grew, periodically breaking out into revolts, which were severely repressed by the occupiers.

In this troubled climate, nationalist demands developed at the beginning of the 20th century, and the first independentist leaders emerged.

Towards Independence

In 1920 the liberal Destour party was created giving the independentist opposition a militant base in Tunisia. Its demands were soon judged to be too mild, however, and in 1934, a rift split the party giving rise to the more dynamic Neo-Destour party led by the young, fiery lawyer from Monastir, Habib Bourguiba (the other faction of the party took the name the Old Destour party).

The banning of the two parties, the imprisonment of their leaders, and the declaration of a state of emergency in 1938 only stirred nationalist feelings up further. Nationalist tendencies gained a new lease of life when the Second World War broke out and the Italian and German troops arrived in Tunisia playing the role of liberators.

The conflict found a new theatre of war in this country between November 1942 and May 1943 when German forces under Rommel fought the Allied troops in Tunisia. A decisive battle took place at Mareth near to Gabès in February 1943 during which the Allies chased the Germans and Italians out of Tunisia definitively.

During the war and the post war period, the last two beys ruled in Tunis: Moncef (1942-1948) and Mohamed Lamine (1948-1957). When the French colons resumed their former posts, and the Tunisians' situation did not change, independence struggles took off again with a vengeance. The French granted a few concessions, hoping to negotiate reforms, but these were judged insufficient by the opposition, particularly the Neo-Destour party.

Habib Bourguiba president

After the failure of the negotiations with Bourguiba in Paris, demonstrations and violent outbursts broke out again in Tunisia up until Bourguiba's triumphal return from exile on 1 June 1955, and until the independentists' success in gaining the suppression of the Protectorate at the beginning of 1956, and the proclamation of Tunisian independence on 20 March the following year.

The bey then nominated Habib Bourguiba President of the Cabinet. The following year the bey was deposed by the Parliament which abolished the monarchy. The Republic was declared on 25 July 1957, and Habib Bourguiba became president. The country entered into a period of reforms which led to the constitution of a secular state, promotion of women, access to state school for all social classes, improvement of social welfare, etc.

The following year, relations between Tunisia and France deteriorated when the French air force bombarded the Tunisian village of Sakiet Sidi Youssef (8 February 1958) which it thought was a base for the Algerian FLN forces. Later the confrontation worsened as France, which had kept the military port of Bizerte, did not hand it back until 1963 after a series of bloody confrontations with the Tunisian population in July 1961.

Following the example of the major politico-economic ensembles forming throughout the world (for example the European Common Market), Tunisia planned to form one with its Maghrebi neighbours. In January 1974, therefore, its signed a treaty of union at Djerba between Tunisia and Libya. The treaty was never effective, however, as tension soon developed with colonel Kaddafi.

One year later, Habib Bourguiba was nominated president for life, but in 1976, an important clause was added stipulating that if the president of the Republic became incapacitated, he would be replaced by the Prime minister.

Black clouds in domestic affairs

In spite of the reforms, inequality persisted and the poorest classes stayed pitifully disadvantaged, which provoked open and fierce conflicts between the unique governmental party (PSD) and the federation of trade unions (UGGT) led by Habib Achour.

When Achour was arrested, riots broke out, for example on 26 January 1978, or "black Thursday", when a general strike was bloodily repressed. In December 1984, the Bread Revolt broke out when bread prices doubled, forcing President Bourguiba to go back on price increases for essential food products.

In the meantime, a commando of Tunisian opponents came from Libya and attacked Gafsa in January 1980. During the same year, Mr Mzali, a fierce advocate of economic liberalism and of the Arabisation of the country, became Prime minister.

The president's pronouncement in favour of a multiparty system on 18 July, 1981, marked an important step towards democracy, particularly when the Tunisian Communist Party was recognised and free elections announced. These were held in November, recompensing the "Supreme Combatant's" initiative: all the seats in the National Assembly were won by Bourguiba's partisans.

In 1985 the international situation worsened. On the one hand the Israelis bombarded the PLO's headquarters in the suburbs of Tunis, and on the other hand diplomatic relations were broken off with Libya after 30,000 Tunisian workers were expelled from the country.

The following year, Mr Rachid Sfar replaced Mr Mohammed Mzali as Prime minister, and the dinar was devaluated by 10%.

Ben Ali comes to power

By the end of the 1980s, the growing Muslim fundamentalist movement had reached Tunisia, and a particularly violent demonstration was organised by fundamentalist students in April 1987. This led to several of their leaders being condemned to death in September of the same year.

On the following 7 November, in accordance with the constitution, Zine El Abidine Ben Ali relieved the 84 year old President Bourguiba of his duties for reasons of ill health, and became President of the Republic. The following year the National Assembly introduced a multiparty system and in July revised the constitution, ending the system of life presidency.

On 2 April 1989, presidential and legislative elections were held. Mr Ben Ali was elected president and his party, the RCD, obtained nearly all the seats in the National Assembly (the fundamentalists gained only 13% of the vote).

After a fundamentalist plot was discovered in May 1991, Rached Ghannouchi's party was banned. The March 1994 elections confirmed Mr Ben Ali's position as President of the Republic.

*The prayer room of the Kairouan mosque
is famous for its "forest of columns"
built from materials recuperated
from diverse Roman and Byzantine vestiges.*

the economy

The Tunisian economy, which experienced an extremely rapid development after independence in 1956, still has a strong agricultural base, even if industry and services have boomed over the last few years.

Today, over a third of the Tunisia's working population is still employed in the primary sector (which represents 18% of Gross National Product). Agriculture is concentrated mainly in the rich traditional regions of the north-east (the Medjerda valley) and in the Sahelian region (from Sousse to Sfax). The southern part of the country, where the Sahara begins, is semi-desert and therefore remains the domain of goat and dromedary herding. A small part of this Saharan region is constituted by oases, where immense palm groves and small market gardens have been developed.

Along with the demographic imbalance between the north and the south, Tunisia is also confronted with an acute rural exodus which is emptying the countryside in favor of the major coastal towns where life appears to be less arduous.

Subsistence farming crops head agricultural production. These essentially include cereals (2.5 million tonnes), and especially wheat, which Tunisia produced 1.580 million tonnes of in 1992 (all of which was consumed locally). Cereal farming has developed in the north and central regions of the country in particular.

The olive country

Olives are amongst the major commercial crops farmed, and are turned into oil in more than 2,000 presses. Tunisia has consequently become the fourth olive oil producer and the second exporting country in the world after Greece. In 1992, the country produced 265,000 tonnes and exports represented 3% of all Tunisia's foreign sales.

Olive growing already existed in ancient times. Right from the first few centuries A.D., the Romans

THE DATE PALM, A PROVIDENTIAL TREE

Few people realise the numerous precious qualities this astonishing tree has, or realise the incomparable services it renders the inhabitants of the desert.

For the traveller who, exhausted after the long walk across the rocky solitudes and the fastidious mounds of the dunes, spots the much awaited green line of the grove, or ghâba on the horizon, the date palm is symbolic of hope and joy. With what avidity the eye feeds on this splash of colour which exudes comfort and life! The line fills out more and more, and little by little all the parts of the "ghâba" become distinguishable, the sight of which fills the soul with an unequalled sense of elation.

Soon, the delicious crowns of leaves can be made out swaying gently from left to right on their tall slender trunks: one by one, your inquisitive eyes scrutinize each clump of greenery displaying all its enchanting grace, as you look for the most beautiful and most sheltered place to pitch camp.

What is an oasis when you take away the palm tree? A solitary

nicknamed El Djem "the olive oil capital". Over the centuries, however, oil production regressed so much that it had almost completely disappeared on the eve of the modern period. At the end of the last century, Paul Bourde, a French agronomist, gave a new boost to the plantations by allotting land around Sfax at a reasonable price. Within a few years, many small land owners had settled in the region and were planting olive trees at a rapid rate. Whilst there were only 400,000 olive trees in Tunisia in 1880, by the 1950s, there were more than 23 million, and in recent years, 55 million.

Today, oil production has spread considerably further than the Sfax region, and is now common in the Sahelian region to the north (El Djem, Mahdia, Sousse), and on the coast between Bizerte and Tabarka and southwards as far as the Isle of Djerba.

In total, olive groves account for 1.4 million hectares, that is a third of the farming land – a really green smudge! Sfax is still nonetheless the "olive capital" with its oil presses and port which sends the precious liquid off around the world. (The Tunisian National Office for Oil is in charge of collecting, stocking and exporting the olive oil).

After Middle Eastern countries like Iraq, the Maghreb is one of the major date palm producers in the world... Algeria is at the top of the league with 5 million palm trees, followed by Morocco (4 million) and Tunisia (3 million).

These providential desert region trees measure from 15 to 30 metres tall and grow in all the hot regions of the world between the 15° and 30° latitudes, "their feet in the water and their heads in the flames". They produce their fruit after about 12 years, and in the major producing countries, 30 to 100 kg of fruit may be harvested per tree, and 3 to 15 tonnes per hectare.

Tunisia produces about 65,000 tonnes of dates per year – a tenth of which are exported – in the southern oases around the el Djérid Chott (Nefta, Tozeur, Kébili, Douz), or

strip of scarcely vegetated pasture, which, without the refreshing shade that the tutelary tree provides, would only exist a short time before its shoots withered away...
The date harvest takes place in the autumn, more or less early, given the numerous varieties of the species. Dates destined for the shops, for example, are gathered before they are completely ripe and are spread out in the sun so they finish ripening as they dry.
There are a very small number of privileged trees that produce camel loads of fruit, that is about four to five quintals. The date is a food that is extraordinarily healthy. Eaten alone with nothing else, it is not enough to feed a man however. Indeed, the poor have to have a little cereal with it, and the nomad some meat and camel's milk from time to time...
DR GUSTAVE NACHTINGAL
Sahara et Soudan.

along the Mediterranean coast (Gabès).

In the Nefta palm grove alone, there are about 400,000 trees. This immense forest needs to be vigilantly looked after by man, who has to supply a lot of irrigation. In Nefta, the palm grove is irrigated by a complex system of little channels which are supplied by 152 springs!

Over two hundred varieties of dates are harvested in the oases, including the succulent *"deglet nour"* ("finger of light"), which is exported the world over. The little dry, firm dates are eaten locally. When they are crushed and grounded, they produce a flour which replaces bread. Crushed in water and fermented, they produce "date wine". Along with the date production, the palms also produce "palm wine" (*laghmi*), fire and building wood, and the leaves are used for making roofs, mats and baskets.

Market gardening and fruit growing is rapidly developing in the north (the Tunis and Cap Bon region), mainly producing tomatoes, citrus fruit, melons, water melons, apricots and almonds (the Tell region and in the steppes).

Foreign visitors will be delighted to discover high-quality Tunisian wines in restaurants, even if these are not yet well known abroad. Wine is produced in temperate regions in northern and central Tunisia, for example in the Medjerda valley, on Cap Bon, and in the Zaghouan, Sousse and Monastir regions. The best known wines include Mornag, Thibar, Koudiat, Saint Cyprien, Château Feriani, etc. Over 200,000 hectolitres of wine are produced each year.

Other cultures include esparto grass, which is used for making paper (100,000 tonnes a year), and cork oak (the Tabarka region).

Sheep and goats

Tunisia is also a rearing country. This activity is particularly widespread in the central and southern regions of the country. There are currently over 7.6 million animals. As the climate tends to be dry, sheep and goats are the best adapted to the vast central regions (the Tell steppes) and southern coast of Tunisia.

In 1992, there were over 5 million sheep and 1.2 million goats. There are fewer cattle, as they are less resistant to the heat – 660,000 heads – and these are mainly reared in modern pilot centres.

Donkeys, mules and dromedaries, which are essentially used for carrying people or goods, are reared by the nomads in the southern Saharan areas (Djérid), using traditional methods, which are not highly productive. The nomad continue to move from the southern pastures to northern pastures as the summer approaches, and vice versa during the autumn, winter and spring when the southern pastures are renewed. Small rearing is developing rapidly: poultry farming is practised in vast modern industrial centres.

Fishing: a multitude of ports

With its 1,300 km of coastline, Tunisia is particularly well endowed in the fishing domain, to the extent that over the years, a port was created every 40 kilometres, and today there are nearly thirty ports (the main ports are at Tabarka, Bizerte, La Goulette, Sidi Daoud, Kélibia, Mahdia, Sfax, Kerkennah, Gabès, Djerba and Zarzis). Tunisia also has a large fishing fleet of over 10,000 fishing boats.

From 1962 to 1992, catches (grouper, gilthead, sole, sardine, mackerel, mullet, bass, octopus) have increased from 30,000 to 100,000 tonnes, and 50,000 fishermen are employed in this sector.

With 17,000 tonnes of fish sold abroad for an income of over 100 million dollars in currency, fishing has become the most important export industry, overtaking olive oil production.

Like its Algerian and Libyan neighbours, Tunisia has rich mineral wealth. Until recently, its largest mining revenues came from the exploitation and sale of phosphates. Producing 6.4 million tonnes annually, Tunisia is the fourth phosphate producer in the world. The crude mineral is extracted from deposits in the Gafsa (Metlaoui, Redeyef and Moularès) and Kef regions, and is then taken to the major chemical plants in Sfax, Maknassy and Gabès where it is transfor-

*Agriculture, fishing and rearing
are the pillars of Tunisia's
economic prosperity
along with tourism.*

med into sulfuric acid, nitrates and fertilizers.

During the last few decades, petrol and gas production has started complementing phosphate production as the El Borma reserves in the Tunisian Sahara, the Sidi Litayem reserves near to Sfax, the Douleb reserves between Thala and Sbeïtla, and the Ashtart and Tazerka offshore reserves out at sea from Sfax and Cap Bon respectively have started to be exploited. In total 5.4 million tonnes of petrol were produced in 1992, compared with 4.9 million in 1989 (petrol reserves have been estimated at 232 million tonnes). Furthermore, natural gas deposits have also been discovered and are now being exploited at El Borma in the south of the country, and at Miskar off the Kerkennah islands, enabling Tunisia to extract over 380 million cubic metres of gas each year (total reserves are estimated at 88 billion cubic metres).

In order to break into the hydrocarbure domain, Tunisia has increased prospecting and drilling throughout the country, built pipelines (linking the Douleb, Sidi Latayem, El Borma deposits to the Skhira petrol port), and gas pipelines between Algeria (Hassi R'Mel), the Tunisian sites and the Skhira, Tunis, and Bizerte ports.

Huge investments have also been made to develop the Skhira and Bizerte petrol ports, and to build the first refinery at Bizerte (a second one is planned on the Cape Serrat site on the northern coast to the west of Bizerte).

Furthermore, new petrol and gas deposits may soon be exploited, either in the Sbeïtla region (High Steppes), at Sabria, south of the chott el Djérid and Laarich, near to Tataouine, or offshore from Djerba and the Kerkennah islands, as well as in the Hammamet Gulf.

This energy policy has paid off as hydrocarbures now represent 20% of Tunisia's export revenues (680 million dinars).

Other minerals include zinc (9,400 tonnes, deposits near to Béja and Jendouba in the north-west), lead (in the north-west of the country), iron (295,000 tonnes in 1992, near to Djérissa in the north-west), salt (at Sousse, Sfax and Tunis), and spar flourine (near to Nabeul).

Like most developing countries, after independence Tunisia launched its industrialisation process with the food and agricultural sector. This was so successful that today, this industry is highly diversified, ranging from oil production to cork, from fish products, paper production, dairy products to animal feed, etc. The country's deeply-rooted craft traditions (carpet making, copper work, pottery, basketry, leatherwork, weaving, etc.) are very much alive today and new export markets have developed.

Tunisia's heavy industry was considerably developed next with the help of foreign investors. Developments have been principally focused on refining the country's mineral wealth (the Bizerte refinery, the Gafsa, Gabès, Zarzis, Sbeïtla, Tunis, and Bizerte chemical plants, the Menzel Bourguiba steelworks, and the Tunis and Bizerte cement works).

Light industry has not been overlooked. Textiles, the clothing industry, car assembly plants, electronics and electrical goods are expanding considerably at the moment.

Africa's foremost tourist country

Tunisia's tertiary sector (services) is booming and is both the country's major employer (36% of the working population are involved in this sector), and the country's major producer (accounting for over 50% of the Gross National Product).

Tourism tops the services sector, with over 4 million European tourists a year (Germans, Italians, French, Spanish). The fully expanding tourist industry has become the country's first "export" activity (guarantying an influx of currency), as its revenues cover over 60% of Tunisia's trade deficit. It is also one of the country's major employers with 44,000 people working in the tourist industry and hotels, and 300,000 people indirectly involved.

Tunisia is now the "blue ribbon" of African tourism, a long way ahead of Africa's other major tourist countries (Morocco, Egypt, Kenya, Senegal).

It owes this success both to all its natural qualities – it is a little, peaceful country, with beautiful beaches and an astonishing cultural and artistic patrimony – and to the dynamism of the public authorities and the private sector who work in close collaboration.

The public authorities – the Ministry for Tourism and the branches of the ONTT (Office National du Tourisme Tunisien) – are in charge of promoting and publicising Tunisian tourism abroad. At the same time, they make considerable efforts to upkeep and restore tourist sites in the country (renovation of the Tunis and Sfax medinas, renovation and creation of diverse museums, etc.)

For several years now, private Tunisian investors have undertaken a bold policy to develop the hotel network, sometimes with the support of foreign loans. They have thus built a lot of quality hotels and holiday resorts, first of all along the Mediterranean coast (Djerba island, Nabeul and Hammamet), and then inland.

Tunisian tourism has taken on a new aspect of late. In addition to the more classic beach networks, inland tourism is being greatly encouraged. The aim is for foreign visitors to discover the wonders of the inland regions, for example to numerous vestiges of Roman towns (Dougga, Bulla Regia, Sufetula, Thuburbo Majus, El Djem, etc.) and the major cultural centres (Kairouan, for example).

The deep Saharan south with its Berber villages, nomads and unusual architecture (the Matmata troglodytic dwellings and the *ksour* in the Tataouine region) is a tourist region to be promoted.

The public authorities are lucky enough to be able to count on the private sector to carry out such tourist developments, which now involve the whole country. The private sector has already most courageously begun building in the regions of the future which are still largely unknown to tourists, like the deep Saharan south or the Tabarka coast right in the north.

Trading and transportation

The Tunisians have not forgotten their ancestors, the Phoenician and then Carthaginian trader-shipowners, and the rich caravaneers who developed trans-Saharan trade between Black Africa and the Mediterranean basin. Nowadays, a great many Tunisians survive on national and international commerce and on the transport industry (roads, railways, sea and air travel). Indeed, in terms of Gross Domestic Product, trade and transportation currently represent four times as much as hydrocarbures and twice as much as fishing and agriculture.

Maritime traffic is important as Tunisia has five major commercial ports (Tunis-La Goulette-Radès, Sfax, Bizerte, Gabès and Sousse) which handled 14 million tonnes of merchandise in 1992. Moreover, the Tunisian merchant navy is equipped with a modern fleet of over 70 ships with a combined capacity of nearly 500,000 tonnes.

Roads play an essential role in Tunisia, which now has a good 20,200 km network, nearly two thirds of which are surfaced. Over 300,000 cars, buses, and innumerable goods vehicles (trucks and vans) use these roads.

The *railways* dispose of a 2,242 km network which serves two thirds of the country (north and centre), and which transports an average of over 30 million voyagers and 10 million tonnes of freight each year.

Air travel is expanding. Tunisia, which up until recently had five international airports (Tunis-Carthage, Monastir, Djerba and Tozeur-Sfax), has recently opened a sixth one at Tabarka, which will help to break the isolation of the north-western region. In 1992, passenger traffic rose to 5.5 million people, and the airlines handled 14,000 tonnes of freight.

site by site

tunis

■ In order to really appreciate Tunis, visitors need to imagine it through the eyes of the Saharan and Sahelian peoples who, for centuries, revered "Green Tunis".

In their eyes it was the Promised Land: after weeks of crossing the desert, they would suddenly come across the sight of streams and cascading waterfalls watering gardens full of flowers, of orchards bursting with fruit trees, and all this water, so rare and so precious in their arid lands, flowing in abundance, to waste even...

Think for a moment of the words nomads from Chad often used to chant: "Take us to the land of Green Tunis... Even if we have no millet, the waters of Tunis alone will be enough to support us... Green Tunis is a paradise..."

In Nigeria it was known as "Tunis the prosperous" and "Tunis the blessed". The town inspired the same magical aura for other West African peoples who, in their folk tales, evoked "this beautiful and rich oasis with its plants and trees so green..."

The sparkling mirror of Tunis Lake

European visitors flying into Tunis will not be disappointed. In the daytime, planes fly over the green hills of Carthage and Sidi Bou Saïd, and over the belt of market gardens around Tunis before landing by the sparkling mirror of Tunis Lake where the colonies of flamingos live.

Flying in over the Tunisian capital at night time is even more magical. The ground twinkles and flickers like a Christmas tree, from the ships anchored in La Goulette port to the checker-board of Tunis's main avenues (Avenues Bourguiba, Mohamed V, de Paris, de Carthage, and de la République)...

Contrary to what most people think, Tunis is not situated on the shores of the Mediterranean, but on the Little Sea (*El Bahira*), a lagoon which is connected to the sea via La Goulette pass.

Salty lakes (*sebkhas*) nestled at the foot of hills are very common in this rugged north-eastern region of Tunisia, for example the lakes of Bizerte, Ichkeul and Ghar el Melh near to the port of Bizerte north of Tunis. The Tunisian capital is also surrounded by a string of natural stretches of water: El Bahira (Tunis Lake), sebkhet Sedjoumi and sebkhet er Ariana.

When Tunis was founded by the Phoenicians several centuries B.C., it was no more than a tiny village.

Later, when the Arabs began their invasions in the 7th century A.D., it was still a very small garrison town tucked behind the high walls of its medina, but there was also the sea port which was just beginning to become important.

Up until the 13th century, the capitals of Arabic Ifriqyya (modern-day Tunisia) were Kairouan and Mahdia. In the 11th and 12th centuries, at the end of the period of unrest caused by the fearsome Beni Hillal nomads' ravages, governors were posted to Tunis by the Almohad sovereigns of Morocco in order to try to restore peace in the country. These governors who founded the Hafsid dynasty, made Tunis their capital and settled in the Kasbah.

When it was designated the capital during Abou Zakariya's reign (1229-1249) in the 13th century, Tunis – successor to Carthage, Kairouan and Mahdia – already seemed too hemmed in and soon began to overrun its too small walls, which were knocked down, and spread outwards to the Bab Souika and Bab Djezira suburbs. During the Hafsids' reign, the Andalousian Muslims – who had been chased out of Spain by King Alphonso XIII – settled in Tunis. This was a blessing for the town, which suddenly unexpectedly acquired an educated elite. Thanks to this elite, Tunis became an influential cultural and religious centre where mosques, zawiyyas, souks, hospitals and medersas sprang up. Furthermore, it became a foremost economic centre thanks to the development of trade, crafts and banking.

A turbulent past

From the 13th century right up to modern times, Tunis' historical path was a turbulent one. In 1270, the French King Saint Louis, leader of the eighth crusade, tried to capture the Tunisian capital in vain before he and his companions died during an

Preceding pages:
Tunisia's turbulent history forced the Takrouna villagers to take refuge on a peak between Hammamet and Sousse. Nowadays they can at last descend into the valley to cultivate their orchards safely.

outbreak of the plague. In the 14th century and again in the 16th century, it was successively occupied by the Merinids of Morocco and by the pirate Barbarossa. This gave Charles Quint an excuse to capture the town in 1535, sending his Spanish troops to occupy it until 1574. The Turks took over next, setting up a regency governed by a dey, a pasha and a bey. In the 17th century, the title of bey was made hereditary, and the bey became all-powerful in Tunisia up until the creation of the French Protectorate in 1881. Under the Protectorate, the country was ruled by a French general resident, and the bey became a purely nominal title. In 1956, Tunisia gained independence, and became a republic the following year, with Tunis as its capital.

Over the centuries, the Tunis agglomeration has expanded outwards from the Medina central core. Its districts have sprung up haphazardly in the surrounding region, hugging the contours of Tunis Lake and sebkhet Sedjoumi. The town has gradually reached and engulfed the little agglomerations to the east (La Goulette, Carthage, La Marsa, Gammarth) and south-east (Ben Arous, Hammam-Lif), forming one vast conurbation.

Tunis currently has 700,000 inhabitants, whereas Greater Tunis (the conurbation) is close to 2 million inhabitants. Its different neighbourhoods tend to be specialised: the Medina and its huge souks, for example, remain the centre of crafts and small commercial trading.

The popular neighbourhoods of Halfaouine and Bab Souika have expanded all around the old town. The ministries are concentrated in the Kasbah district to the west of the Medina, and the major schools and universities are grouped in La Rabta and the University campus districts.

The town centre: the "lower town"

The "lower town" where the new districts were built under the Protectorate stretches east of the Medina as far as the port. This is where the town centre is situated, along with the large hotels, banks, restaurants, and luxury boutiques.

The residential districts (Lafayette, Montplaisir, Cité Jardins) have developed around the Parc du Belvédère, whilst the port and Lake Tunis are surrounded by popular neighbourhoods.

Tunis port, which has been redeveloped several times, is linked to the sea and La Goulette outer harbour by a canal dug in 1890. This enables large sea-faring ships to enter the shallow waters of Lake Tunis and to come right into the town. Trains and vehicles cross the lake via the two parallel causeways made from earth extracted from the canal.

The main Tunis-Carthage international airport was built on the northern shores of this Little Sea, and is surrounded by industrial zones, for example the Charguia zone.

Major urban freeways have recently been developed throughout the Greater Tunis agglomeration, along with a small underground train which links the town centre with the Ariana suburb in the north, the cité Ibn Khaldoun and Bardo in the west, and Ben Arous in the south.

A regional development plan elaborated in 1977 aimed to slow down the growth of the Tunisian capital, as its population had been growing in a completely uncontrolled manner for several decades due to the acute rural exodus.

Avenue Bourguiba, a large promenade lined with ficus trees where thousands of birds nest, is the "Champs-Elysées" of Tunis and is one of the capital's prides with its large hotels, banks and cafés with terraces.

Florists' stalls, news stands, and snack bars have mushroomed on the platform in the middle of the avenue. The east-west Avenue Bourguiba begins at the Tunis port and La Goulette dyke on Lake Tunis and continues westwards via the Place du 7 Novembre 1987, which has a large clock in the middle (and is bordered by the ONTT, the Ministry of Tourism, and the Hotel du Lac). It intersects Avenue Mohamed V, where the Congress Palace and Artisanal Palace are situated, at right angles.

Avenue Bourguiba then continues along its busiest stretch which becomes the Avenue de France before reaching the Porte de France, the main entrance to the Medina.

Vast baroque and rococo buildings inherited from the colonial period can be seen all along this

TUNIS AND ITS OUTSKIRTS

MEDITERRANEAN

SEA

Cape Gammarth

Gammarth
Beach

LA MARSA

Sidi Bou Saïd

Amilcar

ɔud

Carthage

Salammbo

Le Kram

LA GOULETTE

ort

ULF OF TUNIS

Az-Zahra

HAMMAM-LIF

namet

Djebel Bou Kornine

main road, for example the *Munici-pal Theatre*, which looks like a great white cake with a pediment decorated by a group of statues. Modern high-rise buildings have recently been built, for example the *Hotel Africa* and the *International Tunisia*. The terraces of several cafés spill out onto the pavements, notably the *Café de Paris*, the meeting place for the fashionable Tunis crowd. The *Passage du Colisée* commercial centre with its indoor bar and a cinema is also worth visiting. At the western end of the avenue is the Ibn Khaldoun monument in honour of the Berber historian born in Tunis, the neo-Roman style *Saint-Vincent-de-Paul Cathedral*, and opposite, the *French Embassy*. The *Central Market* is situated in the town centre, along with the main post office to the south of Avenue de France. On the Avenue de Paris is the beautiful "Twenties" style *Hotel Majestic*.

A fascinating Medina

The old quarter of Tunis (*Medina*), which is an UNESCO listed site, stretches westwards from the modern town centre after the large Avenue Bourguiba and Avenue de France.

In contrast to the large open spaces of the modern centre, the Medina is a fascinating, swarming, closed-in world which, at first sight, seems to be an inextricable labyrinth.

Armed with a good map and with a few landmarks, visitors will end up knowing it inside out after a few days' walking. There is no point in being worried about getting lost as it is only by going the wrong way and retracing one's steps several times that the hidden beauties will be discovered. Moreover, the Medina is not dangerous: visitors will be more likely to be invited to drink a mint tea than to have their wallets pinched.

Many marvels of Islamic architecture are found in the Medina, including mosques (*jamaa*), palaces (*dar*), Koranic universities (*medersas*), and mausoleums (*tourbet*). There are three main routes which enable visitors to explore them thoroughly: one covers the heart of the Medina with the Central Mosque and the souks, another the south (around Tourbet el Bey), and the third covers the northern part of the Medina (around the Maison de la Poésie).

There are several possible entrances to the Medina, but the most obvious one is situated at the end of Avenue de France, which is the continuation of Avenue Bourguiba. This leads into the little Place de la Victoire. In the centre of this square the Porte de France (*Bab el Bahar*) is situated.

Beyond this very lively little square where the *British Embassy* (with its beautiful blue studded door) is located, two main routes – Rue Jamaa Zitouna and Rue de la Kasbah – cut deep into the heart of the Medina.

The first, which is lined with antique, bric-a-brac and souvenir stalls, leads directly to the Central Mosque. In the first road on the right (Rue de l'Ancienne Douane), is the *Foundouk des Français*, an old caravanserai. Heading back to Rue de la Zitouna, visitors will pass in front of the now abandoned 17th century *Sainte-Croix Church*. Carried along by the flow of the crowds, head back along the narrow street which sweeps under an arch. Visitors will just be taking in the packed terraces of the very charming eateries along the way (very rustic dishes are served here at incredibly low prices. Do not ask for alcoholic drinks) before the street opens out onto a small esplanade where the Central Mosque is located.

The Ez Zitouna Central Mosque

Originally built in the 7th century, the *Zitouna* (Olive tree) *Central Mosque* has been modified several times, notably during the Aghlabid emir Ibrahim ibn Ahmed's reign (856-863). The prayer room has 184 columns, most of which are surmounted by ancient capitals, and its annulated Zirid style dome (9th century) is supported by a drum whose alcoves and stones have beautifully harmonious colours. In the 15th century, a library was built, and in the following century, a gallery with colonnades was added to the eastern facade. During the 17th century the Turks built the colonnade in the courtyard and in 1834, the Hispanic-Moorish style 44 metre tall minaret was built.

The Zitouna was originally Tunis's religious and political centre. Later on, it became a religious centre alone, and developed into a major forum of Islamic influence where Islamic law and theology were taught in the nearby medersas. Nowadays, it continues to be a centre of Islamic learning and Muslims come here for the ritual prayers.

The *Echammaïa medersa* and the 17th century *Hammouda Pacha mosque* with its octagonal minaret lie to the north of the Central mosque. To the south of the Central mosque is the *Mouradia medersa* and the complex of three medersas (Palmier, Bachia and Slimania). All were built during the 18th century and have an interior courtyard surrounded by a gallery with colonnades that leads to the students' lodgings and prayer room. Near to here is the *Kachachine Hammam* (Turkish baths), and the *National Library* which was created in 1814 in the former El Attarine barracks with its interior courtyard and gallery on several floors.

The noble guilds' souks are regrouped around the Central Mosque: the perfumers' souk (*el Attarine*), the material merchants' souk (*el K'mech*) and booksellers' souk (*el Koutbia*). Further to the west of the Zitouna are the jewellers' souks (*el Berka*), and the saddlers' souk (*es Sarrajine*). To the north are the Turkish souk (*el Trouk*), the fez makers' souk (*ech Chaouachia*), the *Souk el Bey*, and the babouche makers' souk (*el Blaghjiya*). Even further northwards is the *souk el Blat*, the copper souk (*en Nahas*) and the grain souk (*el Grana*).

Of all these covered markets, visitors will be particularly interested in the *souk Eltrouk* (Turkish souk) where the carpet sellers are concentrated. Weavers can be seen working here, and it is possible to buy the nomads' *kilims, mergoums,* hangings and shawls.

These traders had the clever idea of installing wonderful terraces on the roofs in order to attract clients. Escaping from the stale air of the souks for a few minutes, visitors can enjoy the superb panoramic view over Tunis. From these belvederes decorated with ceramic tiles, the minarets of the Central and Turkish Mosques can be seen emerging from the sea of roofs, and Bou El Kornine and the Belvédère rise up on the horizon.

Next, it is worth visiting *souk el Berka* (the jewellers' and goldsmiths' souk) where the little indoor square was once a slave market. The slaves were paraded on a platform and auctioned off. In the covered, lit corridors of the market, jewellers have set up tiny, marvellous bijou stalls with painted and decorated windows.

Heading westwards from here, visitors will come across the *Sidi Youssef Bey mosque*, built by a former Tunisian sovereign (17th century), with its octagonal Turkish style minaret, then the 17th century *dar el Bey*, the palace where the government is housed, and former residence of the Tunis beys (it is not open to the public, and it is forbidden to take photos), before coming to the edge of the Medina.

In the past, the *kasbah*, or fortress where the Tunis sovereigns lived for a long time, was situated to the west. The *kasbah mosque* is worth visiting. Built in the 13th century under the Hafsid dynasty, it has a beautiful Almohad style square minaret like the one at the Koutoubia mosque in Marrakech.

On the way back into the Medina through the south-west districts is the *Sidi Boukhrissan Mausoleum* (which houses the tombs of the Beni Khourassan dynasty, who ruled during 11th-12th centuries), the *dar el Haddad* (built in 16th century, it is one of the oldest houses in the Medina), the *el Ksar mosque* (built in the 12th century, with a 17th century minaret), the *dar Hussein* (now the head offices of the Archaeology Institute, this palace has a beautiful courtyard with an earthenware decorated peristyle), and the *hammam Daouletli*.

The poetry centre

A second route takes us right into the southern part of the Medina. The Rue Tourbet el Bey leads to the *kouttab Ibn Khaldoun* and the *Tourbet El Bey* (the mausoleum built in 1780 to house royal family tombs). Further along is the *dar Ben Abdal-lah*, the old palace which houses the museum of Tunisian popular traditions (the wonderful rooms are full of furniture and things which once belonged to the grand Tunis families). A little further still, is the *Teinturiers' (dyers) Mosque*, or *New Mosque (Jamaa Jadid)* built at the beginning of 18th century by bey Hussein, founder of the Husseinite dynasty, and the *dar Othman*, the palace built by dey Othman in the 16th century.

A third route leads to the north of the Medina. There visitors can see the *Sidi Mahrez mosque* (patron of Tunis) with its beautiful white domes and high tiered square minaret, the *Maison de la Poésie* (poetry centre) which has been set up in the dar el Dzira, an old 18th-century palace, the *hammam* on Rue ed-Deheb, and the *dar Lasram*, a former palace, now the headquarters of the "Association de sauvegarde de la Médina de Tunis". To the north of the Medina are the popular districts of Bab Souika and Halfaouine which were made famous by Férid Boughedir's film "Halfaouine".

Belvédère hill to the north of Tunis is considered to be "Tunis's green heart". Lovers and strollers come here to admire the superb views over Tunis, and sports lovers come jogging here. At the foot of the hill, a beautiful stretch of water surrounded by cafés with terraces is a favorite meeting place for local families. In the Belvédère park there is also a *zoo*, the *Museum of Modern Art* (exhibitions of contemporary Tunisian artists' work), a swimming pool and a stadium.

In the *El Menzah district* to the north of the park, there are beautiful Moorish colonial and cubist 1930s-style buildings and villas.

To the south is the Sidi el Béchir district (ex-Montfleury), where the *Jellaz cemetery* is situated, and the Sedjoumi quarter overlooking the *Sebkhet Sedjoumi*.

West of Tunis, the *Bardo Museum* situated in the neighbourhood of the same name, is one of the most beautiful museums in the world. Its collections are devoted to Antiquity (*see later*).

Visitors without a car should take the little TGM train (Tunis-La Goulette-La Marsa) to go and discover the pretty beach resorts around Tunis.

Modern and traditional architecture cohabit harmoniously in Tunis,
which has conserved its old medina
dominated by the beautiful Zitouna mosque (above right),
but which also has main streets
like the elegant Bourguiba Avenue (below right).

bardo (the)

Passing via the causeway across Lake Tunis – where groups of flamingos may be spotted – the railway goes to *La Goulette*, the fishing and commercial port whose beach and innumerable fish restaurants are very popular among Tunis's residents (especially as the town is only 12 km from the capital). It is worth visiting the 16th-century fortress built here by Charles Quint during the Spanish occupation from 1535 to 1574.

The TGM then passes through *Salammbô* and *Carthage*, which were immortalised by the French novelist Gustave Flaubert (*see later*), heads on via *Amilcar* and *Sidi Bou Saïd*, a charming village perched up on the cliffs (*see later*), and terminates at *La Marsa* (former summer residence of the Tunis beys; venue for malouf concerts at Saf-Saf).

Shortly after La Marsa, *Gammarth* is set up on the corniche. Several good restaurants with terraces overlook the sea, for example the "Grand Bleu".

Lying between the Mediterranean sea and the sebkhet Ariana, *Raouad*, north-west of Gammarth, has a wonderful beach which is very popular with holiday makers.

Ez Zahra and *Hammam-Lif* (former beylik town), the first seaside resorts on the outskirts of the Tunisian capital, lie to the south-east of Tunis. Further to the east, is the *Cap Bon peninsula* (*see later*) where the major seaside resorts of *Hammamet* and *Nabeul* have been developed (*see later*).

Taking the RN 3 road southwards out of Tunis, visitors will discover *La Mohamédia* and the vestiges of 18th and 19th-century royal palaces, before coming to a *Roman aqueduct* which used to take water from the *Zaghouan* heights (at the foot of the djebel of the same name) as far as Carthage.

(*See information p. 184*).

■ The only known portrait of the Latin poet Virgil (done in mosaic) and a huge 137 m^2 mosaic, which is possibly the largest in the world, are the two star features of the Bardo palace in Tunis, which has one of the most beautiful collection of Roman mosaics in the world.

This Moorish style palace built in the Bardo district to the west of Tunis, is a superb building in the middle of a park. In the past it was the residence of the Tunis sovereigns up until the creation of the Republic and the deposition of the last bey, Mohamed Ali Amin, in 1957.

The *museum* does not take up the whole of the Bardo which is in fact a group of buildings, one of which houses the *National Assembly* (not open to the public), and an old *arsenal* (currently being restored).

Like the Louvre in Paris, the Pitti Palace in Florence or the Vatican museum, the Bardo is in keeping with the major museum tradition, as most of these are housed in imposing buildings which were once the homes of the ruling families of this world.

The Bardo treaty

During the beys' time, the Bardo was the theatre of some important historic events. It was here that the May 1881 treaty making Tunisia a French Protectorate was signed by Sidi Sakok Bey and General Bréart, who was sent by Jules Ferry.

Today, the museum still shows the traces of its distinguished guests, much to the delight of visitors who cannot fail to notice the beauty of the sovereigns' private suites now converted into exhibition rooms. Visitors can cut across the charming patio decorated with a fountain from the Islamic department, and, looking upwards in the Virgil room, will see the little dome covered with superb lace stuccoes, and the painted wooden coffered ceilings in the former music room.

As the Bardo museum houses items found during archaeological excavations carried out throughout the whole of Tunisia, it has very rich collections of objects and documents that go back to Carthaginian and Roman times, or to the era of the Arab invasions. It is especially famous for its mosaics, however, which were originally from the Roman towns of Bulla Regia, Hadrumete, Uthina, Thuburbo Majus, etc. (a whole morning or afternoon is necessary).

The rooms on the ground floor offer an overview of Tunisian prehistory. Amongst the most remarkable items and monuments are the little female figurines carved out of stone in the Capsian period (end of the Palaeolithic era), and the strange Hermaion monument from El Guettar (near to Gafsa) which dates from the Middle Palaeolithic era (40,000 years). This curious monument dedicated to the spirit of a stream consists of a pyramid of stone balls, carved flints and animal bones.

Also on the ground floor are the remnants of Punic Carthage destroyed by the Romans in 146 B.C. Of particular interest are the rare terracotta representation of the god Baal Hammon, the very famous stele carved with a priest and a child destined for sacrifice, and a few grimacing masks placed in sepultures to ward off evil spirits.

Several rooms are devoted to the Roman and pre-Christian collections, in particular objects found during digs at Thuburbo Majus, Tabarka (ornamental tiling representing the cross section of one of the first Christian churches in Tunisia, dating from 4th century A.D.), and Bulla Regia (statues of Apollo, Aesculapius and Ceres).

The large mosaics and a vast collection of antique statues are displayed on the first floor. In the Carthage gallery, visitors will notice the statue of the emperor Hadrian, as well as the huge one of an empress from Roman Carthage. On the ground are the famous 3rd century Roman mosaics representing Bacchus giving a vine to a peasant, and rural scenes. These came from the Laberii villa in Oudna (Uthina) to the south of Tunis.

The large Sousse room follows on from the Carthage gallery. One of the largest mosaics in the history of Roman art representing various sea deities in coils, and notably the Triumph of Neptune, can be seen on the floor. On the wall, the famous mosaic of lord Julius illustrates the life of a Roman nobleman in the country. In the Dougga room there is another version of the triumph of Neptune, the four corners of which are surrounded by allegories of the four seasons (2nd century A.D.). Another mosaic representing the cyclops forging in Vulcan's lair is remarkable for its realism (4th century). In the little El Djem room, there are still lives of game, fish and fruit, and of the triumph of Bacchus (3rd century).

The Virgil room contains one of the museum's gems: the earliest portrait of the Latin poet surrounded by the Muses Clio and Melpomene (from a villa in Sousse, 3rd century A.D.). A beautiful medallion mosaic representing the deities of the days of the week and the zodiac signs is displayed on the floor (from Bir Chana in the Zaghouan region).

Another first floor room contains the treasure of a Greek boat which was shipwrecked off Mahdia. It contained superb bronze and marble statues of Venus and a young satyr, which have been a little damaged by their time under water.

On the same floor, look out for the famous mosaic of Odysseus tied to the mast of his ship listening to the mermaids singing, which comes from Dougga (4th century), the two mosaics representing the crowning of Venus (Carthage, 4th century, and Ellès, Maktar, 4th century), and the floor tiling showing wild boar hunting scenes, horse races and the marriage of Bacchus and Ariadne.

Diana, the goddess of hunting

On the second floor are funereal objects from the Roman period (glassware, pottery, statuettes) along with some superb mosaics: Venus on the rock, Diana the goddess of hunting, Hercules' Labours, the triumph of Bacchus, and the Four Seasons.

In the Althiburos room there is an unusual mosaic with the drawings of 23 types of ancient ships.

On the way back down to the first floor is the Islamic department which has some beautiful collections of furniture (mirrors, caskets, beds, benches, screens), musical instruments, and ancient weapons.

There are superb calligraphic books, notably the famous blue Kairouan Koran whose *suras* are covered in golden Kufic writing.

(*See information p. 184*).

bizerte

■ Bizerte's strategic position on the Sicily straits overlooking the two Mediterranean basins, has meant that, for many years, it has been as hotly disputed as Gibraltar or the Golden Horn of Istanbul. Over the centuries, it has therefore had quite a turbulent history from the time of the Carthaginians' and Romans' *Hippo Diarrythus,* up until the creation of a French military naval base in the 20th century.

A powerful naval base

At the time of the Protectorate, the French dug a bottleneck canal linking Lake Bizerte to the Mediterranean, which made Bizerte a powerful naval base.

This base in turn harboured part of the Serbian army in 1916, the Russian counter-revolutionary fleet led by the Tzarist general Wrangel in 1921, and finally the defeated Spanish Republicans' fleet in 1939.

During the Second World War, Bizerte surrendered to the Germans in 1942, then was liberated by the Allies in May 1943 – shortly before the Sicily landings – after over 250 air bombings in six months, which caused some serious damage.

As France had still not handed over Bizerte a short while after Tunisian independence in 1956, violence broke out in 1961 during which 3,000 Tunisians died. Bizerte was finally granted its independence in 1963.

Today, it is as if Bizerte wished to settle down to a well-earnt rest from history's turbulent events, finding itself a new and less arduous vocation. One of the several projects being considered would make the town into a 46 hectare free zone, thereby attracting new industrial investors which would give the town's economy a kick start.

In the meantime, Bizerte appears to be a most peaceful town, especially around the Old port by the Medina below the fortress (*kasbah*), dating back to the 13th and 17th centuries. During the summer, children splash around in the water, whilst adults spend hours in the cafés or their brightly painted boats, repairing the fishing nets.

After the Place Slahedine Bouchoucha (look out for the 1642 foun-

*Bizerte, which was once a hideaway
for the Barbary pirates and later a military base,
now offers the peaceful image
of an old port lined with
traditional fishing boats.*

tain and the Rebaa mosque with a square minaret), the *Medina* can be reached via a maze of streets and alleys where visitors can see innumerable shops and workshops a-buzz with activity, or can visit the 17th century *Central Mosque*.

From the ramparts of the *Fort d'Espagne* built by the Turks in 1573 and recently converted into an open-air theatre, there is a wonderful view over the town.

The *Quartier des Andalous* (Andalousian Moors), chased out of Spain in the 17th century, stretches to the north of the Kasbah. This is one of the most picturesque districts with its little arched streets and painted and studded doors. The fish market, Crafts centre, the imposing Congress Palace and the Sidi Salem Fort (13th-17th centuries) should not be missed.

To the north of Bizerte, the Corniche, the town's Riviera, runs along to the cliffs of Cape Bizerte where a number of hotels have been built by the Cape Bizerte beach. After a short detour, the road comes to Cape Blanc whose rocky shores are very popular with scuba divers. The return journey goes via djebel Nador ("the Look-out mountain", 260 m) where the view is splendid.

Industrial suburbs have developed around Lake Bizerte (110 km^2): Zarzouna et Menzel Bourguiba (steelworks and chemicals), whereas oyster farming has developed at Menzel Jemil.

To the south-east of Bizerte are the picturesque villages of *Alia* (mosque and Andalousian streets with archways) on the slopes of djebel Hakima, and of *Metline* (Roman name: *Beneventum*), where the houses appear to be tilting down the hill. From here, visitors can follow the coast to the Remel, Rass Jebel and Raf-Raf beaches set in a region of vineyards and market gardens.

At Rass Sidi Ali el Mekki, there is a little headland. Plane Island lies just out to sea. The cape, which has a marabout and a necropolis, is a place of pilgrimage for Muslims in the region.

Ghar el Melh (the "Salt Hole") at the foot of djebel Nador (325 m), is the ancient port of Farina which served as a base for Charles Quint's fleet when he attacked Tunis in 1541, then as a hideaway for pirates. The orchards and vineyards of this

farming village and fishing port run alongside the lake of the same name.

At the foot of djebel Kochbata in the river Medjerda estuary, *Utica*, the earliest Phoenician trading post, was set up in Tunisia in 1101 B.C., three centuries before Carthage. After Carthage was destroyed in 146 B.C., the Roman proconsular authorities lived there up until the first century A.D. (when they moved back to the reconstructed town of Carthage). It was here that the Roman military chief Cato (great-grandson of Cato the Elder, archenemy of Punic Carthage) committed suicide whilst re-reading Plato's *Phaedo*: he had chosen the loosing camp (Pompey's) whereas Julius Caesar was going from victory to victory. In the past, Utica was a sea port, but the Medjerda river has deposited so much alluvium that the coast has receded several kilometres and the Gulf of Utica has disappeared. Nowadays Utica is landlocked, and lies several kilometres away from the sea.

Archaeological excavation work has led to the discovery of vestiges of the Roman town, including streets and houses (notably the splendid House of the Waterfall), whose floors are covered in mosaics. A huge Punic necropolis containing a number of sarcophagi has also been discovered. A small museum houses the wonderful collection of Punic jewellery, vases, amulets and steles.

Further to the south, the Tunis road crosses the Medjerda river via the Bizerte Bridge built in 1852. From here a little road heads northwards to Kalaat el Andalouss (*Castra Cornelia* under the Romans), a village inhabited by the descendants of the Andalousian Muslims chased out of Spain. The RN 8 then passes via Cebalat and Ariana before reaching the north of Tunis. To the south-west of Bizerte, the road runs alongside *Lake Ichkeul* (120 km^2). This lagoon and marshland at the foot of djebel Ichkeul (511 m) have been made into a natural reserve. It is now a botanical reserve and sanctuary for innumerable aquatic birds.

Continuing westwards towards Tabarka, the road comes to Sejnane (Berber pottery) and, on the coast, to the beautiful beaches of Cape Serrat and Sidi Mechrig, near to Cape Nègre. (*See information p. 184*).

cap bon (peninsula)

■ Cap Bon Peninsula near to Tunis looks like a finger pointing northwards towards Sicily, jutting out into the Mediterranean sea. It is just a hop of approximately one hundred kilometres over the Straits of Sicily, which is a tiny channel linking the eastern and western Mediterranean basins.

This fact alone speaks reams about Cap Bon's strategic importance and the role it has played in history from the time of the Carthaginians up until Rommel's army in the Second World War.

A splendid coastal road

The djebel Sidi Abderrahmane runs along the length of the peninsula like a backbone, forming steep cliffs which plunge down into the Gulf of Tunis.

Visitors driving along the corniche will be enchanted by the wild beauty of the landscape and the views of the coasts of Carthage and the Islands of Zembra and Zembretta.

Apart from Hammam-Lif, Bordj Cédria, Soliman and Sidi Raïs, there are few beaches on the west side of Cap Bon.

Indeed the pleasures of the idle life and the beach are found on the southern side of Cap Bon on the Gulf of Hammamet (the Menzel-Témime, Nabeul and Hammamet beaches).

It takes a day to drive around discovering the whole peninsula if you follow the itinerary below which sets out southwards from Tunis.

After driving along Tunis port and the Bellevue and Mégrine districts, skirt around the Radès port in the suburbs of the capital. This will bring you to *Hamman-Lif*, the closest beach to Tunis, dominated by the picturesque *djebel Bou Kornine* which looks like a sugar loaf.

The Cap Bon peninsula proper begins at *Bordj Cédria* beach and this marks the beginning of the route around the western part of the penin-

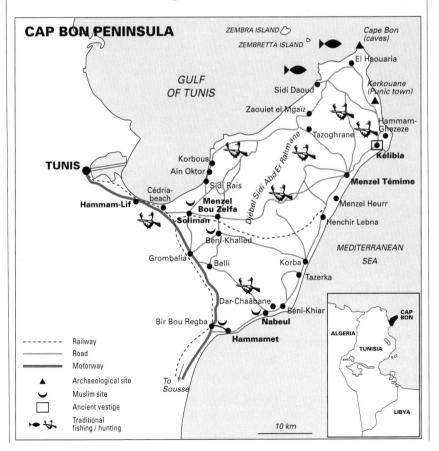

Northern Tunisia's
rich cereal growing lands
were thought of
as Rome's "wheat store"
in ancient times.

sula. At *Soliman* (a village founded by the Arabo-Andalousian refugees in the 17th century), a road on the right leads to *Menzel Bouzelfa* in the heart of a major citrus fruit producing region (festival of the orange tree in the spring time).

If you go straight on rather than turning off to Menzel Bouzelfa, the road leads to *Sidi Raïs* where the superb coastal corniche begins. After *Aïn Oktor* is *Korbous* (*Aquae Calidae Carpitanae* in Roman times), which is both a little family seaside resort and a thermal town reputed since ancient times. Its warm sodium chloride waters and cold sulphurated calcic waters cure rheumatism, arthritis, and some afflictions of the nervous system.

The route then inches its way up the djebel Sidi Abderrahmane passing via Sidi Aïssa and Zaouiet el Mgaïz before coming to *Sidi Daoud*. The "*Matanza*", a bloody tuna fishing ritual, is carried out in this little fishing port at certain times in the year (from May to the beginning of July). Tourists may be able to gain permission to go with the fishermen in order to see this violent and bloody tuna fishing spectacle.

During the culling, which is also practised in Sicily and southern Portugal, the fishermen group their fishing boats around in a circle out at sea. Fishing nets are lowered into this improvised arena and hauled in full of hundreds of tunny fish, some of which weigh up to 250 kg, writhing in their final death throes. The fishermen stab at the fish in a wild frenzy using harpoons, axes and knives amidst a gush of blood and seething foam.

With the Haouaria falconers

In *El Haouaria* on the tip of the peninsula, falconry and sparrow-hawking have been practised for centuries (*see under Haouaria*). A very active falconry club has been set up, and each year, once the birds of prey have been trained, the hunt for game birds commences. The hunting season finishes in great splendor in June with the falconry festival, which attracts more and more spectators every year.

On the nearby beaches, where visitors can enjoy the pleasures of beach life or go scuba-diving, it is worth visiting the caves right by the sea where slaves once extracted the blocks of sandstone used to build Carthage in ancient times. Out at sea, the Islands of *Zembra* and *Zembretta* (the *Aegimures* in Antiquity) were designated a protected marine reserve in 1973.

At Haouaria on the far end of Cap Bon, the road curves back round and heads down towards Nabeul and Hammamet on the eastern face of the peninsula.

En route, visitors should try to stop at *Kerkouane* where rare vestiges of a Carthaginian town have been uncovered. Founded in the 5th and 6th centuries B.C., it was ransacked several times by the Syracuse tyrant Ayatellus, and by the Roman general Regulus before being finally razed to the ground by the Romans at the end of the Punic wars in 140. Bathrooms with hip baths can be seen in the villas, which indicates that the Carthaginians were very advanced in terms of comfort.

Fishing by lamplight

Kélibia, the ancient Roman colony of Clupea founded by Caesar, is dominated by the kasbah, a Byzantine fortified castle built on a rocky headland in the 6th century (150 m). Its fishing port specialises in lamplight fishing. The fishermen attract shoals of "bluefish": sardines, anchovies, mackerels, etc. with lanterns fixed to their boats.

After Menzel-Témime (where there are beaches) and Henchir Lebna, the road cuts through Korba (the ancient Roman colony of Curubis, founded by Caesar), Tazerka, Béni Khiar (where covers and rugs are made using artisanal methods) and Dar Chaâbane (quarries and stone carving) before coming to the beaches of *Nabeul* (*see later*) and *Hammamet* (*see later*) thus completing the circuit around the Cap Bon peninsula.

In the space of a few years, these two towns on the edge of the Hammamet Gulf became very popular seaside resorts on the international tourist market, attracting essentially European holiday makers.

(*See information p. 185*).

carthage

■ Carthage is possibly one of the first towns in the history of mankind to have been martyred, followed in the 20th century by the destruction of Dresden and Le Havre by the British, Warsaw by the Germans and Hiroshima by the Americans. The Carthaginians were probably also amongst the first peoples to have been victims of a genocide.

Indeed, the Romans could not have made a better job of completely razing the town in the spring of 146 B.C. after ten days and ten nights of fierce fighting, fires and carnage. One of the sole survivors of this apocalypse, the Carthaginian general Hasdrubal's wife, preferred to throw herself and her children into the flames rather than to survive.

Then, in a terrifying display of singlemindedness, the Romans buried the ruins of Carthage, filled in the lot and covered the whole site with salt so the grass would not grow back. They then tried to totally obliterate their rival from the memory of mankind, from history, by deporting any survivors and forbidding any references to, or records of the Punic capital.

If it had not been for Julius Caesar and his nephew Augustus, who rebuilt a new Carthage on the original site, the town would have fallen into oblivion for ever.

A twist of irony had it that the Romans' determination to annihilate Carthage in fact had the inverse effect. As is always the case with martyrs, Carthage lived on in myths and legends, so much so that its heros, Hamilcar, Hannibal, Queen Dido and Salammbô have become a part of universal mythology.

Artists, writers, and musicians have immortalised these myths. The Latin poet Virgil began the trend in the *Aeneid*, by giving Aeneas' romantic liaison with Queen Dido an epic dimension. Purcell, the British composer, wrote one of the purple passages of the history of music in 1689: Dido's lament ("Dido and Aeneas"). In the 19th century, the French novelist Gustave Flaubert wrote the romantic tale of the beautiful Tanit priestess Salammbô.

DIDO'S CLEVER TRICK

■ *In the 8th century, Elissa-Dido, Belus's daughter, fled from her brother Pygmalion, the king of Tyre (modern-day Lebanon), when he killed her husband. She settled in Tunisia and founded Carthage (Kart-Hadasht, "the New Town") thanks to a clever trick. Indeed, when she landed on the site of Carthage, the local population agreed to give her a plot of land on the condition that it did not exceed the size of a cow hide. Dido agreed, and had the hide sown into such a great number of fine strips that they delimited a huge area!*

This woman, who was one of Virgil's heroines, was thus able to found a powerful Phoenician colony on Tunisian land that became the centre of a huge maritime and trading empire in the Mediterranean. Much of its wealth came from mining and trading Spanish silver and tin minerals. The Carthaginians' supremacy worried the rising Roman powers, however. After three wars, Rome reduced the Punic power to dust after having captured and destroyed Carthage in 146 B.C. The Carthaginian empire was spent and would not rise again from the ashes.

For a long time, no one really knew where the site of Punic Carthage was exactly.

The Arab historians wrote descriptions of Carthaginian ruins, but these were the ruins of Roman Carthage. In the 19th century, the first excavation works on Byrsa hill, in the suburbs of Tunis between La Goulette and Sidi Bou Saïd, sparked off a great deal of controversy. Some archaeologists even officially stated that the current site of Carthage should be looked for at Bejaïa (on the north-east coast of Algeria)!

Whatever, from 1880 to 1920, excavation work took place on Byrsa hill. First of all the Roman vestiges were uncovered, and then the Punic remains, although these only consisted of tombs. There were no traces of their houses, palaces or temples – once again the town of Hannibal had disappeared. Finally, the first Punic districts were uncovered, but new controversies broke out about the true position of the Punic temples and ports. The question of whether the Carthaginians really sacrificed children to the god Baal Hammon was also hotly disputed.

Even today, experts are divided on this point. Some think that descriptions of child sacrifices to Baal were part of Roman propaganda aimed at discrediting Carthage to legitimatise wiping it off the map. These historians do not deny the reality of the discoveries of ashes and children's bones, but think that these come from the incineration of the corpses of children who had died of illness.

Visiting
the Carthage ruins

In a remarkable twist of fate, Roman Carthage was also to be destroyed, this time by the Vandals (5th century). Later the Beni Hillal Arabs also ransacked the site.

As a result, the Byrsa hill dominated by the former Saint Louis Cathedral, is a heterogeneous archaeological site, a real millefeuille slice, where archaeologists have dug up the remains of columns, statuettes, and wall debris from all periods.

Visitors have to use a lot of imagination to reconstitute what day-to-day life must have been like in these different superimposed towns. It is quite a mystery how such a char-

*All that remains of proud Punic Carthage are a few columns,
a few bits of walls, and several steles
dissimulated amidst the Roman remains.
The old Saint-Louis Cathedral, now converted
into a cultural centre called the Acropolium,
is situated on the top of Bysra hill.*

ming site could have attracted so much violence, as everything is so calm and beautiful around Byrsa hill. An incomparable view of the Gulf of Tunis stretches out at the visitor's feet, with beautiful houses set in grounds with swimming pools that are hidden away in the blossoming, green bushes, with the mingling blues of the sea and the sky in the background.

The museum: Carthage's grandeur

Luckily, the museum built on the hill near the cathedral (abandoned and recently transformed into a cultural centre called the Acropolium), helps to understand the site enormously. As if in revenge for the Romans' anathema of the past, the Carthaginian period is the star attraction, and will fascinate all those indignant that their history books gave the Punic civilisation such a bad reputation.

The Carthage that transpires from all the vestiges, models, aerial photos of the Punic sites and maps of the reconstructed town, is truly grandiose.

It is clear that the Carthaginian civilisation cannot be reduced to the two centuries of Punic wars against Rome (3rd and 2nd centuries B.C.). Nearly a thousand years B.C., the daring Phoenician navigators founded a huge maritime empire in the Mediterranean setting up trading posts all over the place and developing the major sea trading routes between the different Mediterranean countries.

Its huge architectural works indicate that Carthage was a great building empire a long time before Rome, as can be seen from the plans of the Punic port whose foundations still remain at the foot of the hill.

In one of the museum's largest rooms, vestiges of the ancient temples and the cults of the Punic gods Tanit and Baal Hammon, are displayed along with funereal urns and steles.

It is surprising to see that the

VIEW OF CARTHAGE ACCORDING TO FLAUBERT

In his novel Salammbô, *Gustave Flaubert offers us several magnificent descriptions of the site of Carthage during Hamilcar Barca's time.*

"They were on the terrace. A huge mass of shadow stretched before them, seeming to contain vague accumulations, similar to the gigantic waves of a black petrified ocean. But a shaft of light rose up over towards the Orient. To the left, at the very bottom, the white meanderings of the Megara canals began to score the greenness of the gardens. The conical roofs of the heptagonal temples, the stairs, terraces, ramparts, began to stand out against the paleness of the dawn little by little, and all around the Carthaginian peninsula, a belt of white foam oscillated whilst the emerald coloured sea looked as if it were frozen still in the cool of the morning. Then, as the pink sky continued to expand, the tall leaning houses on the sloping land pulled themselves up straight, and huddled together like a herd of black goats coming down a mountain. The deserted roads grew longer; the palms emerging from the walls here and there did not move; the full cisterns looked like silver shields lost in the courtyards, the lighthouse on the Hermoeum promontory began to grow pale. Right at the top of the Acropolis, in the cypress woods, archaeologists who set up the displays have opted for the traditional version of the child sacrifices. They consider that real holocausts were carried out in the Carthaginian towns and that it is certain that live children were thrown onto Baal Hammon's braziers in order to appease the god's anger and to ward off evil spirits.

It would be a good idea to take into account the new theories which completely refute this explanation, and even the very existence of these barbaric rituals in Carthage.

A Punic district

It is difficult to distinguish between the Roman, Byzantine, Arabic and Punic vestiges on Byrsa hill, which is why it is a good idea to go with a guide.

In fact visitors will only see a little district of Punic Carthage near the top of the hill, where the Punic, then Roman acropolis (ancient citadel) was situated. The remains of this group of houses built along rectilinear roads in the 3rd and 2nd centuries B.C. show (as do those at Kerkouane, on the tip of the Cap Bon peninsula) how much the Carthaginians were ahead of their time.

Their houses were covered in decorated stuccoes and the floors with mosaics. Various conveniences gave the inhabitants a high level of comfort considering the period, for example the pipes for evacuating used water and the cisterns for drinking water. (Another small Punic district called the "Magon quarter" has also been discovered by the sea near the Antonine thermal baths).

At the foot of Byrsa hill on the Gulf of Tunis, Salammbô still has vestiges of the ancient Punic ports which were the basis of Carthaginian power during Hamilcar and Hannibal's time.

There are two stretches of water linked to the Mediterranean by narrow channels, now lined with modern villas.

The rectangular strip of water was

Eshmoun's horses, sensing the arrival of the light, pawed the marble floor with their hooves and neighed in the direction of the sun...

The moon rose skimming the waves, and, in the town once again enveloped in darkness, luminous points, witnesses, shone: the shaft of a cart in a courtyard, several rags of hung cloth, the corner of a wall, a golden necklace on a god's breast. The glass balls on the roofs of temples shone here and there like huge diamonds. But vague ruins, heaps of black earth, gardens formed masses darker in the obscurity, and below Malqua, fishermen's nets stretched from one house to another like huge bats spreading their wings. One could no longer hear the squeaking hydraulic wheels drawing water up to the top floors of the palaces; and in the midst of the terraces, camels rested quietly, lying on their stomachs as ostriches do. Porters were asleep on doorsteps in the streets; the shadow of columns stretched forth on the deserted squares; sometimes in the distance the smoke of a still burning sacrifice escaped through the bronze tiles, and along with the aromatic perfumes, the heavy breeze brought the smells of the sea and the exhalation of the walls heated by the sun. Around Carthage, immobile waves glistened, as the moon

(See following page 112)

Special mention must be made of the Tunisian architects' talent.
Inspired by traditional Islamic buildings,
they have provided foreign tourists with hotels
that look like palaces (above the "Dar Djerba" hotel).

the commercial port, the round one was the naval base. During Carthaginian times, a huge circular building containing the arsenals of over two hundred war ships surrounded this stretch of water.

In the middle of the basin, the deserted Admiral's little island still exists. The admiral – the supreme chief of the Carthaginian fleet – had a round pavilion here which gave him a view of the movements of both the ships in the port, and those out at sea.

The "Tophet"

In the little square overrun by wild grasses next to the Punic ports, there is an ancient sanctuary to the goddess Tanit (*Tophet*). Hundreds of Carthaginian steles have been collected in the craters and the vaulted cellar. The guides will explain all the gory details of the ritual sacrifice of Carthaginian children to the god Baal Hammon, who is wrongly known as Moloch. They will even show the "guillotine stones" where the children are said to have been beheaded before they were thrown into the flames in front of their upset but willing parents.

Their version of events is in fact directly inspired by the somewhat sensationalist chapter in Gustave Flaubert's book *Salammbô* devoted to the sacrifices.

It is hard to believe that the terrifying huge statue of the god who devoured children was installed in such a little cellar (whose vault, moreover, dates back to Roman times!).

It appears that in order to attract the tourists, someone thought it a good a good idea to transform the site into a kind of fairground attraction rather than pay attention to historical detail.

The Carthage site is in fact particularly rich in Roman remains. Vestiges of the forum can be seen at the top of Byrsa hill (remains of the columns of the Capitol, or civilian basilica, the oval arena of the Roman

(End of page 109)

VIEW OF CARTHAGE ACCORDING TO FLAUBERT

spread its beams both on the gulf surrounded by mountains and on the Lake of Tunis where phenicopters (flamingoes, NDLR) formed long pink lines amongst the sand banks, whilst beyond, under the catacombs, the great salty lagoon sparkled like a piece of silver. The vault of the blue sky became darker on the horizon, one side in the dust of the plains, the other in the sea mists, and on the summit of the Acropolis the pyramidal cypress bordering the temple of Eshmoun swayed making a murmuring sound, like the regular waves that lapped gently along the breakwater at the foot of the ramparts.
Salammbô went up onto the terrace of her palace, assisted by a slave who was carrying an iron plate of burning coals. In the middle of the terrace there was a little ivory bed, covered in lynx skins with parrot feather cushions, that fateful animal dedicated to the gods, and in the four corners were four long perfume burners full of nard, incense, cinnamon and myrrh...

djerba

amphitheatre where the circus games were held, the circus and Malga cisterns – supplied by the Zaghouan aqueduct –, to the west).

To the north of Byrsa on the Odeon plateau two quiet well conserved ensembles have been uncovered: the *Carthage Roman Theatre* (where the international festival of music, song and dance now takes place) and the neighbourhood of Roman villas, the most famous of which is the *Volière,* which still has its colonnades around the peristyle.

Near by, the *Damous El Karita* is the biggest Christian basilica in Carthage.

By the Punic ports, vestiges of the Dermech basilica have been uncovered, and further northwards, by the sea by the Presidential palace, remains of the Antonine Thermal Baths have been found.

These are amongst the largest baths built under the Roman empire, as can be seen from the recently uprighted *frigidarium* column which is over 15 m high and supported the immense 47 m long, 22 m wide vault of the cold baths along with seven similar columns.

All of Roman and African high society used to meet in these baths which started to be built during the emperor Hadrian's reign, and were completed under Antonine in the 2nd century.

The edifice was built on an east-west axis, perpendicular to the shore, forming two symmetric parts: one for the men and the other for the women. The baths themselves were on the first floor.

In the middle were the meeting rooms, including a huge room with twelve Corinthian grey granite fluted supporting columns.

The cold bath was situated in the south-east, the hot baths in the north-west. In the vast underground cellars crisscrossed by pipes, the personnel stored the fuel for the heating system and cosmetics for the clients (oils, perfumes).

The heating system consisted of an octagonal room with huge walls where the innumerable terracotta pipes carrying the hot and cold water or steam began.

An esplanade and a portico were built around the baths. There were also meeting rooms, shops and public latrines.

(*See information p. 185).*

■ When Odysseus landed on the Isle of Djerba in the *Odyssey,* his sailors, charmed by the strange "lotus" flowers the islanders had given them, did not want to leave.

If they came back today, they would still find them at the entrances of the hotels and holiday resorts offering garlands of flowers. And they would probably still not want to leave as life on the island is so calm and the beaches so enticing....

The Isle of Djerba, which for some years now has been a favorite of European tourism, has a whole string of nicknames: the isle of palms, the isle of golden sands, the isle of Lotophages, the isle of a thousand gardens, the enchanted island, Djerba the gentle, the Mediterranean Polynesia, etc.

Hotels with refined decors

In the past, Djerba was Odysseus' island. Today it is invaded by holiday makers from all over the world. Not all of the island is touched by this holiday fever, however. The innumerable hotel and holiday resorts have mushroomed mainly on the east coast along the Sidi Mahrez, Seguia, Aghir and Ras Taguerness beaches.

This was where *Club Med* built one of its first villages, launching Tunisian seaside tourism in the Fifties. It was such an international success throughout the world that Tunisia is now too frequently identified with Djerba, and Tunisian tourism with mass tourism entirely centred on seaside leisure.

The Djerba island vogue has not diminished today. With 800,000 holiday makers, it has apparently not yet reached a saturation point for the fans of Tunisian tourism. More and more new buildings are being built, and not the least at that! One example is the *Yati Beach* hotel, one of Djerba's most recent, which is made completely out of marble with an interior patio, a refined decor, a large swimming pool and a private beach.

Others will soon be opened, for example the *Royal Garden* (5 star). Given the talent of the Tunisian architects, they cannot be accused of having massacred the coast by making it into a concrete jungle – as is the case in some other Mediterranean countries (Greece and Spain for example). With what is often perfect taste, the architects have invented a seaside architecture that for the most part is rooted in the country's traditions, with its white domes, interior patios and a penchant for decorative touches inspired by the great traditions of Islamic architecture: painted ceramics, mosaics, stuccoes, painted or sculpted wood, and marble.

For those who do not wish to spend the whole of their holiday basking in the sun, Djerba's 640 km^2 territory has a number of surprises in store. Control of the island has been hotly disputed over the centuries, and all of its occupiers have endeavored to make their mark, leaving many a building behind. The Jews, for example, who were chased out of Babylon by King Nebuchadnezzar in the 6th century B.C., brought a fragment of the Jerusalem temple with them and built a splendid synagogue around it.

The Berbers, who had converted to Islam, developed Kharijism here (a split which is also upheld by the Mozabites of Ghardaïa in Algeria) and built a whole series of small mosques. The Spanish and the Turkish pirates (notably the famous Dargouth) who fought over the island left behind forts and the site of a macabre "Tower of skulls".

Along with these vestiges, Djerba has some very lively markets, animated fishing ports, artisanal villages where the inhabitants continue to make pottery of all kinds using age-old traditional methods, and immense olive and fig plantations where a whole population of farmers incessantly work the wells and irrigation channels to bring an abundant supply of water to the surface.

Houmt Souk, the capital of Djerba, is a good place to begin visiting the island. With the development of tourism, the market (on Mondays and Fridays), souks, stalls in the medina, and the Crafts centre are very popular with foreigners, who will also find many restaurants there where they can grab a bite to eat whilst doing their shopping.

Several beautiful mosques are situated near to the souks, for example the *Strangers' mosque* with its little domes, and the *Turks' mosque* which has a tapering minaret, or the immaculately white *Sidi Brahim el Jamni mosque*.

Also worth visiting are the ancient caravanserais (*fondouks*) which have been restored to their original function as stop-over lodgings. The Tunisian Touring Club's Marhala caravanserai has indeed been made into a hotel. In the past the fondouks put up the caravaneers and their animals in their closed buildings to protect them from possible robberies. The stores and stables on the ground floor were for goods and the dromedaries, and the rooms on the upper floors for the voyagers. There was often also a little mosque inside the whole ensemble so that everyone could complete their ritual prayers.

By the sea is the 15th-16th centuries Houmt Souk citadel (*borj-el-Kébir*) where the Spanish took refuge in 1560 when the pirate Dargouth and the Turkish army attacked. The siege ended in a terrible massacre and the decapitated heads were amassed in the "Tower of skulls" which has now disappeared (a simple stele on the beach marks the site). The recently restored fort houses a small museum.

Menzels in the countryside

Midoun, Djerba's second town, is situated in the east of the island near to the fashionable beaches and holiday resorts which are very popular with the holiday makers. It also has some vast souks where crafts goods from all over the country are sold, including Guellala pottery, rugs and covers, copper objects, natural sponges, perfumes, jewellery, etc.

One of the most beautiful mosques on the island can be seen at *Mahboubine*, a little town to the west of Midoun. Its domes and immaculately white cubic buildings look like a modern abstract sculpture. In the middle of the surrounding olive plantations, there are a number of *menzels*, the traditional homes of the Djerba planters. Their blind walls give them the air of a small fortress. Surmounted by vaults and little domes, they usually have an interior courtyard with an impluvium for catching the rain water. Archaeologists have dug up the remains of a Roman town in the area.

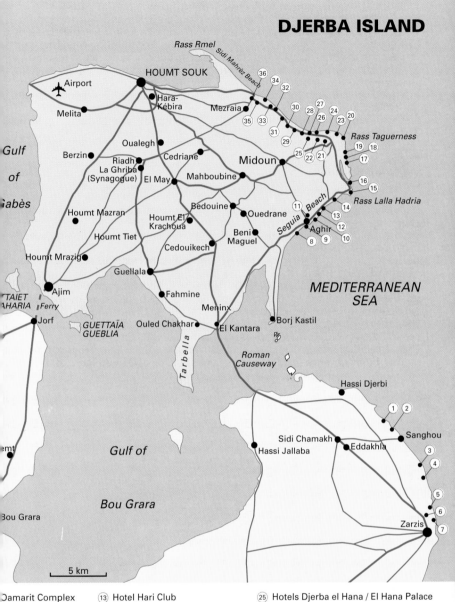

DJERBA ISLAND

Rass Rmel
Sidi Mahrèz Beach
HOUMT SOUK
Airport
Hara-
Kébira
Melita
Mezraia
㊱
㉞
㉜
㉚ ㉗ ㉔ ⑳
㉘ ㉖ ㉓
㉟ ㉝
㉛
㉚ ㉙
Rass Taguerness
⑲ ⑱
⑰
Oualegh
Midoun
㉕ ㉒ ㉑
Gulf
of
Berzin
Riadh
La Ghriba
(Synagogue)
Cedriane
El May
Mahboubine
⑯
⑮
abès
Bedouine
Ouedrane
Rass Lalla Hadria
⑪
Seguia Beach
⑭
Houmt Mazran
Houmt El
Krachoua
⑬
⑫
Beni
Maguel
Aghir
Houmt Tiet
Cedouikech
⑧ ⑨ ⑩
Houmt Mrazig
Guellala
MEDITERRANEAN
SEA
Ajim
Fahmine
TAIET
AHARIA
Ferry
Jorf
Meninx
GUETTAÏA
GUEBLIA
Ouled Chakhar
El Kantara
Borj Kastil
Tarbella
Roman
Causeway
Hassi Djerbi
Sanghou
① ②
Gulf of
Sidi Chamakh
Hassi Jallaba
Eddakhla
③
④
Bou Grara
⑤
⑥
Bou Grara
Zarzis
⑦
5 km

Damarit Complex	⑬ Hotel Hari Club	㉕ Hotels Djerba el Hana / El Hana Palace
Club Sangho	⑭ Hotel Djerba la Douce	㉖ Hotel Méninx
Hotel Zita	⑮ Hotel Djerba Menzel	㉗ Hotel Robinson
Hotel Zarzis	⑯ Hotel Djerba la Fidèle	㉘ Hotels Cédria / Hasdrubal
Hotel Zéphir	⑰ Hotel Tanit	㉙ Hotels des Néréides/Djerba Beach/Le Ksar
Hotel Zina	⑱ Club Meriam	㉚ Hotels 4 Saisons / Dar Midoun
Hotel Amina	⑲ Hotel Aldiana	㉛ Hotels Pénélope / Palm Beach
Hotel Aghir	⑳ Hotels Yati Beach / Rym Beach	㉜ Hotels Abou Nawas / Jasmina / Toumana
Hotel Palmariva	㉑ Hotel Méhari	㉝ Hotels Les Sirènes / Le Petit Palais
Hotel Aladin	㉒ Hotels Plaza / Yadis	㉞ Hotels Médina / Strand
Hotel Sina	㉓ Hotel Aquarius	㉟ Hotels Beau Rivage/ Djerba Orient/ Djazira
Hotel Sidi Slim	㉔ Hotels Dar Djerba / Méridiana	㊱ Hotels Ulysse / Dar Ali

dougga

A small Jewish community still lives in the centre of the island in the villages of Hara Kebira and Hara Srira.

The inhabitants come together to worship in the famous *Ghriba synagogue* ("the splendid") whose interior is decorated with blue earthenware, stained glass windows and old polychrome wainscotting. There is a stone from the old Jerusalem temple and some very old *torahs*. In May, the large pilgrimage to the Ghriba brings together many diaspora Jews.

Other attractions on Djerba include the Guellala pottery workshops, the Ajim fishing port with its sponge market, and a number of olive oil presses dotted all over the island.

From Djerba island, it is possible to get to Zarzis and Gabès (*see later*) on the mainland, or to make long excursions into the Tunisian south, particularly to the Ksour mountains around Tataouine, or to the chott el Djérid (Nefta, Tozeur, Douz).

(*See information p. 185*).

■ All over Tunisia, parts of walls, colonnades, the odd lop-sided triumphal arch, and innumerable fields of ruins, still standing proud defying the ravages of time, are a testimony to the arrogant presence of Ancient Rome, as is the case with the town of Dougga near to Téboursouk to the south-west of Tunis.

Originally a Phoenician colony, then the residence of the Numidian prince Masinissa (in the 3rd century B.C.), *Thugga* – now Dougga – underwent its greatest expansion under the Roman empire in the 2nd and 3rd centuries (especially under Marcus Aurelius, 121-180). It was then inhabited by the Byzantines from the 4th century A.D. onwards.

Its main particularity is that it covers 65 hectares of steep mountainous ground lying at an altitude of 600 m. The Roman town planners had to use a great deal of ingenuity to build on this difficult terrain, and abandoned the large Roman town's habitual checker-board plan.

In its golden era, Dougga had a population of 25,000 to 30,000 inha-

"THE GHRIBA" SYNAGOGUE

■ The Ghriba ("The Marvellous") is thought to be one of the oldest synagogues in the world. Indeed, it appears to have been built in the 6th century B.C. by Jews expelled from Jerusalem.

In 587 B.C., the Jewish people of the kingdom of Judah, who for 17 years had lived under the yoke of the Babylonians, revolted against their king Nebuchadnezzar II.

The Babylonians took over Jerusalem and razed it to the ground, deporting all the Jews to Babylon (586).

This was the beginning of the famous "diaspora", or dispersion of the Jewish people from the kingdom of Juda (Palestine).

Some of these Jews fled to North Africa and settled on the Isle of Djerba. They built a vast synagogue around a stone from the Grand Temple of Jerusalem which the fugitives had piously carried to the island.

Other than this building's historic interest, it can be noted that the Djerba Jews' liturgy has remained almost unchanged over the centuries.

bitants, and 5,000 families.

Some of its monuments are famous for their beauty and their well-conserved state, for example the capitol temple devoted to the divine triad: Jupiter, Minerva and Juno.

When archaeologists began the initial excavation work, they were not expecting to discover such a vast town which, furthermore, was partially buried under modern villages. With the authorities' agreement, they managed – without great difficulty – to expropriate the inhabitants from the site who definitively left the hills to go and rebuild their village down in the valley.

Magnificent temples

The first entrance to Dougga, halfway up the slope, leads into the southern quarters of the town. There is a pointed 21 m storied tower which is a *Libyco-Punic mausoleum* that apparently dates back to the 2nd century B.C. It is thought to have been built by Carthaginian artisans under orders from the Berber king Micipsa, son of Masinissa, in 139 B.C. In the past it was decorated with a stele with bilingual Libyco-Punic inscriptions listing the names of the artisans who built it. Unfortunately, a British consul thought it was a good idea to take it back to the British Museum in London in the last century, and it is still there today.

Further up the hill are the *Cyclops Thermal Baths* (with hot, warm and cold baths, a resting room and a gymnasium with holes for the apparatus). Next to it is an *odeon*, the *brothel* (with a sculpture representing a phallus and female breasts), the public *latrines* with 12 places and a wash basin, then further on, *Septimus Severus' Arch*.

The most impressive monuments are further up the hill, grouped around the interconnecting market place, forum and the poetic sounding *Square of the Winds Rose* ("Place de la Rose des Vents"). The latter has a sundial engraved with

ODYSSEUS ON THE ISLAND OF THE LOTUS-EATERS

■ *... For nine days I was chased by those accursed winds across the fish-infested seas. But on the tenth, we made for the country of the Lotus-eaters, a race that live on flowers. We disembarked to draw water and my crews quickly set to on their midday meal by the ships. But as soon as we had had a mouthful and a drink, I sent some of my followers inland to find out what sort of human beings might be there, detailing two men for the duty with a third as messenger. Off they went and it was not long before they were in touch with the Lotus-eaters. Now it never entered the heads of these natives to kill my friends; what they did was to give them some lotus to taste, and as soon as each had eaten the honeyed fruit of the plant, all thoughts of reporting to us or escaping were banished from his mind. All they now wished for was to stay where they were with the Lotus-eaters, to browse on the lotus and to forget that they had a home to return to.*
I had to use force to bring them back to the ships, and they wept on the way. But once on board I dragged them under the benches and left them in irons. I then commanded the rest of my loyal band to embark with all speed on their fast ships for fear that others of them might eat the lotus and think no more of home. [...] So we left that country and sailed on sick at heart.

HOMER
Odyssey, Book IX
(Penguin Classics, 1951)

Reconstructed by archaeologists stone by stone,
the Dougga capitol is one of the most beautiful
and most famous edifices
built by the Romans in the early centuries A.D.

douz

the names of the 12 winds that blow in Tunisia, notably the Africus (sirocco), the Circius, the Septentrion, and the Auster.

Visitors will notice that the rugged lie of the land forced the architects to abandon the sacrosanct plan of the Roman forum. As it was impossible to build the capitol temple on the Dougga forum itself due to the lack of available space, they built it a little further back on a tiny esplanade. The *market* also had to be built on its own terrace instead of on the forum's platform. Dedicated to divine triad (Jupiter, Juno and Minerva), the *Capitol* has a splendid pediment with a sculpted eagle. The *Temple of Mercury* opens out onto the Square of the Winds Rose and the market – effectively, Mercury is the god of traders and... thieves!

Look out for the strange statue of a Roman emperor which was intentionally sculpted without a head: the opportunistic and highly practical inhabitants of Dougga used to replace the emperor's head each time a new one came to power.

Several of the houses around the forum district were especially adapted to the site. Built on several floors, they had a number of entrances, some of which open out up the street, and others down the street.

The theatre is located to the northeast of the forum. Financed by the rich Lucius Marcus Quadratus, whose name features on a stele, it could hold up to 3,500 spectators. The prompter's pit and three entrances for the actors can still be distinguished on the stage. Other interesting monuments include the temples of Saturn and Minerva to the north, and the temple of Caelestis near to the Severus Alexander triumphal arch. Close to Dougga, to the north of the RN 5 to Kef, are the remains of the Roman town of *Musti* with its 2nd century temples, its basilica, and Byzantine forts. In the past there were two archways over the big Roman road which linked Carthage and Théveste (Tébessa in Algeria near to the Tunisian border). To the east and north of Dougga there are ancient remains of Aïn Tounga, *Tignica* to the Romans, and *Trajan's bridge* over the Medjerda river near to Béja (interesting monuments: the Byzantine enclosure, the Bab el-Aïn gate, and the Kasbah tower).

(*See information p. 185*).

■ The artist Eugène Delacroix would have been enchanted at the sight of Arab cavaliers riding their richly clad thoroughbreds, prancing at full speed, performing dressage exercises and acrobatics, one minute galloping standing on the saddle, sword in hand, one minute upside down, or coming together in formation, riding along in a line like ghost riders amidst the clouds of dust and thundering guns. His delighted eyes would have also noticed the shimmering fabrics, the stallions' gleaming coats, the brightly glinting daggers. A delight that lasts only the duration of the Sahara Festival in Douz.

Along with these equestrian exercises and shows, desert hare dogs (*sloughi*) and mehari races, and spectacular dromedary and ram combats are organised during the festival. Amongst the other spectacles festival goers can see are the traditional Berber recitals and dances. Traditional marriage celebrations dating back to the time of the caravans and "desert lords" are also held.

The fiancees parade through the town adorned in traditional jewellery, perched in the tent-like canopies on the dromedaries' backs.

As these festivities last for only a week during the month of December, foreign visitors coming at other times will have to content themselves to a visit to the market (Thursdays, frequented by the nomads), a camel ride, and a trip to the Zaafrane, Sabria and Kébili oases and the chott el Djérid.

This prettily little town on the edge of the desert was on the verge of falling into the state of torpeur common in all the Saharan oases.

Thanks to its dynamic town council, however, Douz is currently shaking itself up to become the new centre of Saharan tourism, overtaking Agadès in Niger and Tamanrasset and Djanet in Algeria. As these two countries are undergoing prolonged periods of political unrest, desert lovers are no longer at ease rambling in the Hoggar or the splendid Ténéré desert. Over the last few years, therefore, more and more of them are coming to discover the dunes of the Grand Erg Oriental, the Tunisian part of the Sahara desert. This has proved to be blessing for Douz, which is currently building

el djem

hotels to receive this new clientele.

From Douz, there is a circuit that is becoming a classic amongst hikers and desert lovers.

Setting out from the southern part of the town in four-wheel drive jeeps, the trekkers come to the edge of the Grand Erg. In Toual Errebaï at the foot of djebel Kachemel Maguel, they meet up with camel drivers who await the trekkers with a little herd of dromedaries. The dromedaries carry the foodstuff, fire wood, luggage and tents for the whole expedition.

After a first night in tents in the desert, the circuit continues into the desert for four days at a rhythm of 5 to 6 hours walking a day. The main stages are Gour El Kleb to the southwest of Douz, then down to El Méda and back up eastwards towards Ksar Ghilane via Jaffra.

At Ksar Ghilane, the last leg of the trip, the four-wheel drive jeeps meet the trekkers and take them to the Ksour mountains.

(*See information p. 185*).

■ What could be more unlikely than listening to Mozart in a Roman amphitheatre in the heart of Tunisia? This is nonetheless precisely what the little Sahelian municipality of El Djem, halfway between Sousse and Sfax, proposes every summer.

Like a mirage

Any visitor coming here for the first time will think they are seeing a mirage. In the distance on the horizon, a kind of flying saucer looks like it is landing in the middle of the fields. The closer one gets, the more this strange object seems to rise up into the sky, unfurl and turn around like a giant ferries wheel.

Although it is smaller than the Coliseum in Rome, the El Djem amphitheatre is more impressive as it is not hemmed in and hidden by modern buildings like the one in Italy. On the contrary, it towers over the low houses in the little town.

Originally called *Thysdrus*, El

ROME THE BUILDER

■ *Once they had built roads and founded engagingly charming cities, the inexhaustible Roman builders, who wanted to make these lands inhabitable, built water towers, dug wells and cisterns, erected soaring aqueducts across gorges and valleys, and built artificial lakes.*

Life thus spread across the expanses of these solitudes, and there where before there was only dusty desert, the green grace of gardens laughed amidst the song of the fountains. Thanks to the Roman labourers, thanks to the victory of its soldiers and the skill of its artists, acropolises, temples, forums, arenas, triumphal arches, obelisks, baths and markets sprung up in what had been the African desert.

The most imposing Roman ruins remain in Tripoli, Sabrata, Leptis Magna – land of Septimus Severus which he adorned with the most beautiful monuments –, El Djem, Dougga, Timgad, Djemila, Cherchel, Tébessa, Volubilis, Tangier, and a host of other towns. Like a rare and sumptuous cloak thrown across its brown shoulders, the whole of Africa is adorned from the Gulf of Gabès to the shores of the Atlantic.

PIERRE JALABERT
Histoire de l'Afrique du Nord.

*The large, fine sand dunes
and huge palm groves of Douz,
gateway to the Sahara desert,
unfold near to the Chott el Djérid.*

Djem was founded during Julius Caesar's reign several years B.C. The town flourished in the 2nd century thanks to its olive culture which earned it the nickname "the oil capital", which it supplied Rome with abundantly.

The huge Coliseum

El Djem's Roman circus is an amphitheatre or "circular theatre". Second only to the Roman Coliseum in size, it can hold 35,000 spectators.

It was built in the year 200, possibly to replace an old arena dug into an artificial earthen mound. In this flat region, rather than making an artificial hill and digging a crater in it, then lining the crater with terraces as the Greek and Latin architects did traditionally (notably in Pompeii in 80 B.C.), the El Djem architects preferred to use the Coliseum in Rome as their model. Built in 80 A.D., the Coliseum invented a new kind of architecture destined for circus games: the theatre with arcades.

The El Djem builders did not have the vast Roman quarries of travertine stone at their disposal, however. They had to make do with a poorer and, moreover, softer material – dune sandstone – which forced them to change their plans. Instead of creating a delicate architectural style with lots of arches and columns as in Rome – which was possible as they used resistant materials – they were forced to build a veritable circular wall. In order to lessen the chunky aspect, they ingeniously pierced the arcades and embedded pilasters in them as a facade.

Although experts are not a hundred percent sure, it would seem that the traditional circus games the Romans enjoyed so much at the time of the empire, took place in the El Djem Coliseum. Perhaps the first Christian martyrs were fed to the lions here, as many mosaics in Tunisia's Roman villas seem to suggest.

El Djem had its moment of glory in 238 A.D when the very old North African proconsul, Gordian (who was over 80 years old) was proclaimed Roman emperor in the Coliseum during the *Liberalia* celebrations by a group of rebels who were revolting against the heavy taxes imposed by the emperor Maximinus in Rome. The revolt was orchestrated by the farmers and traders half-bankrupted by the drop in olive oil prices caused by overproduction. With his son Gordian II, the new emperor had to fight against the loyalist Roman forces led by the legate Capellian who had Thysdrus and the rebel towns ransacked. When his son was killed in battle, Gordian committed suicide in his Carthage villa. His grandson Gordian III was finally appointed emperor by Rome just after Maximinus was assassinated.

Legend has it that Kahena, the Berber princess who resisted the Arab invasion in the 7th century, was held under siege inside the Coliseum where she had taken refuge. As events in the conflict had taken a turn for the worse, she could have fled via the underground routes that led into the heart of the countryside.

With the arrival of the Beni Hillal nomadic Arab hoards in the 11th century, the town was ransacked and did not recover immediately. The El Djem Coliseum became a stone quarry, enabling a lot of buildings to be constructed in the surrounding towns, notably the Kairouan Central Mosque.

Along with the Coliseum, numerous Roman vestiges have been dug up by archaeologists in El Djem. They have discovered two other smaller amphitheatres, cisterns, thermal baths and numerous villas decorated with superb mosaics (*the Four Seasons, the Abduction of Ganymede, Leda and Zeus in the form of a swan, etc.*). A museum has been built near to the little Coliseum south of the town to protect most of these works of art. Of these gems, it is worth citing the mosaics representing the Muses, circus scenes with lions and the four seasons.

(*See information p. 186*).

AN OIL CAPITAL

El Djem, now a small town with several thousand inhabitants, is situated in the heart of the region where the Tunisian coast bulges out to the east.
Suddenly, on the long straight road between the town and Sousse, an enormous ochre cylinder which, as one gets closer, is dotted with regularly spaced black voids, comes into sight towering high above the grey olive trees and the low white houses. The mass of the construction bears down on the village, and travellers will be surprised that such a colossus was built to entertain the ancestors of the Bedouin who now hold their market at the foot of the arches.
Such amazement is no longer justified since excavation work carried out by the "Institut National Archéologique de Tunisie" has uncovered hundreds of metres of roads lined with sumptuous villas well beyond the limits of the modern town.
Before Sbeïtla, Kairouan, and Sfax, Thysdrus – ancient El Djem – was an oil capital in the 2nd and 3rd centuries. Its bourgeoisie demonstrated its power in 238 when it overturned an emperor who wanted to make them pay what in their opinion were excessive taxes.
It was most probably during this period of splendor around the year 200, that the African Coliseum was built to replace the old arena also uncovered on the same site.

GILBERT PICARD,
Empire Romain
(*Architecture universelle. Office du Livre*).

gabès

■ In spite of the growth of its chemical industry, Gabès, a major oasis by the sea, has not completely lost its character. To the north of the town, vast palm groves and orchards (grenadines, olives, lemons, bananas) stretch as far as the Gulf of Gabès. The palm groves, which provide the town with a real "green lung", have over 300,000 trees producing several varieties of dates, notably the succulent *deglet nour*.

A maritime and caravan port

Gabès' strategic position on the what was known as the Gulf of Syrtis Minor, and its role as a hyphen between the Maghreb and Libya, were appreciated by the Phoenician navigators who set up a maritime trading post here very early on (5th century B.C.). Under the Romans it became a port side town called *Tacapae*.

When the Arabs came in the 7th century, the maritime port of Gabès flourished as it was at the terminus for the trans-Saharan caravans from the Sudan (West Africa), Libya and Algeria.

During the Second World War, Gabès paid a high price for its strategic position between Libya and the Maghreb. In the spring of 1943, fierce fighting took place in the region at Mareth to the south (*see later*) and around the Akarit river to the north between Rommel's Afrikakorps and the Allied forces.

Since the recent discovery of phosphate deposits at Gafsa in the south-west of Tunisia, and the gas and petrol deposits at El Borma in the south, Gabès has become both a terminus for the gas and oil pipelines, and a major industrial port specialising in chemicals (the region's real petrol port is at Skhira, 50 km northwards, however).

The green palm grove belt

The town, which has developed between the confluence of the canalised Gabès river and the El Mania river, has several traditional districts in the town centre which are worth exploring, notably Petite Jara, Grande Jara, Jara (crafts centre), Médina, and el Menzel. To the south of the town on the other side of the Gabès canal, the former *Sidi Boulbaba mosque* – the Prophet's barber – has been transformed into an archaeological and popular arts museum.

Next is the palm grove, the town's real attraction, which can preferably be visited by barouche. Visitors are immersed in a huge shady green belt with a highly complex system of pipes and irrigation channels (*seguias*), where they will also discover market gardens and orchards where the farmers practise a most diversified polyculture ranging from peach farming to henna to tobacco.

Several traditional Berber villages are tucked away in the oasis, for example Aïn Zerig, M'Teurch, El Ménara, Nahal, Bou Chemma, Semassa and Chenini. Finally, there is a Roman dam and the sources of the oued where a pool, bar-dance hall and a zoo have been developed.

A prehistoric site

Near to Gabès (25 km to the north), the Akarit river Mousterian site was uncovered in the 1950s. It dates back to 20,000 to 26,000 years B.C., the time of the Neanderthal man, who was our last ancestor before the arrival of the Homo sapiens. Numerous stone tools (spear heads, scrapers) were discovered there along with zebra and rhinoceros bones.

Gabès is the real pivotal point of southern Tunisian tourism as it is the gateway to the Djerba Island beaches and seaside resorts and the Zarzis peninsula in the south-east. From Gabès it is also possible to head on into Tunisia's deep south via Matmata (troglodytic houses), Médenine and Tataouine (Ksour mountains region). Finally, the western road to the Djérid oases (Tozeur, Nefta, Douz), the frontier posts of the Sahara desert, sets out from Gabès.

(*See information p. 186*).

Set in the old part of the town,
the El Djem coliseum is one
of the biggest amphitheatres
built during ancient times after the one in Rome.

gafsa

There is nothing more delightful and refreshing in the blazing heat than the sight of swarms of children swimming, diving and splashing about trying to outdo each other – a sight that can commonly be seen right in the town centre in the Gafsa Roman pools.

From time to time, the little daredevils bet each other a coin to dive from several metres up into the depths of the pools without a hint of hesitation!

After this little interlude, visitors really should go to see the little *museum* by the pools. There are only a few rooms, but each one is of a rare quality, and there are some particularly interesting Roman mosaics.

Some of these are real masterpieces and give us information about daily life in Provincia Africa at the time of the Roman Empire. Like their compatriots in Italy, the Romans in Tunisia were particularly fond of public circus games. They did not just enjoy the cruel sight of Christians being thrown to the lions, or gladiators cutting each other's throats: the Gafsa mosaics reveal that they also appreciated more peaceful jousts, and in particularly sports like running races, high jump, disc throwing, boxing and pancratias. These various activities are depicted with relish on several of the mosaics. Winning athletes can be distinguished at a prize-giving.

The capital of Tunisian prehistory

This little museum also provides us with a lesson in prehistory, which is most welcome given that Gafsa (*Capsa* in Roman times) is set in the heart of a region particularly rich in prehistoric vestiges.

Whilst digging at the sites near to Gafsa and at Metlaoui, El Guettar, Redeyef, Sidi Mansour and El Mekta, archaeologists uncovered an abundant collection of stone tools from all periods, including acheulian type flint tools from the Lower Paleolithic, many Mousterian tools

THE OLDEST RELIGIOUS MONUMENT IN THE WORLD

In the 1950s, archaeologists made a stunning discovery at El Guettar near to Gafsa in southern Tunisia. During excavation work they discovered a small pyramid-shaped heap of stones 0.75 m tall and 1.30 m in diameter. It looked like the cairns *the herders used to make in the mountains to signal paths. But, as they looked more carefully, they noticed that this conical pile was made out of several dozen quite regular balls, mixed with 4,000 prehistoric carved flint tools, and animal teeth and bones. Moreover, this "construction" was found on the site of an ancient spring and at the time must have been almost completely submerged.*
Built some 40,000 years ago (in the Mousterian period of the Middle Palaeolithic), this strange monument most certainly had some religious purpose. Was it a shrine dedicated to the spirit of the spring? If this was the case, given its venerable age, this would make it the oldest religious monument in the world...
The experts named the strange construction the Hermaion *(Temple of Hermes), as it looks very much like the heaps of stones the Greeks used to build along the roadside in honour of their god Hermes, protector of herders, their flocks, and of travellers.*

hammamet

from the Middle Palaeolithic (the time of the Neanderthal man), and the exceptional El Guettar Hermaion (*see inset "The oldest religious monument in the world"*).

The Kébili sites in the Djérid, and the Gafsa region sites (Sidi Mansour in the north, Lalla and El Guettar in the east) belong to the "strip civilisation" (20,000 years B.C.) typical of southern Tunisia. At that time our distant ancestors fashioned tiny strips of flint (5 cm maximum) with chipped edges.

Shortly before the Neolithic period, the Capsian civilisation – from which Gafsa's former name Capsa comes – flourished in the Gafsa region. There are many sites: Gafsa, El Mekta, Redeyef, Bir Hamaïra (Metlaoui), Bir Oum Ali, etc. These generally consist of heaps of ashes and burnt stones from ancient hearths in which thousands of tools were uncovered along with the remains of feasts, notably snail shells and animal bones.

Gafsa, which is a very old town that goes back to the to the Numidian era B.C., began to flourish again at the beginning of the century when its large phosphate deposits began to be exploited, and again in the last few years due to tourism.

Visitors can go to see the workshops with weaving looms where the famous Gafsa carpets are made using artisanal methods (*haoulis* and *ferrachia*). These are brightly coloured and figurative with naive style figures and animals.

There is a wonderful view of the whole oasis and especially of the 15th-17th centuries Kasbah from the top of the Malikite Central Mosque minaret (*Jamaâ Sidi Yacoub*). From the Kasbah, which was destroyed in 1943 when a German powder magazine exploded, and later restored, visitors can go to the huge palm grove (100,000 date palms) where there are also orchards full of orange, apricot and lemon trees.

Right by the south-east road to Gabès leads to the charming oasis of Lalla. Like Gafsa, Metlaoui, situated to the west, owes its expansion to the mining of its phosphate deposits. Tourists can take the famous "Red Lizard", the beylik train, from Metlaoui railway station to the Seldja river gorges, the huge and picturesque "sabre gash" in the mountains. (*See information p. 186*).

■ Hammamet should be twinned with Saint Tropez in France as they have clearly have a lot in common. Both were founded on a gulf that bore their name, both expanded around a fishing port, and, thanks to the international "jet set", both ultimately became large, fashionable seaside resorts. Their all year round warm climates and the perpetually festive ambiances only accentuate the similarities. Even in the detail common traits can be found. Both towns are jealously guarded by a 16th century citadel whose once formidable ramparts are now the setting for holiday makers' strolls.

In the heart of the Kasbah

Once they have deposited their luggage in one of the town's innumerable hotels, newly arrived visitors will inevitably end up strolling along the large Avenue Bourguiba which runs along the seafront and forms Hammamet's forum. Here, restaurants, hotels and shops lie side by side opposite the medina and the fort. The ebb and flow of the crowd will naturally carry visitors along to the foot of the ramparts of the old quarter. As they look up, they will be surprised to see that the covered ways and lookout towers have now been converted into restaurants and shops (*Barberousse, La Médina*) with superb views over the town and its bay.

The old fort (*kasbah*) is also a belvedere. It can be reached via the steep riding path in the medina. The interior of the citadel, which was originally built in the 16th century and has recently been restored, is a cool and calm haven. In the shade of the tamarind trees, a warder dozes and several cannons lie dormant. Very steep little stairs lead up to the curtain walls and bastion where a Moorish café and a souvenir shop have been opened. The ramparts afford an indiscreet view right down onto the patios and terraces of the beautiful villas next to the medina. People whisper the names of the owners: members of the international nobility and showbiz stars. The artist Paul Klee and the French writers André Gide and Georges Bernanos used to live here part of the time, as, more recently, do the French cinema actor Jean-Claude Pascal and the television producer Frédéric Mitterrand.

Back in the Medina, it is a pleasure to stroll along the labyrinth of twisting little streets. The streets, which are a far cry from the fetid and obscure little alleys of medieval medinas, are painted in radiant pastel colours, like pale blue, pistachio green, and pale pink. Each house is hermetically shut behind wooden doors painted in the same monochrome colours as the walls. Visitors will be struck by the ironworkers' fine skills. All of the doors are similar, but none are exactly the same as they all have different arabesque stud designs. Little secret gardens with fountains, arcades and ceramic decorations are hidden away behind these thick doors and walls.

Visitors may suddenly come across scenes of the Hammamet fishermen's day-to-day lives in the streets. Here a cluster of men chat together on their doorsteps, there women knit, watching over the children playing football out of the corner of their eye. Like in Venice – nicknamed the "Cat Republic" – many tomcats come entwining themselves around your legs, or lie basking in the sun. Everything here spells peace and tranquility. At the foot of the fort, inside the medina, the laden stalls of little souks line the covered alleys and passages. As in all of Tunisia's souks, it is possible to buy rugs, perfume, pottery, basketry and chased copper goods here. Next to the souks is the *Central Mosque* (15th-century minaret) and the *Sidi Abd el-Kader el-Djilani mosque* which was recently turned into a Koranic school.

The *International Cultural Centre*, Tunisia's cultural Mecca, has been opened in the gardens of a sumptuous residence by the sea on the Avenue des Nations-Unies to the west of the town (near to the "Parc Plage" and "Continental" hotels). Acquired by the Tunisian government in 1959, the house was built by a Romanian millionaire Georges Sébastian during the "golden years" of the 1920s-1930s. Today *Dar Sébastian* opens its rooms and ancient theatre to the Hammamet International Festival (in July/August) during which jazz concerts, plays, ballets and shows are held.

The lucky few – film and television stars –
live in these beautiful traditional houses
in the Hammamet medina
with terraces overlooking the Mediterranean Sea.

haouaria

Along with these intellectual and artistic pleasures, Hammamet offers a wide range of sporting activities: swimming, water skiing, sailing, tennis, horseback riding, etc. Since 1992, golfers can enjoy the three greens at the "Cyrus" golf course 10 km from the town. These links designed by the great specialist Ronald Fream have been landscaped in the rustic setting of an olive grove and a natural forest with six lakes.

The circuit around
the peninsula

In the western suburbs of the town, visitors can see experts working on the Puput archaeological site (near the "Tanfous" hotel).

Hammamet is the starting point – or terminus – of a large circuit across the Cap Bon peninsula (*see earlier*) via the Nabeul seaside resort (*see later*), up towards Kélibia, Kerkouane and Haouaria, and then back down to Korbous.

(*See information, p. 188*).

■ Haouaria, on the tip of Cap Bon to the south-east of Tunis, is a little village that has a passion for birds of prey and the art of falconry. Statues, frescoes, clubs, families, and dynasties of falconers: everything here is placed under the sign of the peregrine falcon and the sparrowhawk.

Unlike in the Arab Emirates where falconry is the reserved for princes, in Haouaria it is a resolutely popular leisure activity unique in Tunisia.

Neither petrol emirs, nor descendants of the Middle Ages European cavaliers, the Haouria falconers on Cap Bon are simple working class people who for centuries have passed their skill in training birds of prey on from father to son. Today, over 140 falconers belong to the club founded in 1967 whose headquarters are located in a magnificent clubhouse on the edge of the village near to the beaches and caves.

The falconers are very open to foreign visitors and will kindly take them around the club showing the pictures of the different birds on the

THE "RED LIZARD"
OF METLAOUI

■ *Some visitors take the "Red Lizard" to the Seldja river gorges. This train, a true relic of the past once belonging to the former Tunis beys, still has its Twenties-style wooden carriages and wrought iron platforms.*

Most of them are equipped with comfortable divans, especially the harem carriage where the bey's wives used to admire the landscape whilst tucking into Oriental sweets when on vacation.

These excursions organised by a Tunisian tour operator (for further information ask at Metlaoui station) take place several times a week and are very popular with foreign visitors.

For several hours, passengers can enjoy the impression of being plunged into the past, and experiencing the luxury of a top Oriental dignitary's court, whilst at the same time discovering a region somewhat on the fringes of the "classic" major tourist circuits.

walls or explaining the complex migratory routes taken by the birds each year guided by their mysterious but precise sense of direction.

It is most unusual for the birds to stay in Haouaria, or to faithfully come back to find their masters the following year, but there are exceptions to the rule: in the 1830s, one falconer explains, Cheick Ali Bennar, an inhabitant of Haouaria, kept his sparrowhawk for 30 years, and much more recently, another falconer kept his for over 20 years.

The falconers have to devote a lot of time to these birds and deploy all their psychological secrets to make them hunting birds within the space of a few weeks.

The sparrowhawk, for example, is a highly intelligent animal that becomes a hunter when it is six months old. The falconer must discover a given hawk's temperament, and find ways of training it that will be best suited to its personality.

In general, the falconers control the birds through affection and food (indeed, the best hunters are the birds of prey that eat a lot, digest quickly and are always hungry as this drives them to hunt endlessly).

The Haouaria falconers use fixed or mobile traps to catch the birds. These are usually nets with a live sparrow decoy set up in the mountains during the migration season (beginning of March until the end of April). Once they have been trained, the birds participate in the falconry festival held in Haouaria at the beginning of June. Competitions are organised in order to distinguish the best hunters, and during the general jubilation, the village is the theatre for a whole range of festivities: concerts, traditional dances, etc.

Along with its birds of prey, Haouaria is also famous for its caves. These are in fact vast underground quarries where slaves used to carve out huge blocks of stone in Phoenician, Carthaginian and Roman times. As the caves were by the sea, it was easy to transport the freestone by ship to build many of the region's ancient monuments. During the Second World War, the German Afrikakorps troops took refuge there until their surrender in 1943. A lot of natural sculptures can be seen down in these caves, notably a camel in the process of sitting down. (*See information p. 188*).

■ It is not the fields of cereals that attract tourists to Jendouba, a large farming village in the highly fertile Medjerda valley, but rather this region's ancient vestiges. Indeed, the archaeological excavation sites of *Chemtou, Thuburnica* and *Bulla Regia* are situated near to Jendouba.

Situated north of Jendouba on the Tabarka road, Bulla Regia does not look like anything special at first sight. There are hardly any large triumphal arches or temples, and all that initially catches the eye are some sections of the thermal baths' walls. The site is very important, nonetheless, as the architectural style of the houses is almost unique compared to all the other major ancient Roman towns. In order to adapt to the Tunisian climate, their owners had them built on two floors: the winter apartments were built on the ground floor whereas the summer quarters were built on a cooler underground floor so inhabitants could escape the summer heat. Thanks to the high up little windows, these rooms gained some light without loosing their crypt-like coolness.

Moreover, in addition to the thick walls and their depth underground, these living quarters had a highly ingenious insulation system with their walls peppered with hollow, air-filled pipes.

The Amphitrite mosaic

Not only were these underground apartments comfortable, they were also most finely decorated, as can be seen from the Hunting and Fishing Mosaics and Amphitrite houses in particular. The latter still has a superb mosaic inspired by the mythological scene "Amphitrite astride a sea centaur" which shows the sea goddess accompanied by Neptune and two winged spirits. The mosaics in most of the other villas have been removed and sent to the Bardo museum in Tunis.

The remains of a forum with vestiges of a temple to Apollo, a market, a theatre, and a basilica (1st century A.D.) have also been discovered. It is also worth visiting the little museum built on the other side of the road near to the site.
(*See information p. 188*).

*The Kairouan Central Mosque in the fourth holy Islamic town
is one of the most beautiful
in the Muslim world. Founded in the 7th century,
it was then improved and expanded
by the Aghlabid dynasty in the 9th century.*

kairouan

When the Arab conqueror Uqba ibn Nafi reached the dry steppes in the middle of Tunisia, he stopped and drove his lance into the ground: "This is where we are going to found our settlement, which will become the bastion of Islam until the end of time." Much to the stupefaction of his companions!

– "But this land is completely desolate and there isn't even any water", one of them dared to answer.

– "Be patient!" replied the emir.

This scene took place in 660, a few years after the death of the Prophet Mohammed, at the time when the Arab armies arrived in North Africa bearing the banner of Islam. Uqba ibn Nafi was one of the first to penetrate inland into Ifriqyya (Tunisia), whose coastal regions alone were occupied by the Byzantines at that time.

He arrived from the south with his cavalry, and set up his headquarters in the Kairouan region.

A miraculous spring

Eventually, a miracle occurred. A beautiful trickle of water – obviously a miracle spring – suddenly appeared at the bottom of a well. Even today, nobody questions that it runs underground to join the Zem Zem spring in Mecca several thousand kilometres away!

– "But the region is infested with scorpions and poisonous snakes!" his lieutenants fretted.

Uqba stood up on the plain and, addressing the wild beasts, pronounced the famous anathema: "In the name of the Prophet, we wish to settle here in the town of Allah. Be off with you!" At that, all of the scorpions, snakes and other fearsome animals moved away.... apart from one female scorpion who asked for mercy for her offspring. This was granted on the express condition that they never showed themselves, and never harmed the men in the region.

Since that day, all the scorpions in Kairouan live buried under stones and never sting anyone...

Other legends exalt Uqba's superhuman energy as he conquered in the name of Islam.

It is said that as he galloped westwards along the African coast of the Mediterranean, he was stopped short by the Atlantic Ocean in Morocco. Furious, he rode his horse into the sea right up to its belly and, taking the sky as his witness, exclaimed: "Look everyone, I can spread God's territory no further!"

Uqba set up a military camp in Tunisia as a base for conquering the whole of the Maghreb. The site was judicially chosen: not too close to the coast to be threatened by the Byzantines, and also on the caravan trail linking Egypt and the Maghreb. Moreover, the original name of the camp was "Quairawan", from which the term "caravan" probably came.

As Uqba was an ardent proselyte of Islam, he had the first and only permanent structure built in his camp alongside the tents in 670 or 671, namely the mosque.

The town of Kairouan was thus born. Over the centuries houses and public buildings sprang up and were enclosed by high walls, and the town became not only one of Tunisia's first capitals, but also Islam's fourth holy town after Mecca, Medina and Jerusalem. According to Islamic law, seven pilgrimages to Kairouan dispense worshippers of the obligatory pilgrimage to Mecca.

Today, Kairouan's proud ochre ramparts, and the domes and minarets of its numerous mosques still stand tall amidst the yellowed grass steppes of central Tunisia where herder nomads roam in the summer time.

Surrounded by the salt lakes – *sebkhas el Hani* and *Kelbia* – it presents travellers the fascinating and anachronistic sight of a town straight out of a Medieval tale. No one, not even non-Muslims, can remain indifferent to this town's austere beauty, as the 19th century French writer Guy de Maupassant, the Swiss painter Paul Klee, and, more recently, the French writer Henry de Montherlant and the specialist in Mediterranean history, Jacques Lacarrière, have all discovered.

The appearance of a fortress

Kairouan's main building, the Central *Jamaâ el Kebir* Mosque, dominates the whole town, and it is generally the first building tourists visit. With the exception of the *mihrab* (the niche indicating the direction of Mecca), it bears no resemblance to the primitive building Uqba ibn Nafi had built in the 7th century as the original mosque was in fact twice demolished during the 8th century.

Most of the current building dates back to the 9th century when the Aghlabids, influenced by the superb architecture of the Abbasid caliphate of Baghdad, repeatedly expanded and embellished the mosque. In 836, for example, the Aghlabid emir Ziyadet Allah spent colossal sums of money on adding the main prayer room and the high minaret.

Before entering the mosque, it is a good idea to walk around the outside to get an overall view. Begin from the esplanade in front, or even better, try to go up onto the terrace of one of the neighbouring houses (particularly that of the shop *Tapis des Princes*, on Place de la Grande Mosquée).

Like all buildings from this troubled period during which Tunisia suffered incessant wars, the mosque looks somewhat like a fortress.

With a penchant for brick, the Abbasid period architects built a heavy-looking building whose beauty is austere and bare. It is rather squat, and rectangular shaped, much longer than it is wide (135 m by 80 m).

Surrounded by an almost blind ochre earthen wall that is supported by powerful buttresses, there are seven doors into the mosque. One – on Rue de la Grande Mosquée – leads directly into the prayer room and is reserved for Muslims only. Another, the *Porte Lella Rihana*, which is the most beautiful, was completed in 1924 and has a portico made of ancient columns.

Non-Muslim visitors can enter via a door on the west of the mosque which leads into the main *courtyard*. This is paved with white marble slabs and bordered by a double row of galleries.

To the south of the courtyard is the main *prayer room* which is wider than it is deep. Seventeen carved cedar wood doors lead into the seventeen naves where, before the

THE ART OF FALCONRY

The very ancient art of training birds of prey to hunt was already practised in Asia nearly five hundred years B.C.
It then spread throughout the rest of the world, particularly in Europe where it reached its apogee in the Middle Ages before almost completely dying out.
In the Arab countries, on the other hand, falconry is still very much alive, especially in the emirates of the Persian Gulf where considerable fortunes are spent on buying and training birds of prey.
During the course of history, falconers have mainly used gyrfalcons, merlins, vultures and sparrowhawks.
The European sparrowhawk is a small bird of prey (with a wing span of 60 to 80 cm) about the size of a pigeon. It is grey with a brown underbelly. As it feeds on little birds and sometimes on chicks, for a long time it was considered to be a nuisance by man who hunted it until it was almost completely extinct (today the sparrowhawk is a protected species).
The sparrowhawk is a migrating bird and every year leaves Europe for Africa in the winter, passing via the Gibraltar and Sicily straits in order to avoid flying over the sea for too long.
The most commonly found species in Haouaria are the sparrowhawk (90%) and the peregrine falcon (10%).
Reputed for its speed, the falcon dives down to catch its prey at over 300 km/h.

visitors amazed eyes, a true "forest of columns" unfolds. There are more than 400 marble and porphyry columns, most of which were recovered from the ruins of Carthage, El Djem and Hadrumete. The capitals are Roman, Byzantine or Arabic.

Walking down the central nave – the widest one – visitors will notice that it has two ribbed *domes*.

At the end of the alley is the *mihrab* niche where, legend has it, an angel showed Uqba ibn Nafi the direction of Mecca. It is lined with small 9th-century shiny ceramic tiles. Next to the *mihrab* is the *minbar*, a magnificent pulpit decorated with 250 carved cedar wood panels that is a true 9th-century work of Muslim art. A little further on is the *maksoura* (private area reserved for princes). Between the two is a cluster of five columns which, it is said, leads to heaven if one manages to embrace or slip in between them.

The style of the Central Mosque's *minaret* is typical in the Maghreb, and has spread throughout all of North Africa: a square tower with three storeys. Standing 40 m tall, it is surmounted by a fluted dome with a shaft that supports a golden crescent and three copper balls.

It is possible to go up to the top of the minaret via the 128 step *staircase* which, visitors may notice, are made out of Christian tomb stones. There is a superb panoramic view of the town and its surroundings from the last storey.

The Barber's mosque

The stunning *Barber's mosque* to the west of the town is another of Kairouan's attraction. Its name is in fact rooted in a double misunderstanding as it is a *zawiyya* (a saint's mausoleum, and the seat of a religious brotherhood), not a mosque, and the Prophet Mohammed's companion who is venerated there was never his barber.

Behind every legend is a element of truth, however. Abou Zamaâ el Balaoui was nicknamed "the Prophet's barber" as he always wore a medallion containing three hairs from Mohammed's beard. Today, purists prefer to call this sanctuary the *zawiyya of Sidi Sahab* ("the Companion's mausoleum").

KAIROUAN

To Tunis

Rue des Aghlabites

Boulevard Est

Boulevard Est

Boulevard

Hospital

Rue Sidi Abdelkader

Central Mosque

Rue Ibrahim Ibn el Aghlab

Rue Ali Bey

El Moitz Ibn Badis

Avenue

Rue Kchelfa

Sidi Adb el Kader Zawiyya

Kasbah

Rue de Djerba

Rue el Kadraoui Ibn el Kadraoui

R. Sidi Bou Omrani

Bab el Khoukha

Place de Tunis

R. Dar el Bey

Rue el Kedidi

Rue Salah Soussi

Bab el Tounes

Boulevard Sadikia

Rue

Trois Portes Mosque

El Maalek Mosque

El Bey Bir Barouta Mosque

Zeïtouna Mosque

Bab el Jedid

Belhaouen

Sidi Abid el Ghariani Zawiyya

To Sousse

Rue Sidi Abd el Mounen

Arceaux

Bab ech Chouhada

Rue des

Cultural Centre

Fahrat Hached

A. H. Bourguiba

Rose Mosque

Zouaoui

Rue de Gafsa

Avenue Ali Zouaoui

Governorate

Post office

Avenue de Mahdia

Avenue

Crafts Centre

de la

République

Town Council

Avenue

de Fès

Law Courts

Rue Abi Thameur

To Sfax

Built in the 17th century, this edifice's delicate proportions and refined decor of lacework stuccoes and beautiful floral motif mosaics are ravishing. It includes a series of surrounding buildings, namely the head of the brotherhood's house, the *mokadem*, a Koranic school (*medersa*), rooms for pilgrims, and, naturally, the saint's mausoleum. Unfortunately the general public is not allowed in the interior courtyard nor the different parts of the building.

Golden boats and swans

Visitors should make a detour to see the *Aghlabid basins* near to the Barber's mosque. These are all that remain of the seven huge ornamental lakes built in the Middle Ages.

One, which measures 128 m in diameter, contains over 50,000 cubic metres of water and used to have a little pavilion in the middle where the Aghlabid princes liked to reside.

Another smaller one was fed by a 36 km aqueduct.

It is said that golden boats wove in and out of the swans and perfumed jets of water that the Aghlabid emir Ahmed had had installed in his palace gardens in the 9th century.

In order to fully appreciate Kairouan, visitors should spend a good while strolling in the medina which is surrounded by high walls restored in the 18th century. Several monumental gates lead into the medina, notably *Bab ech Chouhada Djelladine* (the leather traders and tanners' gate), *Bab Tounès* (Tunis gate), *Bab el Khoukha* (the postern gate), and *Bab el Djédid* (the new gate).

In the old quarters, visitors will discover the "mosque with three gates", *Jamaâ Thletha Bibane*, to the east of the Medina. Built by the Aghlabids at the end of the 9th century, its facade is decorated with Arabic inscriptions and floral motifs.

Next to this is the *Bir Barouta*, where a dromedary draws water by making a wheel turn. According to

KAIROUAN DAZZLES PAUL KLEE

In April 1914, Paul Klee (1879-1940), a Swiss artist of German origin, went on a long journey around Tunisia with the German expressionist artist August Macke (1887-1914). When they reached Kairouan, they were dazzled.
On 15 April 1914, Paul Klee wrote in his diary: "So it was not long before we were completely taken by the quite new splendor of this country. Akouda, a fabulous town, greeted us en route, promising so many things – quickly enough for a life perhaps – and disappeared.
At two o'clock, Kairouan. A little French town with two hotels. We quenched our thirst with tea in order to proceed in the dignified manner fitting for discovering such marvels.
First of all, great dizziness. No details, nothing but the ensemble. And what an ensemble! A concentration of the "Arabian Nights" 99% true. What perfumes! How it penetrates, intoxicates, and at the same time makes everything much clearer! Structure and intoxication. They burn scented wood. My true country?" ...
"Colour is within me. I don't need to try to capture it. I know it possesses me for ever, I know it. This is the meaning of this happy hour: colour and I are one. I am an artist."

kasserine/ sbeïtla

legend, this miraculous well is linked to the Zem-Zem spring in Mecca.

Other sites to not be missed include: the *zawiyya Sidi Abid el Ghariani* with its pretty arcaded gallery and fountain (said to have been discovered by Uqba ibn Nafi, and the *zawiyya Sidi Amour Abbada*, or the "mosque of sabres" with its five ribbed domes (it is called this because its patron saint was a reputed dagger maker). Also see the central covered market near to the Porte de Tunis in the west, the Sidi Abd el Kader zawiyya and the Rose, el Maalek and Zeïtouna mosques.

Typical carpets

Kairouan, a major rug making centre, has innumerable family workshops, shops and stores where visitors may admire and buy several specimens of the local production, notably the *zerbiyya* carpets (with brightly coloured knotted stitches), *alloucha* carpets (knotted stitches, made out of sheep's wool or camel hair, beige colours) and the *mergoums* carpets which are woven. Each carpet takes six to twelve months to make. Some, particularly the silk carpets, have over 250,000 knots per square metre (one craftsman alone can rarely make more than 40,000 knots in a year).

Visitors will soon begin to recognise several typical motifs, like the stylistic lustres of the Central Mosque, the Kairouan cross (the four branches of which represent the four holy cities of Islam: Mecca, Medina, Jerusalem and Kairouan), fish (protection from the evil eye), jasmine flowers, and the seasons and days of the week.

A visit to the Kairouan Artisanal Centre will give a deeper understanding of the art of weaving. It is worth noting that most of the major carpet sellers in the medina have terraces on their roofs with ceramic tile benches and doors, like in the Tunis medina. From here there is a superb panoramic view of the town and its surroundings.

Try also to visit the Muslim cemetery on the north-west road where the white tombs – most of which are very old – are movingly simple.

(*See information p. 188*).

■ Near to djebel Chambi (1,544 m), Tunisia's highest point, the large agricultural town of Kasserine where esparto grass is grown, is an excellent springboard for discovering the numerous vestiges of Tunisian antiquity in the High Steppes region.

Along with *Cilium* on the outskirts of the town, *Sufetula*, Tunisia's largest ancient town, is situated near to Sbeïtla in the east.

Before heading there, travellers may first like to visit Cilium where there are several ancient theatres, a triumphal arch, two mausoleums, a Byzantine fort, etc. On the way to Sbeïtla via the N 13, a strange Roman tomb can be seen on the roadside. The front wall of this three storied square tower bears an engraved text, which is a homage to Flavius Secundus. This, along with ruins of another tower a little further on, gave the town the name Kasserine, which means "the two towers" in Arabic.

The Roman town of Sufetula on the river Sbeïtla was founded in the first century A.D. during the Flavian dynasty by veterans of the Third Augusta Legion who were given land in return for their loyal services in pacifying the southern Berber tribes of Tunisia and Algeria.

The town flourished at the end of the 2nd century A.D. during the Libyan Septimus Severus's reign (Tripoli). Later, the inhabitants converted to Christianity and suffered several persecutions under the reigns of the Roman emperors (especially Diocletian) and of the Vandals.

In the 7th century, the Byzantine patrician Gregory made it the capital of the empire independent from Constantinople. At the beginning of the Arab invasion, one of the first battles between Muslims and Byzantines took place here in 747: Gregory was killed and the town razed.

Wealth generated from olive farming

In the past, Sufetula was a large town spread over 50 hectares of land with a population of 9 to 12,000 inhabitants, and was equipped with sophisticated installments: a sewage system, a piped drinking water

The bastions of the Kef afford a wonderful view o[f] set in tiers on the mount

kef (the)

system supplied by several springs and rain water tanks, and an aqueduct-bridge across the Sbeïtla river.

Economically, the town owed its wealth to the olive plantations, and the remains of presses can be seen as soon as one enters the site.

Sufetula still has a number of vestiges from the Roman and Byzantine periods. From the Roman period are the remains of the Septimus Severus and Diocletian triumphal arches, the latter work of art having become the town's symbol over the course of time. The centre of the Roman town is situated at the site of the main forum bordered by the three capitol temples (dedicated to Jupiter, Minerva and Juno, 2nd century) and which were reached via the Antoninus Pius gate (139 A.D.). There are also traces of several thermal baths (with mosaics), a theatre, an amphitheatre and several public fountains.

From the Byzantine and Christian periods, there are the remains of churches (of the martyrs Gervais, Protais and Tryphon, of the bishop Bellator, with beautiful mosaics, and of Vitalis with large baptism fonts), fortified houses and baths.

Archaeological vestiges

Before leaving Sufetula, visitors should go to see the little museum at the entrance where there are some splendid pieces, notably a marble statue of Dionysus riding a panther and a mosaic of Venus.

In the surrounding area to the north, archaeologists have dug up vestiges of *Ammaedara* (Haïdra), the ancient camp of the Third Roman Augusta legion (remains of Christian, Roman and Donatist churches). To the west, they have discovered remains of Bou Chebka, and in the south, near to Fériana, the remains of *Thélepte,* where there is a Christian basilica, a Roman theatre and a Byzantine fort and other diverse vestiges.
(See information p. 188).

■ When the intense heat hits the area, all the inhabitants of the Kef leave their houses in search of the cooler air until late in the night, ambling up and down the main corniche boulevard together in families. This practice, which many foreign visitors are surprised by, recalls the Spanish "paseo". What visitors may not know is that, perched up on the mountain side at an altitude of 750 m, the Kef is a health resort thanks to its high altitude fresh air. Moreover, few visitors will realise that it is possible to go skiing in the whole region during the winter.

Still, the heat is no problem when it means relaxing and savouring the pleasure of an afternoon siesta, and of meeting the very friendly Kef inhabitants in the evening in the town parks, bars, restaurants or at the ice cream and lemonade stalls.

As it is cool in the morning, this is a good time to attack the town's steep slopes and stairways. In the Kef, the town centre and hotels are half-way up the hill, and the principal attractions are at the top. This is in fact quite a treat as each level has a superb panoramic view over the whole region.

The first stop is the little municipal museum in the former *zawiyya Sidi Ben Alissa.* Devoted to popular traditions, it houses numerous collections of day-to-day utensils (cooking utensils, weaving looms, traditional medicine bag, and jewellery).

The room where a nomadic habitation with its large tents, rugs, caskets, bags, water containers, tea pots and hearth has been reconstructed is particularly interesting.

A gem of a mosque

A little further on is an architectural gem: the exquisite little *Sidi Bou Makhlouf mosque.* From the outside it is a harmoniously proportioned sculpture with its annulated domes and little minaret.

Inside, visitors eyes will feast on its intricate lacework stuccos, the splendor of its ceramic covered walls and the cheerful, colourful light shining through its stained glass windows.

The very helpful warders will take visitors up into the little minaret where the pigeons nest. The narrow

kerkennah (islands)

spiral stairway leads up onto the roof where there is a breathtaking view of the town.

Next to the mosque is the old *medersa* (Koranic university) and the annexes which have been transformed into a Moorish café and a hotel. This was a good idea as the bare, cool monk-like rooms are so calm they almost make you want to meditate. In and around the interior courtyard, a sculpted fountain and many statues dotted here and there resemble an open-air stonework museum.

Just above the mosque, perched on the top of the mountain, the powerful crenellated walls of the *Kasbah* built by the Turks stand proud. It is possible to walk around the covered walkways of this ancient military garrison currently being renovated by the ONTT (Tunisian National Tourist Board), and visit the towers with their wonderful view over the town and surrounding area.

History and prehistory

The Kef region is particularly rich in prehistoric and historic vestiges. At Sidi Zine (9 km to the west of Kef) and at Koum el Majène, numerous Acheulian hand axes (belonging to the Acheulian civilisation in the Lower Paleolithic era between 2 million and 400,000 years B.C.) have been dug up. From the animal bones also found, it is strange to think that the region was once inhabited by elephants, rhinoceri, zebras and antelopes. More recent large dolmens with porticoes, dating from 2 to 3,000 years B.C., can still be seen standing at Ellès (50 km southeast of the Kef).

In ancient times, this whole region bore witness the epic lives of the Berber chiefs Tacfarinas, Masinissa and Jugurtha. The latter gave his name to the *Table de Jugurtha*, the tabular mountain 65 km south of the Kef.

Roman remains are abundant in the towns of Musti, Dougga (*see earlier*), Thignica, on the Téboursouk road east of Kef; Althiburos (Medeina), Zannfour, Mactaris, Sufès, Sufetula, Cilium, Thelepte, in the south; and Bulla Regia, Chemtou and Thuburnica in the north. (*See information p. 188*).

■ The Kerkennah islands, a little archipelago off Sfax, have for a long time borne the title of "the last paradise". This must have been ironic, as they most frequently served as a place to send outcasts and outlaws. Hannibal may have taken refuge, or even poisoned himself here in 183 B.C., to escape the victorious Romans. During the Roman occupation, corrupt civil servants were banished to Kerkennah. At the time of the Tunis beys, political prisoners, adulterous women and disgraced courtesans were sent there until the end of their days.

The unyielding, slightly fearsome islanders were never able to enjoy the tranquility prescribed by Saint Fulgence who had a monastery built here in the 6th century. Indeed, over the centuries the islands witnessed the coming and going of the Phoenicians, the Carthaginians, the Romans, the Vandals, the Normands, the Arabs, the European crusaders, the Sicilians, the Maltese, the Spanish, the Turks and the French. The island was even the hideaway of the Barbary pirates and their famous chief Dargouth in the 16th century.

The archipelago is reached by ferry from Sfax opposite (unless you manage to negotiate a ride on a fishing boat or yacht).

After a short one and a half hour crossing, the ferry comes to Gharbi, the southernmost island. Just to the north of Gharbi is Chergui island, the largest and most touristing island.

On the periphery of the archipelago are three islets: *Sefnou, Gremdi* and *Roumédia* (a camel rearing and training centre was been set up on the latter).

Gharbi and *Chergui,* which are flat and covered in palms, pomegranate trees, carobs, fig trees and eucalyptus, have a population of 15,000 islanders who live from sheep rearing, palm wine harvesting, and fishing for octopuses, sponges and fish. In spite of the islands' smallness, a 65 km tarred road has been built on Chergui used by about forty vehicles, most of which are the fishermen's small trucks, and, in the summer, tourists' cars.

Holiday makers will find all the pleasures of the beach on the archipelago, plus totally tranquility and a return to simple activities: walking, sunbathing, swimming, fishing, and scuba diving. These rather wild islands are not – or barely – equipped with modern leisure installments like tennis courts, golf courses, or discos. There are a few beaches to liven up the stay, for example Sidi Frej beach on the north-west coast of Chergui.

Octopus and sponge fishing

The archipelago's prime past times are unquestionably fishing and diving in the Gulf of Gabès waters where fish are abundant. Visitors really should try to make friends with a local fisherman who will take them out fishing.

Sponge fishing, which is in decline due to competition from synthetic products, once furnished all the pharmacists and stores in Europe. Nowadays, thanks to the arrival of the tourists, it is taking off again.

In order to gather these precious sponges, the Kerkennah fishermen set out in twos in their boats. Whilst one rows, the other peers into the water through a glass bottomed cylinder. As soon as he spots one, he pulls it up with a gaff, rather than diving for it, as the sea around the Kerkennah Islands is shallow.

Octopus fishing is more laborious and involves using strings of clay pots that are left to sink to the bottom of the sea. After a few hours, when the fishermen think the octopi will have taken refuge inside the pots, they pull in the rope, bringing hundreds of pots up to the surface.

However, as the numbers of this species are now unfortunately falling dangerously low, the Tunisian government has shortened the authorised fishing period by over two weeks. The octopus fishing season now lasts from 15 October to April and not until mid-May as in the past.

Unlike fishermen on the rest of the continent, the Kerkennah fishermen rarely use dragnets. They prefer to set up their own ingenious trapping systems in the waters.

Having obtained a concession in the sea from the authorities, they install palm grids in fishing ground, forming corridors – or "*bourdigues*" – that lead the fish into the hoop nets in the capture chambers, like the French "*madragues*".

*This movingly simple sailors' cemetery
with its hundreds of little white tombs
lies on the outskirts of Mahdia,
a fishing port on the eastern coast
of Tunisia.*

After a few hours, the fishermen set out in feluccas and pull up the hoop nets one by one in which the gilthead, lamprey, mullet, mackerel and other fish have been caught.

In the summer, "flying" mullet fishing is more spectacular. As soon as a shoal has been spotted, beaters dive into the water and beat the waves with sticks. The startled mullet leap out of the water in all directions, and many of them land in the grids placed on the surface of the water.

Islanders who are not fishermen cultivate vineyards (making muscat wine), olive trees, and especially date palms. As these palms constitute one of the archipelago's sources of wealth, the astute Tunisian tax collectors calculate the islanders' taxes according to the number of palms they own. Along with the date crops, the palms are also a source of palm wine, *laghmi*, which is made by fermenting the sap, and has an alcohol content of between 7 and 8°.

When walking in the palm groves, visitors will discover the picturesque sight of the sap being collected in wooden containers fixed to the trees that have been bled.

The best time to visit the Kerkennah islands is during the summer as this is the marriage period. For 3 to 4 days, all the splendor of the Orient comes alive on the islands.

Sumptuously adorned and hoisted up on a palanquin on a camel's back, the bride-to-be rides around the village to her fiancé's house accompanied by a large cortege of villagers, griots, and musicians.

After the ceremony in the mosque, all the islanders and members of the family who have emigrated to the mainland, or even to Europe, join together for a huge banquet. Sumptuous gifts are drawn out of caskets and exchanged: porcelain and metal crockery, gold and silver damask cloth, etc.

The archipelago has few ancient vestiges, but visitors can visit the Roman wells on Gremdi and the Bordj el-Hissar Turkish fort when travelling around the islands.
(*See information p. 188*).

THE LAST PARADISE: THE KERKENNAH ISLANDS

■ *The two main islands, Chergui and Gharbi, separated by the El Kantara divide, deserve their name "the last paradise".*
Hannibal took refuge there. The Western emperors later made it a place for deporting people. And for centuries the Tunis beys exiled all the harem courtesans they had grown tired of to these hard to reach islands.
Thus, of all the women in the Near East, the ever-beautiful women of Kerkennah, dressed in bright colours, freer here than anywhere else, today live with their faces unveiled, carrying water jars on their shoulders as if they were amphoras as they walk slowly under the palms like Circa princesses, whilst their husbands spin the potter's wheel or fish around their enchanted (or disenchanted) islands for octopus and sponges.

MARCEL SAUVAGE

mahdia

The smart, charming little port side town of Mahdia between Sfax and Monastir, seems to be a simple county town, with no hint of its prestigious historical past. In the 10th century, however, it was the capital of Tunisia (*Ifriqyya*), having supplanted Kairouan at the beginning of the the Fatimids' reign (the same Fatimids whose grand dynasty reigned over Cairo from 969 to 1171). The Fatimids (Ismaelian Shiites) – led by their chief Obeid Allah – took over Tunisia in 909, supplanting the Aghlabid sovereigns.

Proclaiming himself the Mahdi ("God's messenger and savior of the world"), Obeid Allah initially settled in Kairouan in 910 where he had himself declared caliph. He then created his new capital on the Tunisian coast in 921, calling it Mahdia (the "town of al Mahdi").

In 934, his son Aboul Qasim el Qaïm, and in 944, his grandson Aboul Abbas Ismaïl had to contend with the Kharijite Muslims' major insurrections. Led by Abou Yazid ("The man on a donkey"), the rebels initially beat the Fatimids and sieged Mahdia in 944. The town's garrison fought them off, and in 947, "The man on a donkey" was defeated and killed (his corps was mockingly stuffed and paraded on the back of a donkey accompanied by two monkeys). Mahdia's resistance earned it the name "the Invincible", and the Fatimid caliph Aboul Abbas Ismaïl took the title Al Mansour, "the Victorious".

In 972, Mahdia was called "the Conqueror" when its caliph al Moezz Lidin-Allah left Mahdia to go to found Cairo (the Egyptian capital is still known as "al Muiz's Cairo", "Qahira al Muiz" today in memory of its founder.

At the beginning of the 11th century, the Zirids, who had taken over from the Fatimid suzerains in Tunisia, renounced their former convictions and their former allies. They became Sunnite Muslims, recognising the authority of the Abbasid caliphs of Baghdad rather than that of Cairo. In Mahdia, they exterminated all the Shiites in the Central Mosque. As a punishment, the caliph of Cairo sent the pillaging Beni Hillal nomads to ravage Mahdia and the surrounding region.

The nomads were followed by the Genoese and the Pisans who landed and sacked the town in 1088.

In the 12th century, the inhabitants of Mahdia were evacuated by Roger II of Sicily's troops who settled there. It was liberated shortly afterwards, however, by the Berber troops of the Almohad sovereign Abd El Moumin.

Haunt of the Turkish pirate Dargouth in the 16th century, Mahdia fought against the Spanish, then against the Maltese knights.

At the end of the 17th century, the Turks settled in Mahdia, bringing peace to the town once and for all.

A fishing port

Mahdia is now a fishing port harbouring lamprey and dragnet fishing boats, feluccas, and sardine boats. The catches mainly consist of "bluefish": sardine, mackerel, anchovy, and also grouper and gilthead.

A few vestiges of its glorious past still remain, notably the *Central Mosque* built by the Mahdi in the 10th century, which is an austere and majestic building with a very spartan prayer room.

The huge 16th century *Saqifa al Kahla gate,* ("the Dark Porch") leads into the old town (medina) where the remains of an ancient fortress and its large tower and portcullis can still be seen.

Visitors are likely to comes across fishermen mending their nets in the spiralling streets, and craftsmen who specialise in silk weaving in the workshops on Rue de Sidi Jaber (try also to visit the traditional silk weaving museum opened in the old Jami Sfar in the town). Further on at the Place du Caire, there is a beautiful Hanifite mosque, and in Rue Manoubia, the Turkish janissaries' old homes with wooden grills on the windows.

At the foot of the tall lighthouse on the tip of Cape Africa there is an impressive 17th century sailors' cemetery and its Sea gate ("Sour al Bibane").

Visitors can also see several vestiges of the town's ancient ramparts, and the Bordj el Kebir fortress.

It is worth going to see the *Bellaa* ("the Mobile") old port in the nearby rocky inlet which, in Fatimid times, could harbour up to 300 galleys.

(*See information p. 189*).

maktar

mareth

■ Maktar, a modest village in the High Tell south-west of Tunis, could quite well be given the stuffy-sounding title of "the capital of ancient archaeology", its land is so rich in vestiges of all kinds. The village itself was founded several centuries B.C. when the Phoenicians built a fortress on this high plateau to survey and contain eventual raids by the southern Berber nomads.

The Roman town of Mactaris

The town of *Mactaris* developed during the Roman occupation in the 2nd and 3rd centuries A.D. The most fruitful results of excavation work carried out in the region, have been at Mactaris. The ruins, open to the public, include the vestiges of an amphitheatre right by the entrance. Further on is the Forum whose pavings are in a very good state of preservation and which is dominated to the south by the Trajan Triumphal Arch (2nd century A.D.). After the basilica, where there are Byzantine tombs, bear right to get to the temple of Bacchus.

A little further on are the Capitol Thermal Baths and the Young people's Scola with a gymnasium and pool, which prefigured today's Youth Clubs. In the 4th century A.D., it was converted into a Christian basilica (its altar is a pagan sarcophagus). There is another eye-catching building in the same district of Mactaris, namely the tax collectors' office with its niches set in a semi-circle. At the other end of the town are the main Thermal Baths (the best conserved baths in North Africa).

Near to the entrance to Mactaris, there is a little museum housing items found during excavation work: tomb stones in the effigy of the deceased, statues of deities and Roman emperors.

Visitors may discover other ancient vestiges around Maktar. To the north there are the Ellès dolmen with porticoes, and the Zannfour, El Ksour, Kbor Klib, Ksar Toual and Zama Minor (Siliana) vestiges; to the east those of Bou Saadia; to the west, the Althiburos site (Medeina); and in the south, the Sufes (Sbiba) vestiges.

(*See information p. 189*).

■ Mareth is not a tourist spot, but rather a bloody Second World War theatre of war where the Axis forces (the Germans and the Italians) were definitively driven out of North Africa. In order to commemorate the battle, the Tunisian Minister of Defence has just set up a most interesting military museum where, thanks to the numerous diagrams, displays, and films, the Allied forces' "Campaign for Tunisia" which lasted from the end of 1942 to May 1943, can be seen in detail.

Before the war, the French had build a 45 km fortified line (the "Mareth line", dubbed the "Maginot line of the desert") along the Zigzaou river which flows through the Ksour mountains near to Mareth and on into the Gulf of Gabès. At this time, the authorities feared an Italian invasion from their Libyan colony in the east.

After the 1940 armistice, the Italians occupied Tunisia and dismantled the "Mareth line". This was soon rebuilt again by the German Afrikakorps troops under General von Arnim and Marshal Rommel (who had just been defeated at El Alamein in Egypt in October 1942, and had retreated to Tunisia) between the end of 1942 and the beginning of 1943.

For five months, over seven thousand men worked on the new 25 km long Mareth line. It had about thirty blockhouses to protect soldiers and artillery, a line of anti-tank trenches, 100 km of barbed wire and huge mine fields (100,000 anti-tank mines, and 70,000 personnel mines). Two headquarters were also built for Marshall Rommel and General von Arnim right by Mareth.

Backed by the Italian forces, Rommel wanted to stop the British 8th Army led by Montgomery and the French General Leclerc's division from heading southwards from Tripoli in Libya to Tunisia (the Tataouine-Médenine-Ben Gardane front, 20 February 1943). At the same time, the Allied forces under General Anderson were pressing on in central and northern Tunisia.

In February 1943, the Allies attacked the Axis forces at Mareth in southern Tunisia, thus beginning the terrible "Battle of Mareth".

The Axis forces on the ground were considerable, but outnumbered. The Allied forces consisted of

Seen from a plane, the Matmata region of southern Tunisia looks much like a lunar landscape. These craters are man-made, however, and are in fact troglodytic homes.

matmata

160,000 men, 750 tanks, 700 pieces of field artillery, 1,000 anti-tank guns, and 535 planes. The Axis forces, on the other hand had only 76,000 men, 150 tanks, 450 pieces of artillery, 500 anti-tank guns and 123 planes.

As the museum clearly explains: "The Battle of Mareth begun on 16 March 1943 when the 8th Army (British) launched an attack on the Mareth defensive line on two axes: the first axe along the coastal region between Mareth and the coast, and the second axe consisting of a bypass operation around the Tunisian Dahar plateau.

The battle raged during the daytime on 20 and 21 March when the British 8th Army tried to cross the Zigzaou river, but it met with the fierce resistance of the Axis forces led by General Messe.

The battle ended on 28 March 1943 after the British forces' bypass operation via the El Hamma-Tebaga breach was successful, forcing the Axis forces to abandon their defensive positions on the Mareth line and to retreat northwards."

After some furious battles, on 28 March 1943, the Germans and Italians decided to abandon the site to avoid being encircled. They left thousands of dead behind on the battlefields, that the bloodied waters of the Zigzaou river carried into the sea.

The rest of the German army retreated to the Akarit river north of Gabès where this time it affronted all of the Allied forces (Americans, British and French).

The French had just successfully linked up with the others under the command of General Alexander.

The Germans and Italians, who were rooted out from their positions on the Akarit river on 6 April, retreated to Sfax and Sousse and then Enfidaville where the decisive battle was launched on 22 April.

At the beginning of May, the Germans and Italians began to cave in before the Allies who took Tunis then Bizerte. Having retreated to the Cap Bon peninsula, they surrendered on 12 May. From then on, the Germans and Italians had no military forces left in North Africa which meant that the Allies were free to organise the Sicily landing in July 1943.

(See information p. 189).

■ It comes as no surprise to learn that the American director George Lucas shot several of the "Star Wars" scenes at Matmata, the little town in the south-east of Tunisia: the ground is peppered with lunar craters at the bottom of which troglodytic dwellings are buried.

These very unusual rabbit warren dwellings are not at all new. They originally served as underground hiding places and fortresses for Berber tribes in southern Tunisia fleeing the multiple Ifriqyya invaders: Phoenicians, Carthaginians, Romans, Byzantines, Vandals and the Beni Hillal Arab hoards. All the troglodytes had to do was take the well ladders away to render them impenetrable.

Escaping the heat

When peace finally reigned again in the region, it was no longer a matter of the Matmata Berbers defending themselves from other people, but from the weather. Indeed, these underground craters enable the Matmata inhabitants to escape the rigours of the climate: their homes are cool in the daytime whilst the sun blazes outside, and warm at night when the temperature can drop as low as 0 °C (typical climatic variation in the Sahara).

Nowadays, these crater dwellings are reached by a tunnel dug at the foot of the great mounds of earth in which the troglodytic rooms and galleries are found.

Each family's "apartment" generally consists of several vaulted rooms: a communal room with an alcove (recess), a bedroom, granaries and a stable.

The interior is always immaculately white. The highly rudimentary furniture consists of blocks and niches carved in the limestone. Cooking utensils, clothes, gazelle-skin bags containing the family's most precious objects and amulets (Hands of Fatima) and postcards from all over the world sent by tourists who once passed through Matmata, are all hung from the walls of the troglodytic homes. A final cheerful touch is added by the hanging cloths and naive wall paintings.

Most families have installed weaving workshops where they make the traditional *kilims* Berber rugs.

With the arrival of modernity, most of the Matmata Berbers – especially the youngsters – have left their troglodytic homes for modern houses on the surface.

Troglodytic hotels

Only the elders have stayed living down in the wells where they are content to live off the meagre revenues generated by their herds of goats and tourism.

Several of these troglodytic dwellings have been turned into hotels, for example "Les Berbères", the Tunisian Touring Club's "Marhala", and the "Sidi Driss". The latter lodged the "Star Wars" film crew some years ago. Ironically, the inhabitants of Matmata never saw the film.

(*See information p. 189*).

■ The imposing silhouette of the *ribat* watches over the line fishermen, the sunbathing families, and the children diving off the large rock just out at sea. In short, an easy-going sight that takes away any aggressivity or austerity from this centre of Islamic conquest.

Indeed, the monastery towering over the town which is named after it, was occupied in the Middle Ages by a religious order of Muslim warriors as fearsome as the Teutonic knights or the Templars were for the Christians. They knew how to pray, but they also knew how to fight for their faith.

At the time of the monastery's (*ribat*) construction in 797, the Arabs had fought the Byzantines to definitively root them out of Tunisia, and were trying to reduce the Berbers' fierce resistance throughout the whole of the Maghreb.

This turbulent and wild history did not begin with the Arabs, but with the Romans. It was in fact Julius Caesar who founded the entrenched camp (*castrum*) of

SIMONE DE BEAUVOIR IN MATMATA

■ *The promised truck was waiting for me in Médenine. I was the only passenger. The driver was able to recognise the war damaged road to Matmata. In two or three places bridges had been blown up, but he managed to cross the oueds and took me to the remarkable village where ten thousand people live underground...*

The market place was swarming; only men, draped in snowy-coloured burnous, chatty and cheerful; the brown-skinned women with blue eyes, sometimes young and beautiful, but sad looking, were tucked away at the bottom of the wells reached via the caves.

I visited one of these warrens: in the sombre smoky caverns, I saw a half-naked gang of kids, an old toothless lady, two unkempt middle-aged women, and a pretty girl covered in jewellery who was weaving a carpet.

On the way back up into the light, I passed the head of the household on his way back from the market, shining with brightness and healthiness. I felt sorry for my sex...

SIMONE DE BEAUVOIR,
La Force des Choses.

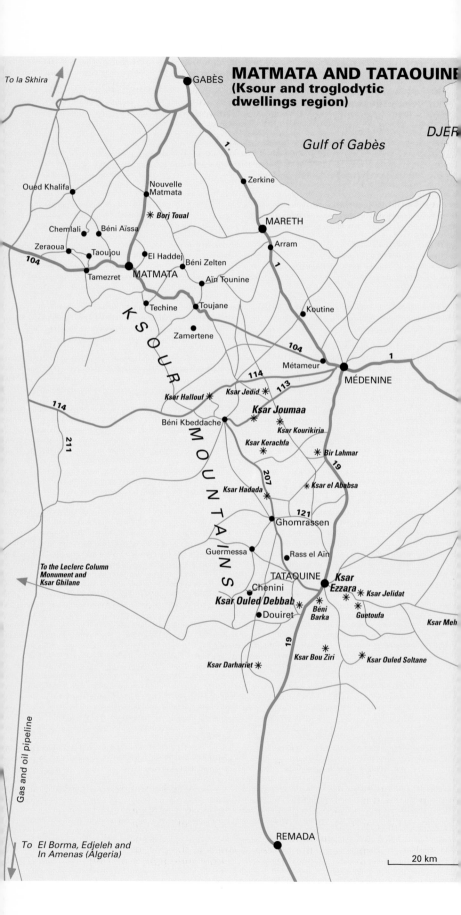

MATMATA AND TATAOUINE
(Ksour and troglodytic dwellings region)

To la Skhira

GABÈS

Gulf of Gabès

DJER

1

Zerkine

Nouvelle Matmata

MARETH

✳ Borj Toual

Oued Khalifa

Chemlali · Béni Aïssa

Arram

Zeraoua

104

Taoujou

El Haddej

Béni Zelten

Tamezret

MATMATA

Aïn Tounine

Techine

Toujane

Koutine

Zamertene

KSOUR

104

Métameur

MÉDENINE

1

114

113

Ksar Jedid

Ksar Hallouf ✳

Ksar Joumaa

Béni Kbeddache

Ksar Kourikiria

114

Ksar Kerachfa

✳ Bir Lahmar

211

19

207

✳ Ksar el Ababsa

Ksar Hadada

121

Ghomrassen

MOUNTAINS

Guermessa

Rass el Aïn

To the Leclerc Column Monument and Ksar Ghilane

TATAOUINE

Ksar Ezzara

Chenini

Ksar Jelidat

Ksar Ouled Debbab

Béni Barka

Guetoufa

Ksar Meh

Douiret

19

Ksar Darhariet ✳

Ksar Bou Ziri

Ksar Ouled Soltane

Gas and oil pipeline

To El Borma, Edjeleh and In Amenas (Algeria)

REMADA

20 km

Ruspina on the Monastir site. Already surrounded by solid ramparts – the remains of which can still be seen today –, the camp was the base for his campaigns in Africa.

Several centuries later when the Arabs set out to conquer the Maghreb, and *Ifriqyya* in particular (Tunisia), they quite naturally took advantage of the Romans' former positions.

Destined to defend the Tunisian coast from possible foreign invasions from the sea (by the Byzantines in particular), the *ribat* was built by the Kairouan Aghlabids (vassals of the Baghdad Abbasids) on the tip of the Monastir peninsula in the 9th century. The fervent Aghlabids also made it into an Islamic religious centre which had its heyday when the Fatimids made nearby Mahdia their capital. During this period, the *ribat* was a place of pilgrimage and an influential Islamic centre.

From its warring past, the ribat has conserved its dense, crenellated ramparts, its covered walkways, and bastions that make it look more like a medieval castle.

It is dominated by a chimney-like tower, the *nador*, from which the soldier monks surveyed the sea and the inland region. During the summer, a sound and light show restores some of the monastery-fortress's former glory.

Also worth seeing is the little Islamic *museum* which houses some beautiful ancient jewellery, glasswork, calligraphic manuscripts and Korans, embroided cloth and even a very ancient medicine cabinet from the Fatimid period (9th century). One of the museum's gems is a magnificent Arabic astrolabe made in Cordoba in 927.

At the foot of the ribat, the *old ribat,* which was almost completely destroyed in the past, has recovered a certain allure since the foundations of its towers and ramparts encircled by a deep moat have been excavated.

The nearby 9th century *Central Mosque* built at the same time as the ribat and in the same ochre stone, completely blends in with this defensive architecture.

To the west is the large Sidi Mezri – patron of the town – Muslim Sailors' cemetery with thousands of white, blue or green tombs and marabouts' domes and the mausoleum of the ex-President Bour-guiba's family who were from Monastir. It is a fine construction flanked by two minarets and a dome.

On the other side of the square behind the ribat and the cemetery, is the *Bourguiba mosque* built in 1963 in a traditional style, with superb decorations and a courtyard with beautiful colonnades around it.

Surrounded by 12th-century medieval walls with crenels and bastions, the Monastir *medina* begins after the Bourguiba mosque. Inside there are several interesting mosques and a souk.

To the east of the ribat is the fishing port, and to the west, the marina. This was made by building jetties from the coast to the old Dagamsi island, making two large basins for yachts (386 moorings). Out at sea from the town, a diving school has been set up on the "Ile des Monastères". Boat trips are organised on the "El Kahlia" to the Kuriat and Conigliera islands.

Heading back up the coast in the direction of Sousse, is the seaside resort of *Skanès* where there are many hotels, holiday resorts, and a golf course (18 holes, 6,000 m) surrounded by palms and olive trees.

By the sea to the south of Monastir, the vestiges of *Leptis Minor* have been excavated near to Lamta. Founded by the Phoenicians in the 12th century B.C., this town became the capital of the Byzacene province in Carthaginian times and prospered thanks to its port which was a major exporter of olive oil.

It was at Leptis Minor that Hannibal landed in 202 B.C. on his way back from Italy at the end of the Second Punic War, and on his way to fight the Roman army led by Scipio which had arrived two years earlier in 204. Shortly afterwards, in 201, the Carthaginian chief was crushingly defeated at Zama, leaving him completely exhausted to the point that he died in 183, and did not participate in the Third Punic War.

After the fall of Carthage in 146 B.C., Leptis Minor obtained the statute of a "free town" from the Romans. Later it became a colony which flourished thanks to its oil trade.

Other vestiges include the remains of *Thapsus* to the west of Moknine by the sea. Further to the south is the port of Mahdia.

(*See information p. 189*).

nabeul

■ Nabeul is indisputably the "ceramics capital" as, when wandering up the main street, you cannot go ten metres without seeing mountains of pots, piles of plates and earthenware tiles.

Along with the leather bags, bird cages and carpets flapping in the wind like banners, all these ceramic goods on sale to tourists have transformed Nabeul into a huge bazaar. And just like in Vallauris in France, the banal – ashtrays, candle holders, copies of "kitsch" amphoras – is found alongside the sublime – goods inspired by the best traditions, particularly the *zelliges* (decorated earthenware tiled panels). The Arabs were undoubtedly masters in the terracotta and earthenware domain. Having learnt this art from the Persians (who learnt it from the Babylonians), they spread it all over the Orient and the Mediterranean basin, notably in Spain where the Majorca workshops gave their name to *majolica* pottery.

Driven out of Spain in the 17th century, the Arabo-Andalusians took refuge in the Maghreb, and in Tunisia in particular, where their potters opened new workshops.

A fascinating "general science lesson"

A visit to one of the Nabeul workshops is the occasion for a fascinating "general science lesson". Visitors will see the red clay or kaolin paste being prepared, the product being made either on a wheel or in a press, the first oven firing, then the painting and glazing, and at last, the final firing giving the finished product.

Many artisans reproduce the ancient ceramic tile patterns that make Tunisian mosques like the "Barber's" mosque in Kairouan, or the recently restored Nabeul mosque, so beautiful.

Nowadays, the ceramic tiles bought by tourists will be used for more profane purposes, like decorating their kitchens, swimming pools or bathrooms.

Nabeul's prolific crafts production is not limited to ceramics alone. The town also produces cane and esparto mats (Rue des Nattiers), orange flower water, and embroidered cloth.

A stop off at the *Errachidia Café* terrace is an absolute must. Squeezed between the bazaars and souvenir shops, this little café right in the town centre is a true haven of peace and refinement. The vestiges of the Roman colony of *Neapolis* founded by Julius Caesar, which gave Nabeul its name, are also worth visiting.

A family-style beach

Other than its craftworks, Nabeul is above all known as a popular, family seaside resort frequented both by the inhabitants of Tunis and groups of European holiday makers.

The town gives onto a large beach on the Mediterranean, to the south of the Cap Bon peninsula.

Summer is not the only time worth visiting Nabeul. In spring, when the orange trees are in bloom, the whole region looks and smells beautiful. It is at this time that the town springs to life for the orange blossom celebrations (end of March/beginning of April).

Around Nabeul are the Béni Khiar weaving workshops (covers, carpets, and burnous "*kachabiah*"), and the Dar Chaâbane quarries where stone is carved into door lintels.

Situated very close to Hammamet (*see earlier*), Nabeul is an attractive and popular seaside resort centred around the old medina and the fort.

It is possible to make the well-known excursion around the Cap Bon peninsula (*see earlier*) from Nabeul. The high points of this tour are the pretty port of Kélibia, the Carthaginian vestiges at Kerkouane and the Haouaria falconers.

(*See information p. 189*).

nefta

■ Nefta, the last stop before the beginning of the Sahara desert, is a very ancient Roman garrison town that was part of the *limes*, the immense line of fortifications that the Third Augusta Legion built in the whole of southern Maghreb to protect itself from attacks by the Saharan nomads.

Spread out along the vast chott, it merits its nickname "the Pearl of Djérid". Indeed, for visitors crossing these desert lands heated white hot by the blazing sun, the sight of this immense green barrier of over 450,000 date palms, induces the most intense sense of aesthetic appreciation, especially when the traveller arrives from the south having spent many days crossing the Sahara.

Before converting to Islam in the 8th century, many Berbers in the Djérid region had been converted to Christianity at the time of the Romans, and then the Byzantines, in the early years A.D. However, the region no longer bears any traces of this conversion. Traces of the Islam are much more obvious, on the other hand. The many marabouts and mosques make Nefta the main religious town in southern Tunisia, the "Kairouan of the desert".

In centuries gone by, the oasis was also an important stopping place for the spice caravans from Cairo and the slave caravans from Black Africa.

The Nefta Corbeille

Nefta harbours a wonder that attracts visitors from all over the world, namely the famous "Nefta Corbeille" (basket), which is a huge basin where the vast palm grove nestles hemmed in by cliffs. Hotel-keepers have taken advantage of this blessing and had most of the hotels built high up on the escarpment giving the clientele a sweeping view of this green wave. Irrigated by one hundred and fifty-two springs (some of which are warm and cold water), and by innumerable wells, during

SIMONE DE BEAUVOIR IN THE GARDENS OF NEFTA

■ *Immediately after the war, the French writer Simone de Beauvoir – companion of the existentialist philosopher Jean-Paul Sartre – went on a long journey around the whole of the Maghreb, which took her to southern Algeria and Tunisia in particular.*
In her memoirs entitled "La Force des choses" ("Force of Circumstances") Simone de Beauvoir wrote:
"The oasis (in Gabès) disappointed me at first: I found myself walking between earthen walls, at the bottom of muddy paths, and, apart from the palms above my head, I could see nothing. And then I slipped into the orchards and experienced the cheerfulness of the fountains amidst the blossoming trees. The gardens of Nefta were even more tender. There was a charming hotel alongside the main square.
Gide had written in the visitors' book: "If I had known Nefta, it would have been her, not Biskra, that I would have loved."

*In spite of the fearsome appearance
of its "ribat" (monastery-fortress),
Monastir is now simply
a peaceful seaside resort.*

the European autumn, the palm grove produces an abundance of the delicious smooth amber and honey coloured *deglet nour* dates ("fingers of light").

It is possible to hire barouches, donkeys or dromedaries to visit the palm grove where there are also a number of orchards full of fruit trees (apricots, peaches, figs, bananas, grenadines, lemons, grapes) and vegetable gardens where chili peppers, carrots, radishes and flowers are grown (carnations, jasmine and roses).

Two rivers run through the Corbeille, serving as swimming pools for the locals (the women swim in the morning, the men in the afternoon).

It is most pleasant to stop at the numerous little covered terraces in the grove and to chat with the Nefta locals whilst drinking a glass of mint tea. This rustic past time enables visitors to find a little warmth in the shade of the date palms and to listen to the sound of the birds singing and the water trickling in the *seguias*

(irrigation channels). On the way out of the grove, go via the "mirage" view point over the chott el Djérid, where it is possible to see optical illusions during the heat of the middle of the day.

Nefta, the holy town of the Djérid, has innumerable religious sanctuaries including *zawiyyas,* mosques and 127 *marabouts* (Muslim saint's tombs). The most famous is Sidi Bou Ali's tomb. Visitors may like to amble along the little streets of the recently restored *medina* where donkeys pass by laden with baskets, in search of the beautiful earthen and pale brick houses decorated with geometric figures and often with old finely worked doors.

Numerous excursions are possible in the surrounding region, for example to the chott el Djérid, towards the Tozeur oasis (*see later*) in the east, or to the mountain oases of Tamerza, Chebika and Midès (*see later*) in the north, beyond the chott el Gharsa near the Algerian border.

(*See information p. 192*).

THE ENCHANTING GRACE OF THE OASIS

■ *The oasis arouses a sense of elation well described by the German explorer Nachtingal when he visited an oasis during the last century:*
" With what avidity the eye feeds on this splash of colour which exudes comfort and life! The line fills out more and more, and little by little all the parts of the palm grove become distinguishable, the sight of which fills the soul with an unequalled sense of elation.
Soon, the delicious crowns of leaves can be made out swaying gently from left to right on their tall slender trunks: one by one, our inquisitive eyes scrutinize each clump of greenery displaying all its enchanting grace, as we looked for the most beautiful and most sheltered place to pitch camp.
The pilgrim knows nothing yet of the movement of life hidden and protected by this wooded massif; he thinks only of the material joys that await him; he is caught body and soul by the spell of the seducing foliage cast over the whole oasis ..."

sfax

■ "The greatest businessmen, the best architects, the most brilliant academics, and the best high school students all come from Sfax..." Such an extravagant elegy of Tunisia's second town could clearly only have been written by a Sfaxian.

There is nonetheless a grain of truth behind this inveterate love all Sfaxians have for their town and which they proclaim ostentatiously, as, over the centuries, Sfax has become a very important economic pole thanks to its chemical, food and farming industries, its flourishing fishing and commercial port, its many shops and its highly rated schools.

One must not forget the architects either, who in Sfax 2000 and in the town's new neighbourhoods, have built high-quality futurist buildings and villas.

Nonetheless, these high flying marks are not enough to satisfy the Sfaxians, who are not the kind of people to accept being second to Tunis in the country.

An age-old rivalry – but always a peaceful one – exists between Tunis and this large southern metropolis. It is above all translated into the inhabitants of Tunis' innumerable jokes taunting the successes – often judged as being too rapid – of their Sfaxian compatriots.

The Sfaxians do not hesitate in returning the compliment, as can be seen from this vitriolic little verse: "People from Tunis have empty heads, empty pockets, but carry heavy loads on their backs. Sfaxians, on the other hand, have heavy heads, bursting pockets, and nothing on their backs".

Since many Sfaxians have now moved to the Tunisian capital, however, this traditional rivalry is petering out. And after all, isn't Sfax the town of the olive tree, symbol of peace and harmony?

The olive-tree town

Sfax's prosperity was initially generated by its olive trees. Even in the days of the little Roman town of *Taparura* – embryo of modern-day Sfax – and under the emperor Domitian's reign (81-96 A.D.), olive growing took off in the Sahel region which became one of "Rome's granaries" along with the rich wheat growing and wine producing lands of northern Tunisia.

As a commercial port, Sfax benefitted enormously from its position as an outlet for the Sahelian olive groves, first of all by extracting the olive oil in its presses, then by exporting the precious liquid to the major Mediterranean markets.

A class of very wealth trader-ship builders who were also landowners and farmers was thus born.

Later, the Sfaxians branched into lucrative spice and silk trading with the Orient. In the modern era when olive oil prices dropped, the Sfaxians, who have always proved to have a great ability to adapt, diversified activities in the region and the town (which nonetheless continued to be a major oil port). In addition to their traditional activities, they branched out into growing and selling fruit and vegetables, poultry farming, pasta making, fishing and fish canning, textiles, building, chemicals, banking and craftwork.

On the eve of independence in 1956, therefore, Sfax was the most industrialised town in Tunisia.

There are practically no vestiges left from ancient Taparura, as its stones were used to build the central mosque and town of Sfax proper (what is now the medina) several kilometres to the south, during the Aghlabids of Kairouan's reign in the 9th century A.D.

Under the French Protectorate (1881 up until independence in 1956), a European quarter developed between the southern end of the medina and the port and railway station.

Sfax's hotels, shops and municipal administrative buildings are located in these large modern quarters crisscrossed by wide avenues (Habib Bourguiba, Farhat Hached, Ali Belhaouane and Hédi Chaker).

In the town centre, the large square at the crossroads of the wide Habib Bourguiba and Hédi Chaker Avenues is surrounded by large cafés and the town hall. This is a large eye-catching neo-colonial Moorish style building which, with its dome and pointed minaret, looks like a mosque.

On the ground floor of this building, several rooms house a little *museum* devoted to antiquities. It is particularly rich in Roman and

Byzantine mosaics ("The poet Ennius and the nine Muses", "Nereid riding on a dolphin", "Neptune surrounded by little fishermen, "Daniel in the lions' den"), frescoes (portrait of a woman and crescent moon, fishing scenes), and diverse objects from excavations at Acholla, Taparura, Lariscus and on the Kerkennah islands including funereal steles, amphoras, oil lamps, sarcophagi and marble ossuaries.

Head southwards along Avenue Hédi Chaker to get to the port of Sfax. The ferry for the Kerkennah Islands leaves from here, and there is also a picturesque fishing port with hundreds of ships rigged with lateen sails and carrying strings of sponges. A little further to the south is the perpetually busy commercial port with its cargo ships and treatment plants. It is here that the phosphates are refined and the bales of esparto, sacks of dates and groundnuts, salt and olive oil are handled for export to destinations all over the world.

Avenue Hédi Chaker also leads to Avenue Ali Belhaouane and the *medina* enclosed by high ramparts which give it an air of a fortified medieval town. *Bab Diwan*, the main gate to the old quarters, is a splendid work of art that looks like a triumphal arch set in the medina fortifications. In order to enjoy the magnificent view of the fortifications and the town, head into the medina and follow the ramparts in a westerly direction. About 100 to 200 m on is the very picturesque *Diwan café* installed on several floors in one of the bastions.

From the Bab Diwan gate, the narrow and jam-packed Rue du Bey heads straight up through the medina's souks and craft workshops, leading to the *Central Mosque*. This was founded in the 9th century, at the same time that the Aghlabids rebuilt the Kairouan mosque. Their Abbasid style square minarets on several storeys are very similar. The Sfax mosque also has a wonderful carved facade.

Also of interest is the *dar Jellouli* on Rue Dribba where a museum of popular traditions has been set up. The term "popular" is inexact, as the museum's exhibits would be better classified as princely traditions. Like all of Tunisia's beautiful palaces, the dar Jellouli is set round an

Several souks and beautiful buildings
like the Central Mosque and the Dar Jellouli palace
lie tucked away behind
the high ramparts of
the Sfax medina.

sidi bou saïd

interior patio with several galleries. This cool haven of peace and beauty stands in strict contrast to the perpetual animation of the neighbouring streets of the medina.

In the museum there are some beautiful exhibits of traditional furniture including, beds set in alcoves, painted wooden cabinets, and low tables. There are also displays of jewellery and sumptuous clothes (richly embroidered and sequined wedding dresses, a sheikh's ceremonial dress with his *jebba*, waistcoats, shirt and embroidered turban, and traditional Sfax and Kerkennah clothing). Displays also include several splendid specimens of Arabic calligraphy and painting on glass (Mahmoud el Feriani was one of the last great glass painters from the "Sfax school").

In the medina, it is also worth visiting the *kasbah*, the fortress built by the cadi El Besri in 849 and which served as a headquarters for the local authorities. Today, the reconverted kasbah is used as an open-air theatre during the Sfax festival in the summer. The Arabic *Borj en Nar* tower (in the street of the same name) built in the 9th century under the Aghlabid dynasty, is now a cultural centre (wonderful view of Sfax from the top of the tower).

Other places of interest include: the central market (Av. Bourguiba), the fish market (Rue du Commandant Béjaoui) and the sponge workshops.

Cruises to the Kerkennah Islands

From Sfax, it is possible to go on a cruise to the Kerkennah Islands (*see earlier*), head to the beaches in the north (Sidi Mansour, Laouza, Chebba) or the south (Nakta), or go on a trip to El Djem and its Coliseum (*see earlier*).

A number of archaeological digs in the outskirts of Sfax have led to the discovery of the remains of ancient towns like *Acholla* in the north, or *Thaenae* to the south of Sfax. Most of the objects found are displayed in the Sfax municipal museum mentioned earlier. (*See information p. 192*).

■ This is without doubt the most beautiful village in the whole of Tunisia. Perched up on the cliff tops, Sidi Bou Saïd's rich houses and white palaces are dissimulated behind the blossoming bushes of their secret gardens. Mimosa and jasmine scent lingers in the air and the reddish bougainvilleas glow like fire. On clear spring and summer days, the ghostly silhouette of Mount Bou Kornine can be made out on the other side of Tunis Bay like a Chinese engraving. By night, the view is magical as the sea and sky blend together and the twinkling lights along the coast seem like part of the Milky Way.

Moments like this make it easy to believe the incredible legend of Saint Louis told here. It is said that when he reached this enchanting stretch of coast with his army of crusaders, the King of France did not fall victim to the plague, but to the charms of Sidi Bou Saïd. Remarried to a beautiful Berber princess, he is said to have spent his last years here living a life of exquisite pleasure and wisdom. He is meant to have changed his name and religion, becoming the Muslim Sidi Bou Saïd, patron saint of the village.

Every tale has a grain of truth in it: the King of France did indeed land at Carthage at the head of the eighth crusade in mid-August 1270, but he died of the plague fifteen days later. At the same time a hermit lived in the hills near to Carthage. This holy sage, the real Sidi Bou Saïd (whose real name was Abou Saïd ibn Khalef ibn Yahia Ettamini el Beji) founded a brotherhood of Sufi sages here in 1207, which was the foundation of the future village that would bear his name.

Great writers like Maupassant and Gide, artists like Macke and Paul Klee, and innumerable cinema and showbiz stars own, or used to own, houses here in Sidi Bou Saïd, which today make the village is a great attraction for Tunisian and foreign visitors.

With its tall staircases and outdoor terrace, the *Café des Nattes*, Sidi Bou Saïd's renowned focal point which serves its famous pine kernel tea, is also the centre of the town and is the departure point for all trips.

On the square and in the Grand-Rue which heads down to the

sousse

famous café, there are art galleries, cafés (notably the *Cheneb*, which has a huge terrace) and craft boutiques which display their brightly coloured carpets outside.

Heading back up behind the café des Nattes, the road passes in front of the mausoleum of Sidi Bou Saïd, the patron saint of the village and of seafarers – notably pirates –, which earned him the title of "Master of the seas" (*Raïs el Abhar*). A beautiful white mosque with a tall square minaret that dominates the whole district is situated next to the Sidi Bou Saïd *zawiyya*.

Higher up is the lighthouse after which the site was first named: *djebel el Manar* ("lighthouse hill"). With the lighthouse keeper's accord, it is possible to go up to the top, albeit disturbing a few pigeon couples en route. Visitors will be impressed by the light's optical system and its ancient clockwork mechanism.

Next to the lighthouse is a movingly simple Muslim graveyard. On the way back down into the village via the steep little streets and stairways, there are many a breathtaking view of the sea, especially if visitors stop off at the *Sidi Chebâane, Dar Zarrouk* or *Chargui* café-restaurants with terraces. Each of these three places has its own charm. The *Sidi Chebâane*, near to an ancient marabout, is more of a family café. The *Dar Zarrouk* is a chic restaurant set in a superb garden with a loggia overlooking the Bay of Tunis. The *Chargui* is popular with tourists, and during the high season, puts on traditional Arab music concerts (*malouf*).

Before leaving Sidi Bou Saïd, visitors really should go to Baron Rodolphe d'Erlanger's former home, *dar Nejma Ezzohra* ("Palace of the Star of Venus"), which has now been converted into a museum. This true Arabian Nights' palace gives an idea of the splendor of the Tunisian princely residences with their gardens, ponds, colonnades, covered marble patios topped by domes with rich lacework stucco decorations. During the Baron's time, Andalousian music concerts were held here amidst burning incense, peacocks and a few tame gazelles.

(*See information p. 192*).

■ Tunisia's third largest town after Tunis and Sfax, the "Pearl of the Sahel" has found a new vocation since the Tunisian tourism boom. Along with its port, industry and commerce, this new activity has meant that Sousse has discovered that it has always had all the ingredients for success: fine sandy beaches, lots of sun, warm, clear water, good hotels and a rich cultural and architectural heritage.

One of the oldest Phoenician colonies after Utica, the site of *Hadrumete* was chosen nearly 3,000 years ago for its excellent natural harbour.

By the 9th century B.C., Hadrumete was already a flourishing trading centre. During the Second Punic War (208-201 B.C.), the Carthaginian general Hannibal chose Hadrumete as his headquarters, and took refuge here after he was defeated by the Romans at Zama in 202.

Along with the other cities who had tied their destiny to that of Carthage, Sousse was severely punished by the Romans. It soon picked itself up again, however, and under the emperor Trajan's reign in the 2nd century A.D., flourished thanks to its port which exported the Sahel olive groves' oil. Unfortunately, in the 3rd century the town rebelled against Rome and the emperor Maximinus with the Thysdrus settlers (El Djem), who had just elected Gordian I emperor. Capellian, Maximinus's legate, beat them and ransacked the rebellious towns.

From the Vandals to the Arabs

In the 3rd century, Sousse became the capital of the Byzacene province following the emperor Diocletian's administrative reform (283-305 A.D.). Under the Vandals, its name changed to *Hunericopolis*. Under the Byzantines' reign, during which it was one of their main North African bases, it became known as *Justiniapolis* and underwent a period of great prosperity.

Destroyed during the Arabs' first invasion at the end of the 7th century, it was rebuilt a century later by the Aghlabids, vassals of the Abbasids of Baghdad. The town again became known by its original Berber name, *Soussa*, and became the emirs' summer residence. Tunisia enjoyed a "golden age" under this dynasty of great constructors who built the Kairouan Central Mosque, and the fortified towns of Sousse (construction of the kasbah and the *ribat* in particular), Monastir and Sfax.

After a short period of occupation by Roger II of Sicily's Norman troops in the 12th century, by the Barbarian pirates, and by the Spanish in the 16th century (who handed it over to the Ottoman Empire), Sousse did not suffer anymore turbulent periods, apart from in the Second World War when it was the target of several air bomb attacks in 1943.

Major attractions: the medina

The medina overlooking the commercial port is the town's main attraction. Hemmed in by 2.5 km of ramparts that date back to 859, the reign of the Kairouan Aghlabid

sovereign Abou Ibrahim Ahmed, it has three fortified gate entrances: *Bab el Jedid* (the "New gate") in the east, *Bab el Khabli* in the south, and *Bab el Gharbi* in the west.

The Place Farhat Hached and the little Place des Martyrs both lead into the medina.

In the old quarters, visitors should go to see the *Central Mosque*, the *ksar er-ribat*, and the *kasbah* and its *museum*.

The *Central Mosque,* which looks somewhat like a fortress, was built from 850 onwards, during the Aghlabid Al Abbès Mohammed's reign, is flanked by two little rounded towers and does not have a tall minaret. Inside, is a long rectangular courtyard bordered by a colonnade. The prayer room, which is wider than it is long, opens out under a portico with nine doors that lead to as many bays. The central nave is surmounted by two little domes.

Near to the mosque is the *ribat*, the monastery fortress that dates back to then end of the 8th century, and which affords a superb panora-

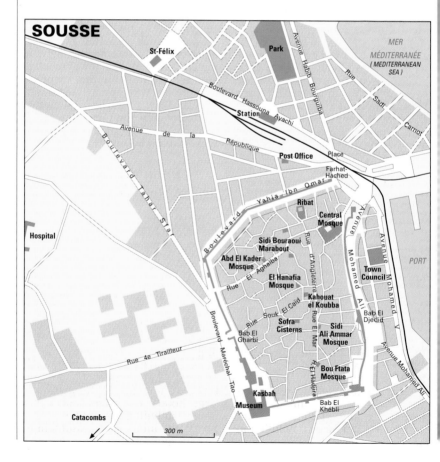

mic view over the town. It was built at the beginning of the 9th century on the site of a very old Christian basilica destroyed by the Vandals, rebuilt by the Byzantines, and destroyed again by the Arabs. Its architectural style, like all buildings in the medieval period, is distinguished by its beauty and its highly majestic spartan allure. This *ribat* is one of the string of fortresses built by the Arabs along the Mediterranean coast from Egypt to Morocco to protect North Africa from the European crusaders.

Like the Monastir ribat which was built at the same time, the Sousse monastery is surmounted by a long chimney-like tower (27 m tall) which enabled the soldier-monks to survey the sea and inland region in case of possible invasions, particularly by the Byzantines.

This lookout tower was added to the fortress during the Aghlabid emir Zidayat Allah I's reign (817-838).

When the ramparts and kasbah were built, the *ribat* lost its military function, becoming a religious centre with a mosque, and the lookout tower continuing the minaret.

Having entered through the splendid fortified gate with its machicolations (a corbelled gallery pierced with openings through which boiling oil could be poured on assailants), visitors come to the large interior courtyard where there are stables and stores. On the upper floors, are the former *mourabitines*'s (soldier-monks) cells.

Today, the Sousse ribat is a cultural centre. Concerts are held in its interior courtyard.

Near to the ribat is the *Zikkak zawiyya* (seat of a religious brotherhood and a mausoleum) with an octagonal minaret, the *Abd el Kader mosque* with its lovely sculpted porch (Rue el Aghalba), the *Sidi Bouraoui marabout*, and the *El Hanafia mosque*.

Whilst strolling through the little streets, visitors will see many an interesting sight, especially on Rue Souk el Caïd where the *Kahouat el Koubba* (a typical café in an old domed marabout), the *el Rabâ* and *el Caïd* covered *souks* are located, and on *Rue du Caïd* stairway where there are many of the traditional craftsmen's workshops. A little further on are the Sofra *cisterns* built during Roman times and restored by the Aghlabid emir Ibrahim in 875.

Rue el Mar, which to the south becomes Rue el Hadjira, passes in front of the *Sidi Ali Ammar mosque* which has a wonderful facade, and the 9th century *Bou Ftata mosque*.

Right in the south-west of the medina towers the imposing bulk of the *kasbah* built by the Aghlabid sovereign Al Abbès Mohamed in 844. It is surmounted by the 30 m tall *Khalef al Fata tower* (*manar*) built in the 9th century.

Inside, the *antiquities museum* is the second most important one in Tunisia after the Bardo in Tunis. It houses an exceptional collection of mosaics from the 1st to 6th centuries A.D. which trace Roman and Byzantine day-to-day life in Tunisia, and also portray scenes inspired by Greco-Roman mythology.

Of particular interest are the little threshold mosaics with animal or sexual motifs which were destined to ward off evil spirits; the major composition in the entrance yard representing the "*Head of Medusa*"; the portrait of the Phoenician sea god Hadad; two versions of "*Jupiter abducting Ganymede*"; "*Dionysus as a child riding a panther*"; "*Neptune's chariot*"; "*Apollo and the Muses*"; "*Orpheus charming the animals*"; "*The triumph of Bacchus*"; "*Venus washing*", etc.

The museum also houses collections of objects and statuettes from the Punic, Roman, Christian and Arabic periods, including a sculpted woman's head from the Antonine period, as well as a charming statuette representing "*Love sleeping*".

To the south of the medina are the *Poet's Roman villa* (mosaics), and the *catacombs*. Running for a distance of 5 km, these consist of 240 galleries and over 15,000 marble tombs and sepultures from the 2nd to 5th centuries. Only the Bon Pasteur catacombs are open to the public for the time being, as the Hermes and Severus catacombs are currently under restoration.

In the town itself, it is worth visiting the *Saint-Felix church* (Rue Constantine) to the north-west of the medina, and the seafront where the Bou Jaafar beach is located. The large hotels, cafés and restaurants have been built along the beach. An extremely modern thalassotherapy centre with bubbling tubs, massage

tabarka

baths, and treatment administered by specialised staff, has been opened in the imposing Abou Nawas Boujaafar hotel. On Sundays, visitors can go to the main market (*souk el Ahad*) on the outskirts of the town which is a food, agricultural and flea market all in one.

The town also has a little pleasure boat port (10 moorings) inside the commercial port. As this is now too small to meet the demands of holiday makers passionate about this maritime leisure, the new and bigger *Port el Kantaoui* (300 moorings) has been developed north of the town inside a marina where there are large hotels and luxury holiday apartments.

A major seaside resort

Port el Kantaoui has now become a major integrated up-market seaside resort whose architectural style is based on that of Sidi Bou Saïd, the charming little town north-east of Tunis (*see earlier*). It has a large range of leisure amenities including an international diving centre, water skiing, golf courses, tennis courts, riding clubs, discos, restaurants, and even a casino (Hana Palace hotel).

Around and about Sousse, tourists can visit the picturesque village of *Akouda* with its pretty little mosque and its Roman remains, the *Sidi Bou Ali* folkloric centre, and *Hergla* further northwards by the sea. This village perched up on the cliff tops was once the Roman town of *Horraca Coella*. Its medieval houses are dominated by the mausoleum of Sidi Bou Mendil who, legend has it, turned his handkerchief into a flying carpet to go to Mecca in the 10th century A.D. The inhabitants of the village exercise a very ancient activity: they plait the esparto *scourtins* (sieves) used to filter the olive oil once it has been pressed.

Sousse is a perfect spring board for visiting the rest of this Sahelian region. From here it is possible to make the trip to the holy town of *Kairouan* (large mosque and 3 zawiyyas), to *Monastir*, *El Djem* (large Roman amphitheatre) in the west, and to *Mahdia* and *Sfax* in the south (*see relevant chapters*).
(*See information p. 192*).

■ It was in Tabarka, the little port side town and seaside resort on the northern coast of Tunisia, that the world famous saying "Don't sunbathe idiot" was launched. In the Seventies, the Tunisian authorities decided to promote a new kind of seaside holiday by adding a major cultural festival to the traditional joys of lazing on the beach and other seaside activities. Today this festival held in July has become the major "Fête du corail" (Coral festival) during which theatrical shows are put on, coral craft products sold and a fairground set up.

An up-market seaside resort

Tabarka has changed a great deal since: huge building sites transformed it into an up-market seaside resort which would become the pivotal point of future tourist development on the "Coral Coast". Surfaced roads already linked Tabarka to the rest of Tunisia and its brand new international airport opened to charter planes from all over the world.

By the end of the Eighties, and during the Nineties, therefore, a seaside tourist complex with 10,000 beds was built around the traditional little fishing port of Tabarka. Luxury hotels, and marinas with yachting ports and waterfront residences came to complete the picture. All this added to Tabarka's vocation of being one of the largest water sports centres in Tunisia, as it already had an important diving centre which proposed underwater photography and fishing.

On land, other top-of-the-range sports like tennis, riding and golf are also available. A large 18-hole golf course with a school – with its own 9 hole course and practice area – stretching over 110 hectares of undulating ground by the sea was recently inaugurated.

It is also possible to go hunting here as Tabarka is the starting point for the large wild boar hunting trips in the Khroumirie mountains and the Mogods. Wild boar hunting has been traditionally practised by the inhabitants of the region for centuries, and they know the large cork oak forests and scrubland of the hills around Tabarka inside out. Along with boar, they also know how to hunt game birds, hares and jackals.

With the numerous leisure activities available, Tabarka hopes to become one of Tunisia's major tourist resorts on a par with Hammamet or Djerba. Thanks to its particularly clement climate, the resort also hopes to operate all year round.

Originally the Phoenician trading post of *Thabraca* ("shady place") by the el Kebir river, and then a Roman colony that owed its development to Julius Caesar, Tabarka underwent its most prosperous period in the 3rd century A.D. Its wealth came from the wild beasts it supplied for public games, and also from its iron and lead mines and stone quarries used for building the palaces of the rich Romans who settled in Tunisia.

This vocation in the luxury industries was confirmed later when a school of painters, sculptors, ceramicists, and mosaic artists converged in Tabarka.

Bastion of Christianity in North Africa in the early centuries A.D., it later converted to Islam and became prosperous again under the Fatimid dynasty in the 10th century A.D. Several centuries later, Tabarka became a major commercial port and was the object of interminable quarrels between France and Italy, both of whom wanted to control the exploitation of its very rich coral banks.

The Tabarka needles

When walking around the town, visitors will discover several interesting places, like the Genoese fort dominating the Tabarka islet (occupied by the Tunisian army, not open to the public), the old Port and the fishing port where the many little fishing boats set out to sea (it is possible to come to an agreement with the owners who will take passengers on trips for a small fee). Visitors will also come across the ancient Christian basilica set in an ancient Roman cistern and converted into a museum, the Sidi Messaoud tower, the bordj el Jedid, and the market (on Fridays).

Along the coast to the west, erosion has sculpted the rocks into large, sometimes strange shaped needles and spurs, whereas in the east, there is the large sandy Montazah beach where most of the big hotels have been built.

Many excursions are organised to the little *La Galite* archipelago 60 km out to sea from Tabarka. The archipelago is made up of several little islands and islets including la Galite, la Gallo, la Gallina, le Plastro, la Fauchelle and le Galiton. Several families of fishermen and viticulturists live on La Galite island, which is the largest in the archipelago. Roman tombs and some Punic remains have been excavated here.

Visitors will find several lovely beaches along the Coral Coast. To the west is the rocky beach of *Melloula* near the Algerian border. To the east, the rocky *Berkouchech* beach (9 km from Tabarka), or the vast *Jebara* beach on the edge of a eucalyptus forest – at Aïn Sobh –, or the rocky *Cape Nègre* beach dominated by the remains of a Roman fortress (near to Sidi Mechrig), and finally the very beautiful deserted *Cape Serrat* beach.

Inland, there are many possible excursions in the Mogods and Khroumirie mountains covered in cork oaks. The little town of Aïn Draham lies at an altitude of 800 m in the mountains back to back with the djebel *M'Tir* (1,210 m). The biggest market in the western Khroumiries is held here.

Hot water springs

The Medjerda valley's huge Beni Mtir dam was built south of Aïn Draham in a wonderful landscape of prairies of forests.

The Aïn Babouch pass heading towards the Algerian border leads to the Hammam-Bourguiba. The sulphurous hot springs' (50 °C) properties, already known to the Romans, are good for respiratory afflictions. (*See information p. 193*).

*Midès, with its eroded limestone gorges,
is the wildest of the "mountain oases"
in southern Tunisia
near to the Algerian border.*

tamerza/ chebika/midès

■ Visitors may well think they are seeing things as they cross the chott el Gharsa north of Tozeur. The ghostly caravans and strangely beautiful towns with cascades and palm groves that suddenly appear in the midsts of this deathly landscape are well and truly mirages. Contrary to what people normally think, these are not mental hallucinations caused by fever and thirst, as a camera will record and reproduce them on film.

According to scientists, in the heat of the sun, the white hot air forms superimposed layers of an irregular density. Some of them have the effect of mirrors and magnifying glasses at the same time.

Therefore, the slightest stone or crust of salt is reflected in these layers of air which magnifies, refracts and deforms, like when a stick is half immersed in water. The palm trees on the horizon? Most of the time they are in fact a few clumps of grass with the light behind them that have been magnified by this optical phenomenon.

Mountain oases

After the mirages and risks of being buried under the sand in the chott el Gharsa, the heights of djebel el Negueb appear on the horizon near the Algerian border. It is here that the Berber populations of the "mountain oases" of Chebika, Tamerza and Midès have taken refuge for centuries.

First stop: *Chebika* at the foot and on the slopes of the djebel. This little ochre earthen village set on the mountain side was part of the Roman *limes* – the huge fortified line running from Libya to Morocco across the whole of southern Maghreb – in the early years A.D. Today, the little Chebika oasis stretches out above a little palm grove crisscrossed by tiny *seguias* (irrigation channels) which form mini-waterfalls.

After this refreshing stopping place, travellers must affront the steep slopes of the winding road up to *Tamerza*. It is certainly worth the effort, as the higher one gets, the more splendid the panoramic views are over the whole chotts region and down into the el Khangat river gorges.

Several signposts indicate where the waterfalls are in the gorges, which can be reached via goat tracks. Surprise: little souvenir stalls and refreshment stands await the traveller selling cold water and mint tea, Berber carpets, stuffed animals (scorpions, sand snakes), fossils and minerals (geodes, gypsum flowers).

A panoramic view over the river

The Berber village-refuge of Tamerza was once the ancient Roman military post of Ad Turrès on the *limes*, and later, the seat of an ephemeral Christian bishopric during the Byzantine era. The village, situated on the el Khangat river bed, prospered until it was devastated by the 1969-1970 catastrophic floods. The remains of the town were abandoned and a new characterless agglomeration that is of little interest to visitors was built a short distance away. The river and the ancient town, however, – restored by the ONTT – still attracts visitors who can admire them from the terraces of the Tamerza Palace. This upmarket hotel, whose architectural style is inspired by that of the Saharan *ksour*, is set at the top of the canyon. Inside are tastefully decorated rooms and suites, and notably a swimming pool built on the terrace, and a panoramic restaurant overlooking the river gorge. At night the view is quite magical, particularly as the Tunisian authorities had the good idea of lighting the remains of the old village.

Five kilometres away from Tamerza right by the Algerian frontier, *Midès* is the last and wildest mountain oasis. Even though tour operators do include it on their routes, it is sometimes forgotten or avoided by tour guides in a hurry to take their parties back to the Mediterranean coast. This is a pity as the village is by the Midès gorges which are a unique natural attraction in Tunisia. Here the mountain torrents have hollowed the soft limestone, sculpting out bowls, spinning tops, amphitheatres, millefeuilles, and even a submarine. Visitors will discover these marvels with the help of a guide who will lead them along the breathtaking goat tracks.

The Berber tribes have always used this wild environment as a

tataouine

natural defense against attackers. They built their villages here as they thought the region impregnable. The 1969 and 1980 floods finally got the better of their earthen citadel however, and they were forced to move their houses further back and higher up.

Palm groves and market gardens stretch out at the foot of the escarpments. There is also a campsite ("la Porte Bleue"), a drinks' stand, and a crafts shop selling Berber carpets and dyed cloth, minerals and fossils.

The mountain oases festival

Every year the Tamerza Festival is held in April-May, bringing together all of the mountain oases. There are exhibitions of local Berber arts and traditions, folk concerts and ballets, parades, theatrical shows, football matches, horse displays and donkey excursions throughout the whole of the region.
(*See information p. 193*).

■ When someone is annoyed with somebody else, they will usually – rudely – tell them to go to... Tataouine. This is because for ages Tataouine has been synonymous with the end of the world in the collective imagination. Indeed for decades, this little southern Tunisian town on the edge of the Sahara did meet up to its desolate and terrible image that the colonial era did much to perpetuate as it was here that the famous "Bat'd'Af" (Bataillons d'Afrique) or "biribis" barracks were situated.

All those considered strong-headed or who had had brushes with the law in civilian life were sent to these semi-deserted regions of southern Tunisia to undergo a harshly disciplinarian spell of military service!

In peacetime, the soldiers were made to break up stones in the blazing sun to make roads. In times of conflict, it was the "Bat'd'Af" which was sent to sought out the dissident Berber tribes hidden away in the djebels.

Today, thanks to the advent of pla-

IN THE LAND OF THE "BAT' D'AF"

■ *Tataouine, the former French garrison town destined to control Tunisia's Saharan borders during the Protectorate, was famous for its "Bat' d'Af" (Bataillons d'Afrique).*
Set up by the King of France Louis-Philippe during the conquest of Algeria in 1832, the African light infantry battalions recruited a lot of "hot heads", who had usually been in trouble with the law or with disciplinary courts.
Many novelists and filmmakers have recorded their harsh living conditions in Southern Tunisia, and also in Algeria and Morocco where there were other garrison towns like Tataouine with their barracks, bars and prostitutes.

One of their marching songs went:
"... from Gabès to Tataouine,
from Gafsa to Médenine,
Rucksack on back, Battalionaires
keep on marching in the dust...!"

*In order to escape the different invaders who attacked Tunisia
over the centuries, the Berber tribes people
retreated into the southern mountain ranges
where they built high altitude villages and mosques
(left: Chebika and women from Chenini.
Above: mosque and graves of the "Seven Sleepers" in Chenini).*

nes and tourism, Tataouine is no longer that ill-famed, far-flung hellhole. Visitors will not need a jeep nor organise a whole expedition to get there. A good surfaced road links the town to Djerba or Gabès within a few hours.

Moreover, Tataouine has spruced itself up, and visitors arriving from Djerba or Tunis will be welcomed by this fresh-looking little town.

Do not miss the *Club Sangho!* This hotel is the ideal base camp for excursions all round the region, and is a real oasis for regaining one's strength after each "rough ride" regional tour. It is a sheer delight to soak in the large pool, rest in the air-conditioned pavilions and to enjoy the top-quality service after scouring the rocky, dusty goat tracks of the deep South!

The ksour
region

Visitors come to the Tataouine region like passionate gold prospectors in the quest of a few splendid nuggets: the *ksour* (plural of *ksar*). These are the strange citadels, almost always built like birds' nests high up in the djebels, on the peaks, or on the tabular cliffs.

It was in the fortified villages of this unyielding, dry and rocky region that the Berber populations came to take refuge from pillaging nomads and in particular from the Beni Hillal Bedouin nomads who were chased out of Egypt by Al Mostansir, the Fatimid caliph of Cairo, in the 11th century.

Most of the ksour dispose of storied earthen granaries ("ghorfas") that look like honeycomb.

The threat of raids continued right up until the last century, especially as the caravan trail from sub-Saharan Africa to Ghadamès (southernmost tip of Tunisia), Gabès and Tunis in Tunisia, and to Libya (Tripoli), crossed the region.

Nowadays, most of the ksour have been abandoned, or are lived in by old people who will not later be replaced by their children.

From Tataouine, which is a good base for visiting the ksour, first of all head towards the south and southeast.

A few kilometres from the town, visitors will come to *Ksar Ouled Soltane*, now deserted but surrounded by a little modern village, and *Ksar Ezzara* (inhabited by an old blind couple).

Another most fine example – the *Ksar Ouled Debbab* – is situated to the south-west and west of Tataouine in the Ksour mountain chain.

A little further on from the ksar at *Douriet*, one of the halts on the caravan trail, there is a drystone citadel that totally blends in with the mountain. The citadel, which is now abandoned by its inhabitants, is used as a granary (ghorfa) by the villagers who live in the valley where they farm instead of just herding as in the past.

The much visited *Chénini Ksar* north of Douiret lies in ruins. Like all the ksour, it was built high up to protect it from the frequent attacks by nomadic pillagers. Perched up on the cliff tops, it forms an amphitheatre and some of its troglodytic dwellings have terraces.

In Chénini there is a little whitewashed roughcast mosque, part of which is underground, and the cemetery where the *tombs of the Seven Sleepers* – and their dog – are found.

According to a legend, which is written down in the Koran (sura XVIII, "The cave"), seven young Christians from Ephesus were walled up in a cave by the Roman emperor Decius. They are said to have miraculously slept for nearly two hundred years and were astonished to find when they woke that their money was no longer valid when they tried to buy food in a neighbouring village. They therefore asked God to let them die.

A camel hump
hill

West of Tataouine and north of Chénini, *Guermessa* was built on a camel hump shaped hill dotted with stone houses, some of which are troglodytic. The village is essentially inhabited by elderly people and women as the menfolk have abandoned their traditional activity as shepherds to go to find fortune in Tunis, usually as porters. They only come back for traditional celebrations or to get married to local girls.

Continuing on towards the north,

thuburbo majus

is *Ghomrassen*. Here the remains of the *kaala*, a fortress perched up on the escarpment like a birds' nest, can be seen with its ghorfas. It has now been abandoned by its inhabitants who have developed a modern town (5,000 inhabitants) in a steep-sided valley (visitors must go to the spice market there). Right by Ghomrassen, Ksar Haddada has been turned into a hotel and its ghorfas (wheat granaries) now serve as bed and breakfast accommodation. Visitors will be struck by the beautiful ochre and white roughcast and the complexity of circulating inside due to the multitude of streets, vaulted passages, steps and terraces which give this ksar the air of a modern theatre.

On the way to Médenine from here, visitors can stop off at the *Ksar Joumaa* which affords a superb view over the whole region.

A Saharan frontier post

Ksar Kédim, which is still in the Tataouine region, is a fortified village that was built on the escarpment by the Zenet tribe. It has an underground route that linked it to the wells in the valley in case of sieges.

On the edge of the Sahara, further to the west from Tataouine, is the *Ksar Ghilane* desert frontier post. Here, remains of the *limes tripolitanus* fortifications built by the Romans throughout the whole of southern Maghreb to defend the region from the desert nomads' incursions, can be seen. The *limes* were abandoned later and replaced by the ksour.

Although a difficult area to exploit for mainstream tourism, the deep Tunisian South from Tataouine to the heart of the Grand Erg Oriental has an attractive future in store as a Saharan tourism should develop in this region nestled between Algeria and Libya, enabling desert lovers who can no longer go to Algeria or the Ténéré, to trek in the wonderful dunes near to Ghadamès (main Tunisian oases in the deep South: El Borma and Bordj el Khadra).

(*See information p. 193*).

■ The ancient town of *Thuburbo Majus* south-west of Tunis, truly merited its old nickname "Respublica Felix", the "Happy Republic". Indeed, founded during Augustus' reign, in the early years A.D., it was set in the rich Miliane river valley amidst vine, cereal and olive growing lands that constituted part of "Rome's Breadbasket". The town enjoyed its greatest period of prosperity under the emperor Hadrian in the 2nd century A.D., however.

The considerable remaining vestiges give us a good idea of the Roman city's rich past, for example the sumptuous houses sometimes equipped with heated bathrooms and decorated with mosaics, some of which evoke the vine and cereal cultures. There are also the remains of majestic public buildings like the *Capitol* with its large stairway and Corinthian columns.

Around the forum were the *Temple of Peace* and the charming little *Temple of Mercury*. Further to the south was the *Market Place* , the *House of the Labyrinth*, and then the *Petronii portico*.

There are also several bath houses (the *summer* and the *winter thermal baths*), a *palaestra*, or place for sports, a temple of Baal and another temple dedicated to Aesculapius, god of healing. It should also be noted that there is a church dating back to the beginning of the Christian era.

From El Fahs, by Thuburbo Majus, head eastwards to *Zaghouan*. This town, which has been a spa since Phoenician times, is situated on the slopes of the djebel of the same name (1,295 m). The springs here used to feed Carthage in ancient times thanks to a 90 km aqueduct, considerable remains of which can be seen near to Mohamédia. During the emperor Hadrian's time (2nd century A.D.), a temple dedicated to nymphs was built around the springs. The remains can still be seen today, but unfortunately not the statues.

Further to the south of Zaghouan towards Enfidaville and the Gulf of Hammamet, make a detour to the perched town of Takrouna. Built on the top of a peak at an altitude of over 200 m, this little completely white Berber village overlooks the Enfida plain, its fields and orchards.

(*See information p.193*).

tozeur and the chott el djérid

■ The image of the sea always springs to mind when approaching Djérid as this sparkling salt lake shimmers before the travellers' eyes, bordered by the dark green fringe of palms that signal the the Saharan sandy ocean to come.

Over the centuries, Berber populations have abandoned their nomadic existence to settle and farm these desolate noman's lands.

With a stubborness that can only be saluted, they dug artesian wells all around the chott in order to tap the Sahara's immense water tables. This miraculous water transformed these arid stretches into fertile land. A string of oases thus developed alongside the chotts and for centuries now, they have supported the highly fruitful date plantations.

The "land of palms"

Nestled in vast palm groves, Tozeur, Nefta, Kébili and Douz have become part of the "land of palms" (Djérid). They owe their prosperity to the market gardens and date palms which produce over two hundred kinds of date, the most succulent of which are the *deglet nour* ("fingers of light").

Their wealth also came from the fact that they were situated along the major caravan routes which engendered the major commercial trading links between the black empires of sub-Saharan Africa, and the Mediterranean basin.

From the south came gold, salt, ivory, wild animals for the Roman games, and slaves. In return, from the north came rich cloths, daggers and a variety of goods.

In Roman times, all the oases served as bastions on the *limes* frontier, the huge fortified line built during the first centuries A.D. from Libya to southern Morocco via Djérid and the high plateaus of southern Algeria.

The Romans feared that North Africa would be invaded by the Saharan nomadic peoples who were always rebelling.

From the 19th century up until the granting of independence in the Maghreb, the French colonial forces, who faced the same danger, sent the African Batalions and the French Camel corps to a string of forts so

*Tozeur, near to the Chott el Djérid,
is one of the main oases
in southern Tunisia
on the edge of the Sahara desert.*

they would be ready to rapidly intervene against the insurgent Berbers' possible attacks.

During the last century, the beautiful Djérid region was nearly the victim of the French commander Roudaire's extravagant project. Inspired by the legend of Lake Triton – the modern day chott el Djérid – according to which the Argonauts sailed here from the Mediterranean in their quest for the Golden Fleece, Roudaire wanted to dig a canal linking the Gulf of Gabès to all the Algerian chotts thereby making a huge inland sea.

The idea was even more preposterous given that it was founded on the false understanding that the chotts were depressions below the sea level. Modern geographers have proved the opposite, however, and Djérid, for example, lies at an altitude of 20-30 m.

The Tozeur oasis provides a classic example of the evolution of the deep South's history. Called *Thusuros* under the Romans when it was part of the *limes*, it later became a flourishing caravan port in the Middle Ages.

With the arrival of the Arabs, Tozeur became a major Islamic religious centre and an important forum of Islamic culture. Many of the educated Muslims studied in its *medersa* (Koranic university).

During French colonisation, it housed a garrison of French legionaries. Nowadays, since caravan trade has dwindle to a halt, Tozeur has turned almost exclusively to agriculture. Over the last few years, however, new horizons are emerging thanks to the development of tourism in southern Tunisia. Foreign visitors, who get here by road or by the thriving Tozeur international airport, now find very good standard hotels in the town, and new ones are constantly being opened.

The restored old town

One of the first attractions for tourists is the recently restored 14th century old town (*medina*). Its architecture, which is particularly stunning in the Oulld el Hadef district, can be classed amongst the marvels of Islamic art.

Walking along the vaulted passages, visitors will see the light ochre brick houses whose facades are decorated with geometric motifs and whose windows are set in Moorish arches (horseshoe form).

In the little *museum* set up in the old *Sid Assa zawiyya*, there are displays of day-to-day objects of the past (caskets, arms, coins, bridal dresses, old doors).

Still in the town, the *Dar Chraïet museum*, which is named after its founder, is a reconstruction of the architecture and decor of a Tunisian palace. From room to room, visitors will see display cases of jewellery, clothes, painted caskets, ceramic crockery, sacred calligraphic books, and absolutely beautiful ancient trinkets. Like in wax-work museums, dummies have been placed in the rooms to give an idea of the beys' court, traditional marriages, or the work of craftsmen (cobblers, hatters, weavers, tailors).

Ali Baba and Sheherazade

After the museum, au *Arabian Nights attraction park* has recently been built. Its themes are mainly inspired by Arabic culture: Sinbad the Sailor's voyages, tales from the "Arabian Nights". Dressed in the shimmering uniforms of the ancient sultan's soldiers, the guides take you to Ali Baba's cavern (which opens automatically when visitors say the pass word "Open Sesame!"), the harem, the slave market, or to the sultan Shahriyar and the beautiful Sheherazade's suites. En route is a nomads' tent, an elephant park and a waterfall that cascades down into a pond where there are ducks.

Before going to visit the palm grove, it is worth going to stroll around the town to see the beautiful brick *mosques* (for example the Sidi Abid mosque), go to the market or the main street – Avenue Bourguiba – to bargain for one of the innumerable Tunisian carpets hanging in front of the souks.

The *Tozeur palm grove* with its 200,000 date palms watered by 200 springs, is another of the towns main attractions. To get an overall view of the grove, go up to the Belvedere rocks overlooking this huge green sea or, even better, fly over it in a hot-air balloon (balloon trips organi-

zarzis

sed by Aéroasis, opposite the Continental hotel).

It is possible to hire a barouche to drive round the palm grove trails where visitors will come across children splashing about in the streams, and where they can stop off in the market gardens or plantations to drink some palm wine (*laghmi*).

The mathematician Ibn Chabbat (13th century) who invented the oasis' complex irrigation system, is venerated by the inhabitants of Tozeur. He was the one to make the water of several springs converge into a veritable river at Ras el-Aïoun which then divides into innumerable channels (*seguias*).

The Sidi Abou Lifa marabout can also be seen in the palm grove dominated by a very ancient juniper bush.

Strolling in paradise

Included on every tourist circuit, the *Paradis* is a tropical botanical garden where over 50 varieties of rose are said to grow along with innumerable other tropical plants like bougainvilleas and orchids.

There is also a little *Saharan zoo* in this garden of Eden where, along with the lions, jackals, mouflons, ostriches, and fennecs, there are a number of reptiles including sand vipers which the warders amuse themselves by pulling out of the snake pit and throwing at the scared tourists' feet. Shortly afterwards, they are up to more tricks, this time giving the dromedaries bottles of Coca-Cola which they gulp down greedily whilst people take photos.

In the bar, which is also a souvenir shop, they sell excellent plant syrups: violet for coughs, pomegranate for sore throats, and rose for cardiac problems.

In December the International festival of the oases takes place in Tozeur. During the festival the dates are picked, floats and traditionally dressed inhabitants parade, folk dances and traditional music concerts are held.

Visitors should also go to see the nearby Nefta oasis on the banks of the chott el Djérid (*see earlier*), and the "mountain oases" (Chebika, Tamerza, Midès, *see earlier*) to the north-west of Tozeur.

(*See information p. 193*).

■ Linked by a Roman road to neighbouring Djerba, the Akara-Zarzis peninsula benefits from its neighbour's extraordinary tourism boom. The peninsula has a number of recently built high-quality hotels like the *Club Sangho*, the *Oamarit complex*, and the *Zita* and *Zéphir* hotels. Other hotels are currently under construction and will soon come to join this line along the eastern face of Akara between Zarzis and Ras Marmour.

Less invaded by holiday makers than Djerba, Zarzis will appeal to all those who prefer to spend their holidays calmly lazing in the sun, far from the crowds. They will find the same white sand beaches and inland, the same olive tree plantations stretching beyond the horizon.

Recent excavation works have shown that *Sebkhet el Meleh,* south of Zarzis, was already inhabited in the Neolithic age, 4,000 years B.C. About twenty village camps were grouped around this stretch of water that used to be part of the Mediterranean. The population lived from rearing, fishing, and farming, as can be seen from the very rich stone tools that were found here (hundreds of blades, arrow heads, and polished stone axes).

At the time of the Roman occupation in the early centuries A.D., the olive culture took off so successfully in the Zarzis region (which was first of all called *Zita*, then *Gergis*) that a pipeline was built – ancestor of the modern oil pipelines – to carry the oil from the plantations to the ports.

In the 18th century, the olive growing culture attracted the Akaras nomads from Libya to Zarzis (Jarjis). They settled here, and still live on the peninsula today growing not only olives, but also citrus fruit and early vegetables (asparagus) thanks to the numerous wells dug in the peninsula and to the water harnessed in the Ksour mountains, further to the west of Médenine.

The Akaras also fish for sponges and fish. They set out in their boats from the Zarzis and El Marsa ports – on Birhet el Bibane lake – to fish in the waters of the Gulf of Gabès which are considered to be the most richly populated in the world. Along with sponges and the tasty "Biban groupers", they also catch tunny fish, bonnitos, mullets...

(*See information p. 193*).

practical
information

Tunis

NAME: Thénès or Tinès (Punic), Tounès (Arabic).

LOCATION AND ACCESS: In north-eastern Tunisia, by Lake Tunis. 71 km south of Bizerte, 175 km east of Tabarka, 63 km north of Hammamet (by motorway), 142 km north of Sousse, 154 km north of Kairouan, 269 km north of Sfax, 394 km north of Gabès, 353 km north of Gafsa, 446 km north of Tozeur, via an excellent network of tarred roads.
– *By air:* Tunis-Carthage airport, which is used by the major international airline companies (Air France, Tunisair, Alitalia, Lufthansa, Ibéria, Tap-Air Portugal, BA, KLM, Sabéna, Swissair, etc.).
– *By rail:* Railway network covering most of Tunisia. Departures from Tunis: TGM line Tunis-La Goulette-Carthage (station at Tunis port, avenue Bourguiba), main lines: Tunis-Gabès, Tunis-Gafsa-Metlaoui, Tunis-Jendouba, etc. (station at Place de Barcelone, Tunis).

DIALING CODE: 01.

CARE HIRE: *Hertz* (Head office, route n° 8, La Charguia-Tunis, tel. 790 211; Tunis-Carthage airport, post 3496, tel. 236 000 or 231 822; in town: 29 av. Bourguiba, tel. 248 559).

TOURIST INFORMATION: *Office national de tourisme tunisien,* 1 avenue Mohamed V, 1002 Tunis, tel. 341 007, telex: 14 381, fax: 350 997. *Commissariat régional au tourisme,* 29 rue de Palestine, 1002 Tunis, tel. 249 403 or 288 720, telex: 15 347. *Automobile-Club de Tunisie,* 29 avenue Habib Bourguiba, Tunis, tel. 243 921. *Touring-Club de Tunisie,* 15 rue d'Allemagne, Tunis, tel. 243 182 or 243 114.

ACCOMMODATION: See list at end of guide.

YOUTH HOSTELS: Headquarters of the Association tunisienne des Auberges de la Jeunesse at 10 rue Ali Bach Hamba, BP 320-1015 Tunis RP, open Monday to Saturday from 08.30 to 12.00 and from 15.00 to 18.00, tel. 246 000.

RESTAURANTS: *Dar El Jeld, Chez Nous,* l'*Astragale, Baghdada, César, la Mamma.*

LEISURE: Sports: pools, tennis courts; discos, cinemas; museums: the Bardo, Dar Abdallah (Popular arts and traditions, Tunis medina).

ART GALLERIES: *Gorji, Yahia, Galerie de la Médina, L'Air libre, Maison de la Culture Ibn Rachik, Galerie de l'Information.*

AMENITIES: Banks/bureau de change (av. Bourguiba), newspapers (newsstands av. Bourguiba), service stations, bookshop, food stores, supermarkets, central market, pharmacies, hospitals (Habib Thameur, Aziza Otmana, Charles Nicolle, Ernest Conseil, Militaire, Aboulkacem Echabbi, Polyclinique), doctors.

Bardo (the)

LOCATION AND ACCESS: Outskirts of Tunis, 4 km west of the town centre.

VISITS: Open from Tuesday to Sunday from 09.30 to 16.30. Closed on Mondays. Entrance fee.

ACCOMMODATION: Hotels in Tunis (see list at end of guide).

SOUVENIRS: Various books, post cards.

Bizerte

NAME: Hippo Diarrhytus (Roman), Benzert (Arabic), Bizerte (French).

LOCATION AND ACCESS: Chief town of the governorate, on the north-east coast of Tunisia, 65 km north-west of Tunis, 136 km north east of Tabarka. Direct trains from Tunis, or from Tabarka via Mateur. Tunis-Carthage airport. *Tunis Air,* 76 avenue Habib Bourguiba (tel. 432 201).

DIALING CODE: 02.

ACCOMMODATION: See list of hotels at end of guide.

TOURIST INFORMATION: *Commissariat général au tourisme:* 1 rue de Constantinople, tel. 432 897/703.

SOUVENIRS: Carpets, wrought iron, statuettes and pottery, olive tree wood objects, jewellery.

TRAVEL AGENTS: *Via Bizerte,* avenue d'Alger (tel. 432 901), *Tourafric,* avenue Habib Bourguiba (tel. 432 315), *Tunisia Line Service,* rue Ibn Khaldoun (tel. 431 944), *Transtours,* 7 rue d'Alger (tel. 432 174), *International Voyages Services,* avenue Habib Bourguiba (tel. 432 885).

AMENITIES: Post office (PTT, av. d'Algérie, rue el Medda, place Pasteur), banks (*BCT, BNT, STB, UIB, UBCI, BS, ATB, BH*), pharmacies, hospital, service stations, market, various shops, car hire (*Hertz,* place des Martyrs, tel. 433 679).

Cap Bon

LOCATION AND ACCESS: Peninsula to the east of Tunis.

Preceding pages:
*These charming, rustic scenes,
themselves an incentive to travel,
can be witnessed
more or less all over Tunisia.*

DIALING CODE: 02.

ACCOMMODATION: See list of hotels (in Korbous, Soliman, Kélibia, Haouaria, Bordj Cédria, Nabeul, Hammamet) at end of guide.

AMENITIES: Service stations, post office, shops, banks.

SOUVENIRS: Rugs, pottery, basketry, citrus fruit, stone carvings.

FESTIVALS: Orange festival in Nabeul (March), Sparrowhawk festival in Haouaria (June), Hammamet festival (July-August), the Menzel Témime amateur musicians festival (June), the Nabeul festival of comic arts (July), the Dar Chaâbane summer festival (July), the Tazerka sea festival (July), the Kélibia Journées des Arts plastiques (July), the Grombalia vine festival (August-September), the Hammamet and Ghezaz-Kerkouane cultural festival (August).

Carthage

NAME: Deformation of « Kart Hadasht » (« the new town »), the name used by the Phoenicians in the 9th century B.C.

LOCATION AND ACCESS: In the outskirts of Tunis (21 km north of the capital), on the Gulf of Tunis. Excellent tarred roads from Tunis to Carthage. International Tunis-Carthage airport used by the major international airline companies.

DIALING CODE: 01.

ACCOMMODATION: Several hotels (see list at end of guide).

Djerba

NAME: Jerba or Djerba (Arabic), Meninx (Phoenician).

LOCATION AND ACCESS: The Isle of Djerba is situated in the south-cast of Tunisia on the Gulf of Gabès. Its capital Houmt Souk is located 108 km east of Gabès, 326 km east of Tozeur and the chott el Djérid, 245 km south of Sfax, 372 km south of Sousse, 513 km south of Tunis. Excellent surfaced roads. Ferry at Ajim (fee paying; every 15 mns in the tourist season).
International airport on north-west of the island (tel. 650223).

DIALING CODE: 05.

HOTELS: A great deal of hotels, holiday clubs, boarding houses, etc. (see list at end of guide).

RESTAURANTS: *Haroun* (fish and seafood specialities), Houmt Souk port (tel. 650488); *Les Flamants roses,* île des Flamants roses (swimming in the sea and boat trips, tel. 650488).

SOUVENIRS: Craft goods (pottery, carpets, jewellery, perfumes), and sponges, in the Midoun souks, in Houmt Souk and in the hotel boutiques.

LEISURE: Karts Handermann and Hafez (near to the Djerba lighthouse).

TOURIST INFORMATION: *Commissariat régional au tourisme,* Houmt Souk (tel. 650016/581/544). *Syndicat d'initiative,* Houmt Souk (tel. 650915). *Syndicat d'initiative,* Midoun (tel. 657114).

AMENITIES: Banks (*ATB, BS, BNT, BT, BIAT, CFCT, STB, UIB*) in Midoun and Houmt Souk, regional hospital in Houmt Souk, hospital in Midoun, pharmacies, food stores, service stations, restaurants, markets (Midoun and Houmt Souk souks), car hire (*Hertz,* place Mongi Bali in Houmt Souk, tel. 650196; Djerba-Mélita airport, post 8, tel. 650233; Dar Jerba, tel. 657158).

Dougga

NAME: Thugga (Punic).

LOCATION AND ACCESS: 110 km south-west of Tunis via the RN 5, 72 km east of Kef, 8 km from Téboursouk.

DIALING CODE: 08.

ACCOMMODATION: In Téboursouk.

Douz

LOCATION AND ACCESS: Oasis near to the chott el Djérid, 55 km south of Tunis via Gabès, 117 km east of Tozeur, 132 km south of Gafsa.

DIALING CODE: 06.

TOURIST INFORMATION: *Syndicat d'initiative,* place de la République, tel. 490930 or 940.

ACCOMMODATION: See list at end of guide.

AMENITIES: Post office, shops, service stations, banks.

SOUVENIRS: Carpets, minerals (gypsum flowers), stuffed animals, dates.

FESTIVALS: Sahara Festival (December).

El Djem

NAME: Thysdrus (Punic).

LOCATION AND ACCESS: 205 km south-east of Tunis, 63 km south of Sousse, 64 km north of Sfax.

DIALING CODE: 04.

TOURIST INFORMATION: *Relais Julius* (30 beds, pool).

AMENITIES: Post office, service stations, shops.

SOUVENIRS: Carpets, jewellery, antiques (Soussi Brothers shops, near to the Coliseum).

Gabès

NAME: Tacapa (Roman).

LOCATION AND ACCESS: Chief town of the governorate, 405 km south of Tunis, 140 km south of Sfax, 150 km east of Gafsa, Railway station, maritime port.

DIALING CODE: 05.

ACCOMMODATION: See list of hotels at end of guide.

TOURIST INFORMATION: *Bureau de tourisme,* place de la Libération, tel. 270 254, *Syndicat d'initiative* (opposite hotel Néjib).

AMENITIES: Post office, service stations, restaurants, various shops, car hire (*Hertz,* 30 av. Ibn El Jazzar, tel. 270 525), pharmacies, hospital, banks.

SOUVENIRS: Gabès carpets, dates.

Gafsa

NAME: Caspa (Roman), Justiniana (byzantine).

LOCATION AND ACCESS: Chief town of the governorate. Altitude 330 m. 360 km southwest of Tunis, 200 km south of Kairouan, 95 km north-east of Tozeur, 145 km northwest of Gabès. Railway station. Tozeur international airport.

DIALING CODE: 06.

ACCOMMODATION: See list of hotels at end of guide.

AMENITIES: Post office, bars, restaurants, service stations, pharmacies, shops, banks.

SOUVENIRS: Typical Gafsa carpets.

*Set on the Cape Bon cliffs near to Tunis,
Korbous is a little thermal spa town
where people have been coming to "take the waters"
since times of old.*

Hammamet

NAME: Siagu (Roman).

LOCATION AND ACCESS: South of the Cap Bon peninsula, 10 km south-west of Nabeul, 64 km south of Tunis by motorway, 85 km north of Sousse by motorway. Railway station: routes to Tunis and Sousse.

DIALING CODE: 02.

TOURIST INFORMATION: *ONTT (Office National du Tourisme Tunisien),* av. Habib Bourguiba, tel. 280 423.

ACCOMMODATION: See list at end of guide.

LEISURE: Pool, tennis courts, beaches, water skiing, golf, horse riding, thalassotherapy (at the Sol Azur hotel).

FESTIVALS: International festival (July-August at the International Cultural Centre, av. des Nations-Unies, tel. 280 030).

SOUVENIRS: Carpets, perfumes, pottery, embroidery.

AMENITIES: Post office (av. de la République), service stations, car hire (*Hertz,* av. des Hôtels, tel. 280 187), dispensary, pharmacies, shops, shopping centre, market (on Thursdays), bank.

Haouaria

LOCATION AND ACCESS: On the tip of the Cap Bon peninsula, 100 km north-east of Tunis.

DIALING CODE: 02.

ACCOMMODATION: In Korbous, Kélibia, Hammamet, Nabeul.

FESTIVALS: Sparrowhawk festival (June).

Jendouba/ Bulla Regia

LOCATION AND ACCESS: 160 km west of Tunis, 65 km south of Tabarka, 56 km north of Kef.

DIALING CODE: 08.

TOURIST INFORMATION: In Tabarka, *Commissariat régional au tourisme,* 32 av. Bourguiba, tel. 644 491.

ACCOMMODATION: In Aïn Draham (see list of hotels at end of guide), Jendouba, and Béja.

Kairouan

NAME: Qawran (the « fortified town » in Arabic).

LOCATION AND ACCESS: Chief town of the governorate, 160 km south of Tunis, 67 km south of Sousse.

DIALING CODE: 07.

ACCOMMODATION: See list of hotels at end of guide.

TOURIST INFORMATION: *Syndicat d'initiative,* place du Commandant Mohamed el Béjaoui, tel. 220 452.

AMENITIES: Post office, service station, shops.

SOUVENIRS: Typical Kairouan carpets.

Kasserine/Sbeïtla

NAME: Cillium (Roman), Kasserine, « the two towers » (Arabic).

LOCATION AND ACCESS: 270 km south-west of Tunis, 107 km south-west of Kairouan, 77 km north of Gafsa.

DIALING CODE: 07.

ACCOMMODATION: See list of hotels at end of guide.

Kef (the)

NAME: Sicca (Punic), Sicca Veneria (Roman), El Kef («the Rock» in Arabic).

LOCATION AND ACCESS: Chief town of the governorate. Altitude: 780 m. 170 km south-west of Tunis, 120 km south of Tabarka, 120 km north of Kasserine. Railway station.

DIALING CODE: 08.

ACCOMMODATION: See list of hotels at end of guide.

AMENITIES: Post office, pharmacies, restaurants, shops, service stations.

Kerkennah (Islands)

NAME: Kyronnis (Greek), Cercina (Roman).

LOCATION AND ACCESS: Off-shore from Sfax, ferry from the Sidi Youssef port, at the western tip of Gharbi Island (every two hours from 06.00 to 20.00 in the summer; in winter four return journeys from 07.00 to 17.00).

ACCOMMODATION: See list of hotels at end of guide.

AMENITIES: Post office (in Ramla, tel. 281 000), Ramla hospital (tel. 281 052), Béhiri pharmacy (tel. 281 074), bank (UIB).

SOUVENIRS: Natural sponges.

Mahdia

NAME: « Town of the Mahdi » (in Arabic).

LOCATION AND ACCESS: On the eastern coast of the Mediterranean, 200 km south of Tunis, 60 km south-east of Sousse. Railway station.

DIALING CODE: 03.

ACCOMMODATION: See list of hotels at end of guide.

AMENITIES: Post office, pharmacies, food store, numerous travel agents, banks.

RESTAURANTS: L'Espadon, Neptune, le Lido, le Quai.

Maktar

NAME: Mactaris (Numidian), Colonia Aelia Aurelia Augusta.

LOCATION AND ACCESS: 160 km south-west of Tunis, 105 km west of Kairouan.

DIALING CODE: 08.

ACCOMMODATION: Mactaris (24 beds).

Mareth

LOCATION AND ACCESS: 33 km south of Gabès, 40 km north of Médenine.

DIALING CODE: 05.

ACCOMMODATION: Hotels in Gabès and Médenine.

TOURIST INFORMATION: In Gabès (av. Farhat Hached, tel. 270 254).

Matmata

NAME: Matmata is the name of a Berber tribe which was later given to the town.

LOCATION AND ACCESS: 450 km south of Tunis, 43 km south of Gabès, 60 km west of Médenine.

DIALING CODE: 05.

ACCOMMODATION: See list of hotels at end of guide.

AMENITIES: Post office, service stations, shops.

TOURIST INFORMATION: Syndicat d'initiative, Guide: Najib Driss.

SOUVENIRS: Berber carpets.

Monastir/Skanès

NAME: From the French « monastère », or « monastery » (see text).

LOCATION AND ACCESS: 165 km south-east of Tunis, 24 km east of Sousse, 80 km east of Kairouan. Railway station at Sousse. Skanès-Monastir international airport, tel. 61 314.

DIALING CODE: 03.

ACCOMMODATION: See list of hotels at end of guide.

RESTAURANTS: Le Grill, le Chandelier, le Central, la Rosa, le Captain, Calypso, Panorama, King's, le Rempart.

AMENITIES: Post office, various shops, pharmacies, hospital, coach station, service stations, car hire (Hertz, airport post n° 8, tel. 261 314), numerous travel agents, congress building, banks.

TOURIST INFORMATION: Commissariat régional au tourisme, in Skanès (tel. 461 205 or 089, 462 894), at airport (tel. 463 0216).

Nabeul

NAME: From the Roman Neapolis (also the root of the name Naples in Italy).

LOCATION AND ACCESS: Chief town of governorate. On the south coast near to the Cap Bon peninsula. 67 km south-east of Tunis by motorway (as far as Hammamet) and by road, 10 km north-east of Hammamet. Railway station (Tunis libre).

DIALING CODE: 02.

TOURIST BOARD: ONTT (Office National du tourisme tunisien), av. Taïeb Meiri, tel. 86 800 or 737.

ACCOMMODATION: See list at end of guide.

SOUVENIRS: Ceramic goods, mats, embroidery, woven rugs and covers, orange flower water. Boutiques and Office national de l'artisanat shop on av. Habib Thameur.

*Beautiful holiday homes
are dotted all along the coast
overlooking the sea north of Tunis.
They are part of Carthage, Gammarth and La Marsa.*

AMENITIES: Post office, hospital, pharmacies, shops, market (Friday mornings), car hire (*Hertz*, av. Habib Thameur, tel. 285 327), banks.

Nefta

NAME: Aggasel Nepte (Roman).

SITUATION AND ACCESS: 23 km west of Tozeur, 116 km south-west of Gafsa, 112 km west of Kébili and 233 km west of Gabès. Tozeur international airport.

DIALING CODE: 06.

TOURIST INFORMATION: *Syndicat d'initiative*, avenue Bourguiba, tel. 457 184.

ACCOMMODATION: See list of hotels at end of guide.

AMENITIES: Post office, service stations, shops, pharmacies, hospital, banks.

SOUVENIRS: Carpets, minerals, stuffed animals.

Sfax

NAME: Taparura (Roman).

LOCATION AND ACCESS: 270 km south of Tunis, 130 km south of Sousse, 135 km northeast of Gabès. Railway station. El Maou airport, tel. 41 700.

DIALING CODE: 04.

ACCOMMODATION: See list of hotels at end of guide.

TOURIST INFORMATION: *Bureau d'information touristique*, place de l'Indépendance, tel. 24 606.

AMENITIES: Banks (*STB, UIB, BIAT, BNT, BT, ATB, UBCI, BS*), post office (av. Bourguiba, tel. 224 722), food stores, markets, pharmacies (tel. 220 549/258/740, 222 486 or 224 700), Hédi Chaker hospital (route d'El Aïn, tel. 224 422/511), service stations, car hire (*Hertz*, 47 av. Habib Bourguiba, tel. 228 626), *Tunis Air* (av. de l'Armée, tel. 228 628), *Air France* (av. Taïeb Méhiri, tel. 224 847), numerous travel agents.

RESTAURANTS: *Le Corail, Turqui, Hannibal, l'Oriental, Baghdad, Bec Fin, Carthage, Chez Nous, le Printemps, la Sirène.*

SOUVENIRS: *Office national de l'artisanat*, rue Hamadi Tej, tel. 96 826.

FESTIVALS: Sfax Fair in June (on corner of Bourguiba and Boukhari avenues).

Sidi Bou Saïd

NAME: Abbreviation of the Muslim saint's name who lived here. His full name was Abou Saïd ibn Khalef ibn Yahia Ettamini el Béji.

LOCATION AND ACCESS: 20 km north-east of Tunis.

DIALING CODE: 01.

ACCOMMODATION: See list of hotels at end of guide.

FESTIVALS: Kharja religious festival in honour of Sidi Bou Saïd (July).

SOUVENIRS: Carpets, pottery, bird cages, perfume.

Sousse

NAME: Hadrumete (Punic), Colonia Ulpia Trajana Augusta Frugifera Hadrumetina (Roman), Harinicopolis (Vandal), Justiniano (Byzantine), Soussa (Arabic).

LOCATION AND ACCESS: Chief town of governorate. 140 km south of Tunis, 127 km north of Sfax, 57 km east of Kairouan. Railway station (tel. 221 955). Skanès-Monastir international airport (tel. 260 300).

DIALING CODE: 03.

TOURIST INFORMATION: *Commissariat régional au tourisme*, avenue Bourguiba, tel. 225 157/158/159. *Office national de tourisme tunisien*, the Port el Kantaoui marina (tel. 241 799). *Syndicat d'initiative*, place Sidi Yahia.

ACCOMMODATION: See list of hotels at end of guide.

AMENITIES: Market, shops, pharmacies, post office (av. de la République, tel. 24 750). Two hospitals : CHU Farat Hached, rue Ibn El Jazzar, tel. 221 411 and CHU of Hammam Sousse, tel. 241 411 and a clinic (les Oliviers, tel. 242 711). Car hire (*Hertz*, av. Bourguiba, tel. 225 428). *Tunis Air* (av. Bourguiba, tel. 227 955) and numerous travel agents.

SOUVENIRS: Carpets and dyed cloth, porcelain, traditional furniture (caskets), copper goods, leather bags, jewellery, olive oil.

FESTIVALS: Sousse international festival (July-August), Mediterranean olive tree festival (in Kalaâ Débira, December), Sidi El Kantaoui festival (in Hammam Sousse, July).

Tabarka

NAME: Thabraca (Phoenician).

LOCATION AND ACCESS: In north-western Tunisia, 16 km from the border, 170 km from Tunis via Mateur.

DIALING CODE: 08.

ACCOMMODATION: see list of hotels at end of guide.

AMENITIES: Post office, service stations, shops, car hire (*Hertz*, résidence Corallo, tel. 644 570).

SOUVENIRS: Carpets, cork and olive wood goods, coral jewellery, Sejnane terracotta pottery and statuettes.

TOURIST INFORMATION: *Commissariat régional au tourisme*, 32 avenue Bourguiba, tel. 644 491.

FESTIVALS: Coral Festival (July-August).

Tamerza/Chebika/Midès

NAME: Ad Turres (Roman) for Tamerza, Ad Speculum (Roman) for Chebika and Madès (Roman) for Midès.

LOCATION AND ACCESS: In south-western Tunisia (Djérid region), by the Algerian border, 65 km north-west of Tozeur, 95 km west of Gafsa. Railway stations at Gafsa and Tozeur. Tozeur international airport.

DIALING CODE: 06.

ACCOMMODATION: See list of hotels at end of guide.

SOUVENIRS: Carpets, minerals, stuffed animals.

FESTIVALS: Tamerza festival (April-May).

TOURIST INFORMATION: In Tozeur, *Commissariat régional au tourisme*, avenue Abou el Kacem Chebbi, tel. 250 503/088.

Tataouine

LOCATION AND ACCESS: 510 km south of Tunis, 50 km south of Médenine.

DIALING CODE: 05.

ACCOMMODATION: See list of hotels at end of guide.

AMENITIES: Post office, pharmacies, shops, banks, market, service stations.

SOUVENIRS: Carpets, pottery, basketry.

Thuburbo Majus

NAME: Colonia Julia Thuburbo Majus, Colonia Julia Aurelia Thuburbo Majus, Respublica Felix Thuburbo Majus (Roman), Henchir el Kasbate (Arabic).

LOCATION AND ACCESS: 3 km north of El Fahs, 60 km south-west of Tunis.

ACCOMMODATION: In Tunis.

Tozeur and the chott el Djérid

NAME: Thusuros (Roman).

LOCATION AND ACCESS: In south-western Tunisia, by the chott el Djérid. 450 km south-west of Tunis, 95 km south-west of Gafsa, 90 km west of Kébili, 210 km west of Gabès. Railway station (Tunis-Sfax-Gafsa line). International airport.

DIALING CODE: 06.

ACCOMMODATION: See list of hotels at end of guide.

TOURIST INFORMATION: *Commissariat régional au tourisme*, avenue Abou el Kacem Chebbi, tel. 450 503/088. *Syndicat d'initiative*, avenue H. Bourguiba, tel. 450 034.

AMENITIES: Post office, shops, banks, hospital, pharmacies, car hire (*Hertz*, av. Bourguiba, tel. 450 214, fax : 450 214), service stations.

SOUVENIRS: Berber carpets and dyed cloths, mats, Berber jewellery, dates and syrup (rose, violet, pistachio, pomegranate, banana), stuffed desert animals (scorpions, lizards, vipers), minerals (gypsum flowers).

Zarzis

NAME: Zita, Gergis (Roman), Jerjis (Arabic).

LOCATION AND ACCESS: On the Akara peninsula, near to the Libyan border in south-eastern Tunisia. 52 km from Houmt Souk (Djerba Island), 46 km north of Ben Gardane, 545 km south-east of Tunis. Djerba-Mélita airport 65 km to the north.

DIALING CODE: 05.

ACCOMMODATION: See list of hotels at end of guide.

SOUVENIRS: Pottery, carpets, perfume, jewellery, basketry.

the journey

before leaving

■ Tunisian tourism has been booming for several decades, and the country now has all the ingredients necessary for making successful holidays. First of all, it is close to Europe, and travel is inexpensive (airplane ticket prices are constantly falling thanks to charter flight companies). With its 1,200 km of coastline along the Mediterranean, Tunisia enjoys an idyllic climate and has many beaches attracting seaside holiday fans. Moreover, Tunisia offers enough curiosities for those who like going exploring.

Other advantages include the low cost of living, which enables tourists to spend their family holidays here without breaking the bank (more and more travel agents are offering week-long package tours including travel and full board and lodgings at the price of a weekend by train to any of the seaside resorts in Europe).

In order to cope with the massive influx of tourists, the public authorities and Tunisian private investors have made remarkable efforts in providing structures by building both top quality hotels and sports facilities, including golf courses, tennis courts, pools, etc. The ONTT's (Office national du tourisme tunisien) astonishing work in restoring the country's architectural patrimony – palaces, mosques, medinas, ribats, medersas, etc. – also deserves a mention.

Some people may be tempted to turn their noses up at a destination they consider too "common". They would in fact be failing to recognise the Tunisian architects' artistic talent in building fine hotels and holiday complexes inspired by the most beautiful old buildings (beylik palaces, traditional Berber villages, or mosques) on the most splendid sites by the sea (Djerba, Hammamet), in the heart of the vast Saharan palm groves (in Tozeur and Nefta), in the mountains (in Tamerza and Tataouine) or in historic town centres (Sfax, Sousse).

No one can blame Tunisian hotel owners for having achieved such good value-for-money service that they can now pride themselves on opening these palaces up to the general public! Still, if visitors really do want to avoid the flocks of holiday makers, they should carefully choose their season and region, preferably travelling in the springtime, autumn or winter. It is also a good idea to opt for the inland circuits, notably the deep south, where visitors can enjoy the sublime solitude of the vast Saharan spaces.

Which season?

Thanks to its Mediterranean climate, it is possible to visit Tunisia all year round. For seaside holidays, however, it is best to travel between the spring and autumn in order to fully enjoy the heat, which is not excessive on the coast where gentle sea breezes blow.

If travelling in the central and southern regions, on the other hand, it is better to avoid the summer as it is extremely hot. In the winter and spring, temperatures in the Tunisian Sahara desert are ideal: its is relatively hot during the daytime, but cool at night which is most refreshing.

Formalities

No specific vaccinations are required. Some health organisations do recommend, however, that visitors to hot countries be vaccinated against typhoid, hepatitis A and B, meningitis, tetanus, and polio.

Visitors require a valid passport when entering Tunisia. Non-European visitors must check for visa requirements. Visas can be obtained from the Tunisian embassy and can take up to three weeks to obtain. Customs allow visitors to bring their personnel effects and sporting equipment into the country, along with 200 cigarettes (or 50 cigars, or 400 grammes of tobacco), and a bottle of spirits.

THE TUNISIAN CLIMATE (average temperatures in °C)

	Jan.	Feb.	Mar.	Apr.	May	June	July	Aug.	Sep.	Oct.	Nov.	Dec.
Tunis	15	16	18	21	25	29	32	33	30	25	20	16
Djerba	16	18	21	24	26	29	32	33	32	28	23	18

Preceding pages:
Holiday makers visiting Djerba and Zarzis are more and more frequently tempted to leave the beaches and their sunbathing to venture down into southern Tunisia where they can discover the picturesque village of Matmata, amongst other sites (photo).

Information on Tunisia

The first place to gather information is the *Office national du tourisme tunisien* (Tourist Board) where staff will kindly give road maps, city maps, brochures and booklets, along with different travel companies' brochures. In Tunis and in all the Tunisian towns and airports, the ONTT has offices giving tourist documentation and information.

- The *ONTT* in Britain: The Tunisian National Tourism Office, 77a Wigmore Street. London, W1H 9LJ. Tel.: (0171) 224 5561, fax: (0171) 224 4053.
- The *ONTT* in the USA: Embassy of Tunisia, 1515 Massachusetts Avenue, Washington D.C. 20005. Tel.: (202) 234 6644.
- The *ONTT* in Canada: Embassy of Tunisia, 515 Oscannro Street, Ottawa, 10 KES 3P8, Ontario. Tel.: (613) 237 0330.

Furthermore, the Tunisian embassy in your country is likely to have a Cultural service with further information.

In Paris, the *Institut du Monde arabe* (1 rue des Fossés-Saint-Bernard, 75005, Paris, tel. (33) 1 – 40 51 38 38), periodically puts on thematic Tunisian exhibitions, concerts and films.

Specialised bookshops

In London, books on Tunisia and maps of the towns and country may be found in *The Travel Bookshop*, 13-15 Blenheim Crescent, London W11 2EE, tel. (0171) 229 5260, fax: 0171 243 1552; *Africa Book Centre*, 38 King Street, London WC2E 8JS, tel. (0171) 240 6649, or in other major bookshops.

In Paris, a wide range of books can be found at *L'Espace IGN* (Institut géographique national), 107 rue La Boétie, 75008 Paris, tel. 43 98 85 00; *L'Astrolabe*, 46 rue de Provence, 75009 Paris, tel. 42 85 42 95; *L'Harmattan*, 16 rue des Ecoles, 75005 Paris, tel. 43 26 04 52; *L'ABC du Voyage*, 14 rue Serpente, 75006 Paris, tel. 46 33 80 06, *Itinéraire*, 60 rue Saint-Honoré, 75001 Paris, tel. 43 36 12 63; *Ulysse*, 26 rue Saint-Louis-en-L'Isle, 75004 Paris, tel.

43 25 17 35; and in other large bookshops.

Any of the following maps are particularly useful: Michelin (Algeria and Tunisia), IGN (2 sheets: Sfax and Tunis, 1/1,000,000), Kummerly and Frey (1/100,000), or the Freytag and Berndt map (1/800,000) which also has a cultural guide.

Clothing and sports equipment

It is often hot when travelling in Tunisia during the spring and summertime, especially in the south, so visitors should take light cotton summer clothes, and avoid synthetic materials. Good walking shoes are necessary for excursions. Other indispensable items include a swimming costume, sunglasses, and a hat for protect from the blazing sun.

In the autumn and winter, overcoats and anoraks are not needed, but a light raincoat and umbrella are advisable, along with slightly warmer clothes: shirts, light jackets, jumpers (especially in the Tunisian Sahara where it can be very chilly at night).

Taking photos or filming: bring your camera (plus different lenses: wide angle, 50 mm and zoom), camcorder, and enough films or tapes (these can be bought in the airport duty-free shops on departure).

Scuba-divers should think about bringing underwater photographic equipment as Tunisia's sea beds are often very picturesque.

Health and hygiene

A little *medical kit* is always a good idea. It should contain: some mercurochrome, antiseptic lotion or surgical spirits, sterilized compresses and plasters, scissors, cotton wool, a serum for poisonous bites, mosquito repellant and an anti-histamine cream (for calming itchy insect bites), suntan lotion and after-sun for calming sunburn, aspirin, talc, Intetrix or other medication for upset stomachs, and Alka-Seltzer. People taking regular medication at home should remember to bring sufficient quantities with them. Most European medication can be found in the pharmacies.

getting to tunisia

By boat

Several companies offer car-ferry services across the Mediterranean (passengers and their cars). The main route from Marseilles (France) to Tunis, is operated by the French company *SNCM* (*Société nationale maritime Corse-Méditerranée-Ferrytanée*) and by the *CTN* (*Compagnie tunisienne de navigation*). Ferries depart from La Joliette sea port in Marseilles, and arrive after a 22-hour crossing at the Tunis-La Goulette port. Other companies provide services from Italy (Genoa, Naples and Palermo) to Tunisia.

Addresses: *SNCM*, 12 rue Godot-de-Mauroy, 75009 Paris, France (information and reservations: tel. 49 24 24 24, telex: 211 168, fax: 49 24 24 09). In Tunis: *SNCM-Ferrytanée*, 47 av. Farhat-Hached, Tunis, tel. 246 536. *Navitour*, 8 rue d'Alger, Tunis, tel. 249 500. *CTN*,12 rue Godot-de-Mauroy, 75009 Paris, France, tel. 47 42 17 55; 3, rue du Président Carnot, 69002 Lyons, tel. 72 41 84 84; 21 rue Mazenod, 13002 Marseilles, tel. 91 91 55 71: 5 av. Dag-Hammarskjoeld, Tunis, tel. 341 777, telex: 12475. In Britain, travel on the SNCM and CTN lines can be booked through *Southern Ferries Ltd*, 179 Piccadilly, London W1V 9DB, tel. (0171) 491 4968.

By plane

It takes 2 hours 45 minutes to fly – the safest, most comfortable and quickest way to travel – from London to Tunis (Carthage airport, 8 km from the town centre).

Most of the major European airline companies fly to Tunisia's six international airports (Tunis-Carthage, Monastir-Sousse/Bourguiba, Sfax-Thyna, Djerba-Zarzis, Tozeur-Nefta and Tabarka) several times a day or per week.

British Airways, Tunisair and *GB Airways* regularly fly from London to Tunis. *Air France, Tunisair* and *Air Liberté* run regular flight services from Paris in France to Tunis. In Britain, it is also possible to fly to Tunisia from the Birmingham, Manchester, Newcastle and Belfast airports. Tunisair and Air France also fly from the French towns of Lyons,

TUNISIA TODAY

TOWNS

Number of inhabitants

⬤ over 500 000

⬤ from 200 000 to 300

● from 50 000 to 100 00

● from 10 000 to 50 000

• less than 10 000

~ Permanent waterway

- - - Temporary waterway

Sebkha, chott, garaa

RELIEF

ALTITUDES in metres

over 1 000

from 600 to 1 000

from 400 to 600

from 200 to 400

from 0 to 200

below sea level

0   100 km

Nice, Marseilles, Strasbourg, Lille, Bordeaux and Toulouse. These airline companies fly not only to Tunis, but also to Monastir-Sousse (3 times a week to Bourguiba airport), Sfax (twice a week to Thyna airport), Tozeur (once a week to Nefta airport), the Isle of Djerba, in the south (3 to 4 times a week to Djerba-Zarzis airport) and to the new Tabarka airport in the north-west of the country near to the Algerian border.

If there are no places left on these flights – planes are often fully booked during the peak summer season in July and August –, it is also possible to reach Tunisia via Belgium, Switzerland, Germany or Italy. From Belgium, *Sabéna* flies to Tunis and Monastir. From Switzerland, *Swissair* flies from Geneva to Tunis. From Germany, *Lufthansa* flies from Frankfurt to Tunis, Monastir or Djerba. From Italy, *Alitalia* flies from Rome to Tunis.

If you fly via Paris, be sure to check which airport you take off from on your ticket or with your travel agent: *Tunisair* flies from Orly-Sud airport, whereas other companies may fly from Roissy-Charles-de-Gaulle (terminal 1 or terminal 2A, 2B, 2C or 2D).

Individual travellers should check-in at least 45 mns. before the flight departure time, groups 60 mns. When flying back from Tunisia, get to the airport 2 hours before the flight.

Travel classes and reductions

The major international flight companies offer three classes of seats on each flight: first (F), business (J), and economy (Y) class. Travellers wishing to benefit from reduced fares and advantageous conditions offered to young people, large families, elderly people, and groups, will be in economy class.

These reductions, which are only offered at certain times of the year, entail certain constraints: you must buy and reserve your ticket on the same day, not change the departure and return dates (otherwise you will risk having to pay the full price), and unused return tickets cannot be reimbursed.

Be sure to reconfirm the return flight (whatever the cost of the ti-cket!) with your flight company at least three days before the date of departure.

Agencies abroad and in Tunisia

Tunisair: In Britain: 24 Sackville Street, London, W1X 1DE, tel. (0171) 734 7644. In Tunisia: Tunis agencies, 48 avenue Habib-Bourguiba, tel. (01) 259 189; 113 avenue de la Liberté, tel. (01) 288 100; Houmt Souk agency (Djerba Island), tel. (05) 650 239.

British Airways: In Britain: Speedbird House, PO Box 10, Hounslow, Middlesex TW6 2JA, tel. (0181) 759 5511 (Head office & general enquiries). In Tunisia: Tunis, tel. (1) 243 941. In USA: BA place, 1850 K Street NW, Initial Square Building, Washington DC, 20006, tel. (703) 661 8898.

GB Airways: In Britain: Ian Stewart Centre, Beehive Ring Road, Gatwick Airport, W Sussex RH6 0PH, tel. (0181) 897 4000 (reservations via BA).

Air France: In France: 119 avenue des Champs-Elysées, 75008, Paris, tel. information: (1) 44 08 24 24, reservations: (1) 44 08 22 22. In Britain: Colet Court, 100 Hammersmith Road, London W6 7JP, tel. (0181) 750 4366. In USA: 125 W 55th Street, N.Y. 10019, tel. (212) 2470 100. In Tunisia: 1 rue d'Athènes, Tunis, tel. 341 999; reservations: (0) 355 442.

Sabéna: In Britain: 36 Piccadilly, London W1, tel. (0181) 780 1444. In Tunis: Hôtel Abou Nawas, avenue Mohamed-V, tel. 259 845 or 259 922.

Swissair: In Britain: Swiss Centre, 10 Wardour Street, London W1V 3HG, tel. (0171) 439 4144. In Tunis: Le Colisée, 45 avenue Habib-Bourguiba, tel. 342 122.

Lufthansa: In Britain: 10 Old Bond St, London W1X 4EN, tel. (0171) 408 0442. In Tunis: Hôtel El Mechtel, boulevard Ouled-Haffouz, tel. 894 411.

Alitalia: In Britain: 205 Holland Park Avenue, London W11 4XB, tel. (0171) 602 7111. In Tunis: 17 avenue Habib-Tameur, tel. 247 944.

Some agencies offer flights on the regular airline routes (*Airtours, Club Med, Horizon, Thomas Cook, Panorama, Cadogan, Nouvelles Frontiè-*

res, *Aspects of Tunisia, Belleair, Cosmos, First Choice, Prestige, Sky Tours, Thomson, SunWorld, etc*).

Charter flights are offered on fixed days and have certain conditions attached, for example, the return ticket must be purchased, reservations and payment have to be made on the same day, and only one flight is available per week.

Package tours

A number of travel agents offer trips to Tunis (*Wigmore, Nouvelles Frontières, Ferrytour, Jet Tours, etc*), the oases (*Nouvelles Frontières, Panorama, Jet Tours, etc.*), and the major Tunisian seaside resorts: Tabarka, Gammarth, Hammamet, Skanès, Monastir, Port El Kantaoui, Djerba, Zarzis (*Club Med, Nouvelles Frontières, Panorama, Cadogan, Wigmore, etc.*)

Driving holidays

Coach, minibus and jeep tours enable visitors to go on a complete tour of Tunisia or visit a particular region. Amongst the travel agents offering such holidays are: *Cosmos, Panorama, Nouvelles Frontières, Club Sangho, Ferrytour, etc.*

Trekking in the deep south

Specialised travel agents offer 8 day walking and camel riding holidays in the deep south of Tunisia (*Club Aventure, Explorator, Itinérances*). In Tunisia contact *Douz Voyages*, tel. (05) 495 179.

Golfing holidays

Several European tour operators, including *Panorama, British Airways Holidays, Golf Holidays International,* and *Jet Tours* , organise golfing weekend trips and holidays. Their packages include air travel, accommodation in top quality hotels, and courses of different levels (beginners, improvers...) with qualified coaches. These trips are organised in Tabarka, Monastir, Hammamet and Port El Kantaoui. *Panorama Holiday Group Ltd*, 29 Queens Road, Brighton, Sussex, BN1 3YN, tel. (01273) 746877. *British Airways Holidays,* Astral Towers, Betts Way, London Road Crawley, W Sussex, tel. (01293) 611311. *Golf Holidays International,* Bridge House, Orchard Lane, Huntingdon, Cambs, PE18 6QT, tel. (01480) 433000. *Jet Tours*, 38 avenue de l'Opéra, 75002 Paris, tel. 47 42 06 92.

Hunting holidays

Small game hunting (game birds) and big European game hunting (wild boar) have been developing for several years now, particularly in the northern and central regions of Tunisia on Cap Bon, in the Tabarka region, and around Zaghouan and Sbeïtla. Hunting weekends and trips are organised both by international tour operators and by local Tunisian companies. These companies will organise the whole hunting trip, from getting the necessary hunting permit and paying taxes and insurance, to organising accommodation, hunting shoes, and providing the guide, beaters and dogs.

Addresses: *Jet Tours Chasse et Pêche*, 19 avenue de Tourville, 75007 Paris, tel. 47 05 01 95; *Tunisie Voyages*, 62 rue d'Iran, Tunis, tel. 01-287 451; *Agence de Tourisme et de Transit*, 45 avenue Bourguiba, Tunis, tel. 01-258 200; *TVT Rapid Voyages*, 8 rue Camille Desmoulins, Tunis, tel. 01-288 459; *Caravane Tours*, 60 rue Nahas Pacha, Tunis, tel. 01-240 194; *Tourafric*, 52 avenue Bourguiba, Tunis, tel. 01-341 488; *Loisitours*, 2 rue Tatouan, Tunis, tel. 01-281 640; *Ariana Voyages*, 93 avenue Bourguiba, Tunis, tel. 01-715 126; *International Voyages Services*, 35 avenue Bourguiba, Bizerte, tel. 02-32 855; *Via Bizerte*, avenue d'Algérie, Bizerte, tel. 02-32 901.

Several specialised hotels: le *Lido* in Nabeul (tel. 02-85 104), *Les Mimosas* in Tabarka (tel. 08-44 376), *Les Chênes* in Aïn Draham (tel. 08-47 211), *Beauséjour* in Aïn Draham (tel. 08-47 005), *Cilium* in Kasserine (tel. 07-70 106 or 682).

getting around tunisia

By plane

The domestic flight company *Tuninter* runs services from Tunis to the main Tunisian towns (several flights a day to Djerba, 1 to 2 daily flights to Sfax, two weekly flights to Tabarka, and several weekly flights to Tozeur); from Djerba (several daily flights to Tunis); from Sfax (1 to 2 daily flights to Tunis); and from Tozeur (several weekly flights to Tunis and Tabarka).

Address: *Tuninter* in London (contact Tunisair) 24 Sackville Street, London W1X 1DE, tel. (0171) 734 7644; in Tunis, tel. 701 717.

By road

The Tunisian roads are generally excellent. There are over 30,000 km of main roads and tracks, and 7,500 km of secondary roads. Most of these roads are tarred.

Several motorways are currently being built. Some have already been completed in the Tunis agglomeration, for example the bypass on the Tunis-La Goulette causeway. The major national motorway already linking the capital to Hammamet (65 km), has just been prolonged 92 km to M'Saken (near to Sousse). Current construction work will extend it southwards to Sfax, then Gabès.

The Tunisian highway code imposes a speed limit of 40 to 50 km/h in built up areas, 90 km/h out of towns, and 70 km/h on the Isle of Djerba.

Car hire

All the major international car hire companies are represented in Tunisia (Avis, Budget, Europcars, etc.). *Hertz* has the greatest number of cars (600 hire vehicles) and the most extensive network in the country (20 agencies, or "stations" throughout the country).

Hertz offers its clients a great deal of advantages, starting with a wide choice of type of vehicle, ranging from Citroën AXs, Renault Super 5s, Peugeot 205s, to Mercedes 190s, Peugeot 605s, to Renault 21 and 25s.

TUNISIA (Communications, tourism)

COMMUNICATIONS

International airport

Port

Sea route (ferry)

Motorway-Highway

Main road

Secondary road

Track

Railway

AGRICULTURE AND REARING

Olive growing zone (southern limit)

Forest

Vineyard

Oasis

Fruit trees

TOURISM

Seaside resort

Thermal spa

Oasis

Troglodytic dwelling

Museum or historic residence

Major ruins or vestiges

Forts and ramparts

Crafts centre

Golf course

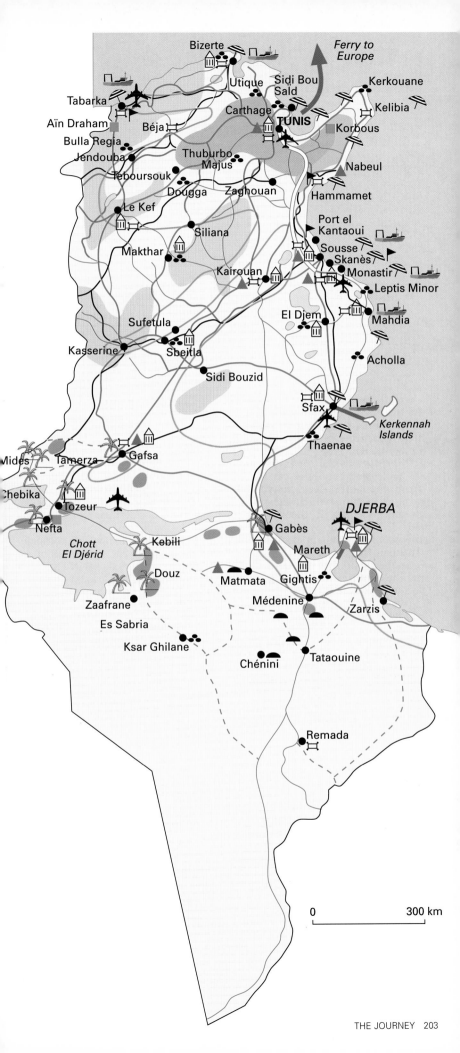

Beja										
106	**Bizerte**									
422	465	**Gabès**								
182	225	240	**Kairouan**							
105	211	388	173	**Le Kef**						
318	340	137	136	287	**Sfax**					
194	213	264	57	230	127	**Sousse**				
68	136	507	250	121	386	262	**Tabarka**			
544	587	122	362	510	259	386	629	**Tataouine**		
424	530	218	292	319	283	349	440	340	**Tozeur**	
104	71	394	154	168	269	142	175	516	446	**Tunis**

All these cars can be hired either by the day and by the kilometre, or for several days with unlimited millage (unlimited third-party insurance included).

Moreover, as the *Hertz* network is so widespread, clients can benefit from the "hire here, leave elsewhere" system, which means it is possible to pick up the hire car in Tunis, Djerba or where ever, and then return it in almost any other Tunisian town.

In the event of an accident, clients can be sure to find a nearby garage to quickly repair the car.

Addresses of the Hertz stations in Tunisia:

In Tunis: La Charguia, Head office, route No 8 (reservations: tel. 790 211; fax: 780 082). Tunis-Carthage airport, tel. 236 000 or 231 822 (ext. 34 96). Town centre: 29 avenue Habib Bourguiba, tel. 248 559. *In Bizerte:* place des Martyrs, tel. (02) 433 679. *In Takarka:* résidence Corallo, tel. (08) 644 570. *In Nabeul:* avenue Habib Thameur, tel. (02) 285 327. *In Hammamet:* avenue des Hôtels, tel. (02) 280 187. *In Sousse:* avenue Habib Bourguiba, tel. (03) 225 428. *In Monastir:* Airport, Post No 8, tel. (03) 261 314. *In Kairouan:* avenue Ibn El Jazzar, tel. (07) 224 529. *In Sfax:* 47 avenue Habib Bourguiba, tel. (04) 228 626. *In Djerba:* Houmt Souk, tel. (05) 650 196, place Mongi Bali, tel. (05) 650 196; Djerba-Mélita airport, post 8, tel. (05) 650 233. *In Tozeur:* avenue Habib Bourguiba, tel. (06) 450 214, fax: (06) 450 214.

Public transport

Seventy-six regular coach routes set out from Tunis and the main towns and run throughout Tunisia.

In the capital, the *SNTN* (*Société nationale des transports*), runs an extensive bus service along 155 bus routes (4,500 km).

Furthermore, the private company *TCV* (*Transports en commun de voyageurs*) offers its users a minibus service (about ten buses) from the suburbs to the town centre (the fare is higher than the bus fare, but these minibuses are more comfortable).

Tunis is currently the only town in Tunisia to be equipped with a metro ("tube") service. This is in fact an "overground" service, which is more like a tramway than a metro, but does have its own lanes (like bus lanes). Run by the *SMLT* (*Société du métro léger de Tunis*), it is a 30 km network with several lines: the northern line goes to Ariana (the airport), the western lines go to the Bardo, the University campus, and the cité Ibn Khaldoun, and the southern line goes to Ben Arous.

Taxis

A great deal of urban taxis circulate in the main towns, especially the "petit taxis", (which are not licensed to take more than 3 passengers, carry large luggage or to leave the agglomeration).

The "grand taxis" are allowed to leave the agglomeration (be warned!: the return journey is billed even if there are no passengers left). There are also the cheap communal taxis ("voitures de louage") which only leave once they are full (4 to 6 passengers), and which assure regular services between several of the towns.

Road and street maps

Tunisian road maps can be found in the main town bookshops once on site (see earlier section "Information on Tunisia" in the "Before leaving" chapter). Street maps of most of Tunisia's towns are graciously given by the various tourist boards.

In Tunis, the ONTT distributes general maps of Tunis and of the Medina. A 1/12,500 map of the capital and a 1/100,000 map of Tunis and its suburbs (Editions Turki) is sold in bookshops.

Some travel agents and car hire companies will give clients general maps of Tunisia.

Travelling by train

Tunisia has over 2,000 km of railways and a modern, comfortable train service (first class carriages are air conditioned, but passengers must reserve seats several days in advance).

The main line departs from Tunis (station at Place de Barcelone) and heads southwards to Gabès via Hammamet, Sousse, and Sfax. Branch lines go to Nabeul, Monastir, and Mahdia (the last two towns are linked to Sousse by a little electric train – the "métro léger" – which also goes to Ksar Hellal and Moknine).

Several other lines go to the north (Bizerte, Tabarka, Dougga, Jendouba) and to the south (Gafsa, Metlaoui).

If you buy a ticket and intend to stop off at several places en route,

---

EMBASSIES AND TOURIST BOARDS

■ EMBASSIES OF TUNISIA:
Belgium: *Brussels, 278 av. Tervuren, 1150. Tel. (322) 7 71 73 95.*
Canada: *515 Oscannro Street, Ottawa, 10 KES 3P8, Ontario. Tel.: (613) 237 0330.*
France: *Paris, 25 rue Barbet-de-Jouy, 75007. Tel. 45 55 95 98, fax: 45 51 25 20.*
Great Britain: *29 Princess Gate, London SW7 10G. Tel.: (0171) 584 8117.*
Switzerland: *Berne, 63 Kirchenfeldstrass, 3005. Tel. (41) 31 352 82 26.*
USA: *1515 Massachusetts Avenue, Washington D.C. 20005. Tel.: (202) 862 1850.*
TOURIST BOARDS:
Belgium: *Brussels: 60 Galerie Ravenstein, 1000. Tel. (322) 11 42, fax: 511 36 00.*
Canada: *Embassy of Tunisia, see above address.*
France: *Paris: 32 avenue de l'Opéra, 75002. Tel. 47 42 72 67, fax: 47 42 52 67. Lyons: 12 rue de Sèze, 69006. Tel. 52 35 86.*
Great Britain: *77a Wigmore Street. London. W1H9LJ. Tel.: (0171) 224 5598.*
Switzerland: *Zurich: Bahnhofstrasse 69, 8001. Tel. (01) 211 4830, telex: 045 813 374, fax: 212 13 53*
USA: *Embassy of Tunisia, see above address.*

*With its medieval medina
surrounded by tall walls
and its modern districts,
Sousse truly deserves its nickname,
the "Pearl of the Sahel".*

you must also ask for a "bulletin d'arrêts".

From Tunis, the little *TGM* train (*Tunis-La Goulette-La Marsa*) crosses Lake Tunis and goes to the northern beaches via Carthage and Sidi Bou Saïd (station at the end of Avenue Bourguiba, near the port).

The highly picturesque "Lézard Rouge" ("Red Lizard") is the former Tunis beys' train, which has come back into vogue thanks to the travel agents, and offers trips around Metlaoui, notably in the Selja river gorges, in its Twenties-style carriages.

Hot-air ballooning

An unusual way of discovering Tunisia, and especially the deep Saharan south, is by hot-air balloon.

The Tunisian company *Aéroasis* in Tozeur proposes balloon trips over the palm groves, the chott el Djérid and the dunes of the Grand Erg Oriental. Address: *Aéroasis*, 4

rue Imam Errassaa, 1002 Tunis, tel. 788 466. In Tozeur, offices opposite the Hotel Continental, tel. (06) 452 361; and in Nabeul, tel. (02) 220 161.

Tourist information

In all of Tunisia's main towns, there are tourist information bureaus that provide all the information, brochures, and maps necessary for organising trips around the country.

In Tunis: *Office national du tourisme tunisien – ONTT*, 1 avenue Mohamed V, tel. (01) 341 077, telex: 14 381, fax: 350 997; Tunis-Carthage airport, tel. (01) 236 000. *Commissariat régional au tourisme*, 29 rue de Palestine, tel. 289 403.

In Aïn Draham: *Bureau de tourisme*, Babouche post, tel. (08) 47 150.

In Bizerte: *Commissariat régional au tourisme*, 1 rue de Constantinople, tel. (02) 32 897 / 703.

In Djerba: *Commissariat régional au tourisme*, Houmt Souk, tel. (05)

USEFUL TELEPHONE NUMBERS

■ In Tunis:
Airport: 236 000
Tunisair: 259 189 or 288 100
Air France: 341 999
Tourist Board: 341 077
Station: 244 440
Emergencies (national no.): 197
Fire brigade: 198
Ambulance service: 190
Ambulances: 341 250/280 or 281 913
Pharmacies: 252 507 or 347 224

In Djerba:
Tourist Board: 650 915
Taxis: 650 205
Rescue services: 650 528
Hospital: 650 018 or 657 280
Police: 657 311
Pharmacy: 650 707
Airport: 650 233

50 016/544/581. *Syndicat d'initiative* of Houmt Souk, avenue Bourguiba, tel. (05) 50 915. *Syndicat d'initiative* of Midoun, avenue Farhat Hached, tel. (05) 57 114.

In Douz: *Bureau de tourisme*, rue Farhat Hached, tel. (05) 90 930/940. *Syndicat d'initiative*, place de la République, tel. (05) 90 930/940.

In Gabès: *Bureau de tourisme*, place de la Libération, tel. (05) 70 254. *Syndicat d'initiative* (opposite Hotel Néjib).

In Gafsa: *Bureau de tourisme*, place des Piscines, tel. (06) 21 664.

In Hammamet: *Office de tourisme*, avenue Bourguiba, tel. (02) 80 423.

In Kairouan: *Syndicat d'initiative*, place du Commandant Mohammed el Béjaoui, tel. (07) 20 452.

In Mahdia: *Bureau de tourisme,* tel. (03) 681 098.

In Monastir: *Commissariat régional au tourisme*, zone touristique de Skanès, tel. (03) 461 205 or 089, 462 894 (Tourisme Service, tel. 467 999). *Tourism bureau* at Monastir airport: tel. (03) 463 016.

In Nabeul: *Commissariat régional au tourisme*, avenue Taïeb Méhiri, tel. (02) 86 800.

In Nefta: *Syndicat d'initiative*, avenue Bourguiba, tel. (06) 57 184.

In Sfax: *Bureau d'information*, place de l'Indépendance, tel. (04) 224 606.

In Sousse: *Commissariat régional au tourisme*, 1 avenue Bourguiba, tel. (03) 225 157 (Tourisme service, tel. (03) 229 999). *Syndicat d'initiative*, place Sidi Yahia. *Office de tourisme*, Port El Kantaoui-La Marina, tel. (03) 241 799.

In Tabarka: *Commissariat régional au tourisme*, 32 avenue Habib Bourguiba, tel. (08) 44 491.

In Tozeur: *Commissariat général au tourisme*, avenue Abou el Kacem Chebbi, tel. (06) 50 503/088. *Syndicat d'initiative*, avenue Bourguiba, tel. (06) 50 034.

Suggested tour routes

– *1 day*: Tunis (visit the town centre in the morning: avenue Bourguiba and the souks in the Medina; the Bardo museum in the afternoon).

– *2 days*: Tunis and its outskirts (the Medina and the Bardo museum on the 1st day; La Goulette, the Punic and Roman remains at Carthage, Sidi Bou Saïd, La Marsa, Gammarth on the 2nd day).

– *3 days*: Tunis and its outskirts (see above).

– *5 days*: Tunis, its outskirts (Carthage, Sidi Bou Saïd in the north-east; Nabeul and Hammamet on the Cap Bon peninsula in the south-east). Also visit the Roman site at Thuburbo Majus south of the capital.

– *10 days*: the north (tour: Tunis and its outskirts, the northern coast from Bizerte to Tabarka). Descend to Le Kef (via Roman towns of Bulla Regia, Dougga, Makthar). Visit Kairouan, Sousse-Monastir, return to Tunis via Hammamet.

– *15 days*: the deep south (Saharan circuit via the oases): Tozeur (palm grove and belvedere), Nefta (the "Corbeille"), the "mountain oases" (Chebika, Tamerza, Midès). Cross the chott el Djérid to get to Douz via Kébili. Descend southwards to Ksar Ghilane, then the "Ksour mountains" (Chenini and Tataouine). Back up to Gabès via Médenine and Matmata (troglodytic dwellings). Return to Tozeur via Gabès, El Guettar, Gafsa, Metlaoui (trip on the "Lézard Rouge" train).

– *A month*: a combination of the tour in the north (Tunis, Cap Bon peninsula, Tunis region and Carthage, Sidi Bou Saïd, Gammarth, La Marsa, a tour in the northern mountains from Bizerte to Tabarka), and a tour in the deep south (Djérid, Matmata, Tataouine), plus a stop-over on Djerba or Zarzis.

the trip and daily life

Formalities

When visitors arrive at Tunis port or airport, they will be asked to show a valid passport (a valid national identity card is sufficient if on a group holiday and if it is accompanied by a plane ticket). Non-European visitors must check to see if they need a visa. Passport control officials will distribute a little slip of paper (a kind of entrance visa) which must be carefully kept with your passport then handed back when you leave the country.

Customs allow visitors to bring all their personal effects and sports equipment, along with a bottle of spirits and the equivalent of 200 cigarettes.

When leaving Tunisia, the frontier banks and bureau de change can only reconvert 30% of the sum originally converted into dinars, and can only change a maximum of 100 dinars. It is therefore recommended to change small sums of money as and when needed (it is best to pay large sums of money by credit card).

Make sure you keep the bank or bureau de change receipts when you change your money into dinars as you may be asked to produce them when you leave the country.

Currency and haggling

The official currency is the Tunisian dinar, which is divided into 1,000 millimes. Just to give an indication, 1 dinar (DT) was worth approximately £0.70 sterling in 1995, but the exchange rate does vary.

All the major credit cards are accepted in the main hotels, large restaurants, airline companies, travel agents, souks (especially when buying carpets). Service stations, small restaurants and hotels, and market stalls do not accept them yet.

Visitors can withdraw emergency money in banks in most of the major towns if they present a credit card and proof of identity. Cash point machines in the main towns do not work with foreign credit cards, even when they have a "Visa" sign.

As the cost of living is relatively low in Tunisia, foreign visitors will be pleasantly surprised to find that they can spend their holidays in most advantageous conditions. Hotels and restaurants are between a third and half the price of equivalent establishments in Europe, not to mention the particularly competitive airline and package tour prices. Visitors ought to take advantage of the opportunity to buy some souvenirs, especially carpets which are cheaper than in Europe.

As in all the African countries, haggling is a "national sport" in Tunisia, and can be quite a game in the souks. As the initial price asked for will always be up to double the item's real value, do not be afraid to bring the price down by suggesting much lower prices. The negotiation will then be underway, and each party has to make successive concessions, thus reducing the divide until an average price is reached that everyone is happy with. A game punctuated with a few minor *coups de théâtre* will often end up around a mint tea with newfound friends.

Taking photos

A photo permit is not required in Tunisia (beware, however: visitors are not allowed to photograph official buildings like the governmental palaces, ministries, airports, barracks...). Visitors will sometimes be asked to pay what is generally a very modest fee if they want to take pictures inside mosques and museums. Visitors wishing to photograph day-to-day scenes in Tunisia should always kindly ask for permission from the people concerned. In the souks in the main towns, the traders are so used to being photographed that they themselves will show you the best place to take a picture (in the Tunis and Kairouan medinas, the carpet sellers have installed very pleasant terraces on the roofs which afford panoramic views of the town).

Time differences and opening hours

During the winter, there is an hour's difference between Britain and Tunisia. When it is one p.m. in Tunis, it will be midday in London. In the summer, the time is the same.

Administrative offices are open

Combining utility and pleasure,
the innumerable irrigation canals in the Nefta palm grove
in southern Tunisia are used both
for date growing and as swimming pools by the children.

from 08.30 to 13.00 in the morning, and from 15.00 to 17.45 in the afternoon on Mondays to Thursdays, and from 08.30 to 13.00 on Fridays and Saturdays. Banks open from Monday to Friday, from 08.00 to 12.00 and from 14.00 to 18.00.

In the summer, the Tunisian administrative offices, banks and some service companies practise the non-stop working day (in operation from July onwards). At this time, staff start working very early in the morning at 07.30, and finish in the early afternoon at about 13.30...

Museums tend not to adopt these hours and are generally open morning and afternoon. The main mosques (in Tunis and Kairouan) can only be visited in the mornings, and are not open to the public on Friday, the prayer day.

Public holidays and market days

Tunisian public holidays coincide with civil celebrations, or with Muslim and Christian celebrations.

Amongst the main Tunisian civilian celebrations are: New Year's Day (1 January); 18 January (anniversary of the Revolution on 18 January 1952); 20 March (Independence Day); 9 April (Day of the Martyrs, commemoration of the events of 9 April 1938); 1 May (Labour day); 1 and 2 June (national holidays: Victory day and Youth day); 25 July (anniversary of the declaration of the Republic, 25 July 1957); 13 August (Women's day); 3 September (anniversary of the Neo Destour party); 15 October (evacuation of Bizerte by the French, 15 October 1963); 7 November, President Ben Ali's rise to power.

As it is a Muslim country, Tunisia also celebrates the many Islamic religious festivities whose dates are variable (the date is officially specified several days before the event): the Hegira New Year; Mawlid an-Nabi (the Prophet Mohammed's birthday); Id al-Adha (commemoration of Abraham's sacrifice of a lamb); Ramadan (the thirty-day fasting period whose dates are fixed yearly according to the moon). At the end of Ramadan, large celebrations are held all over the country.

Market days:
–Monday: In Aïn Draham (south of Tabarka), El Djem (Sahel), Houmt Souk (Isle of Djerba), Kairouan (centre), Mahrès (east coast, south of Sfax), Maktar (north-west of Kairouan), Mareth (south of Gabès), Tataouine (south-east).

–Tuesday: In Béja (west of Tunis), Cédikouech (Djerba Island), Ghardimaou (near to Jendouba, north-west), Kasserine (west), Ksar Hellal (near to Monastir), Menzel-Témime (Cap Bon).

–Wednesday: In Ajim (Isle of Djerba), Guellala (Isle of Djerba), Jendouba (south of Tabarka), Nefta (Djérid).

–Thursday: In Bousalem (west of Béja), Douz (Djérid), Gafsa (north of Djérid), Hammamet (Cap Bon), Houmt Souk (Isle of Djerba), Menzel Bouzelfa (Cap Bon peninsula), Siliana (south-west of Tunis), Téboursouk (west of Tunis).

–Friday: In Jemmel (near to Monastir), Jebiniana (north of Sfax), Ksour-Essaf (south of Mahdia), Mahdia (east coast, south of Moknine), Mateur (south of Bizerte), Midoun (Djerba), Nabeul (Cap Bon), Oueslatia (north of Kairouan), Rass Jebel (near to Bizerte), Sfax (east coast, south of Sousse), Tabarka (north-west coast), Testour (south-west of Tunis), Thala (north of Kasserine), Zaghouan (south of Tunis), Zarzis (near to Djerba).

–Saturday: In Ben Gardane (south of Zarzis), El Fahs (south of Tunis), El May (Isle of Djerba), Monastir (east coast), Thibar (near to Jendouba).

–Sunday: In Ajim (Isle of Djerba), Enfidaville (south of Hammamet), Fernana (north of Jendouba), Guellala (Isle of Djerba), Hammam-Lif (east of Tunis), Ksar Hellal (near to Moknine), Sfax (east coast), Sousse (east coast).

Tunisian telecommunications

Tunisian telecommunications are modern and direct. It is possible to telephone or fax from anywhere in Tunisia to Europe in excellent conditions. The cost of national and international calls is generally cheaper than in Europe.

To call Tunisia from Europe or elsewhere, dial the international dialing code, followed by 216 (the code for Tunisia), the dialing code for the given town, and then the number.

When calling from Tunisia, dial 00 (international dialing code), then the code of the required country (44 for Great Britain, 1 for the USA and Canada, 61 for Australia, 64 for New Zealand, 27 for South Africa....), the code of the town and the correspondent's phone number. In Tunis, the main post office on avenue Charles de Gaulle is open every day from 08.00 to 18.00, apart from on Sundays (09.00 to 11.00).

Medical treatment

Health care is generally good throughout Tunisia where there are 150 hospitals, polyvalent centres and dispensaries, and thirty or so clinics. Every town has satisfactory sanitary infrastructures. Moreover, foreign visitors who fall ill can be quickly treated as a doctor is especially posted to one or several of the hotels in every seaside resort (contact the reception who will call the doctor straight away).

There are also a lot of pharmacies in Tunisia (over 1,000), some of which are open 24 hours a day. If necessary, consult the lists printed each day in the main Tunisian newspapers (for example "La Presse").

In the event of a serious accident or illness, your repatriation will be covered by your holiday insurance policy taken out with your travel agent. Visitors not travelling with an agent are advised to take out their own insurance policy.

Foreign embassies

Below are the addresses of some of the embassies in Tunisia:

–*Britain*: British Consular Services, 141-143 avenue de la Liberté, Tunis, tel. 793 322; – *United States*: 144 avenue de la Liberté, 11002 Tunis, tel. 782 566; – *Canada*: 3 rue du Sénégal, Place d'Afrique, Tunis, tel. 798 004 or 796 577; – *South Africa*: BP 251 1082 Cité Mahragène, Tunis, tel. 800 311.

KEN VILLAGE

■ *On the coastal road heading southwards between Hammamet and Sousse, a village has been created in an authentic Tunisian architectural style to serve as a cultural exchange and international meeting centre.*
Ken (which means "long ago"), is a training village where young people come to learn revalued ancient artisanal techniques. Artist-creators are also welcome to come and work here, making this futuristic complex, which is nonetheless firmly rooted in traditions, a real centre of the Arts.
In addition to the craft works centre, which is Ken's living museum space regrouping pottery, weaving, carpet making, decorative woodworker, and wood painting and sculpture, there is also a modern art gallery, permanent exhibitions of goods made on site, a restaurant, a Moorish cafe, and even a pool and barbecue area where parties are organised in the evenings.

Village "Ken" – Route de Sousse km 82 – BP no. 5 – 4010 Sidi-Khlifa (Bouficha) – Tunisia – Tel. (216) 3 252 110 – Fax. (216) 3 252 112.

Riders often take place in fantasias
performed during the numerous
traditional festivities
held all over the country.

leisure and festivities

■ As the Tabarka festival slogan puts it so aptly, "Don't sunbathe idiot!".

Having said that, however, this little Mediterranean country with its innumerable beaches, warm waters, and permanently fine weather will certainly make you inclined to laze around in the sun, feet paddling in the water. Visitors should get a grip of themselves, however! Especially when they even but slightly realise the immense diversity of the leisure activities available in the country, and when they just begin to list the enormous wealth of tourist attractions. Indeed, in Tunisia, one is spoilt for choice.

Visitors can doze in the Djerba or Hammamet sun, or visit the Tunis, Sfax or Sousse medinas, hunt in the Khroumirie, or go ballooning over the Sahara. They could try coral fishing in Tabarka, or sponge fishing in the Kerkennah Islands. Others may like to go and discover the wonders of Kairouan's Islamic art. Or play a round of golf in Hammamet, go horse riding in Djerba, or listen to an opera in the El Djem coliseum...

Beaches and sun bathing

Below is a short list of Tunisia's beaches and seaside resorts classed according to the region for all sun-bathing fans:
– The "Coral Coast" in the north: the Melloula beaches (on the border with Algeria), Tabarka (large seaside resort), Berkoukech (rocky beach 9 km east of Tabarka), Jébara in Aïn Sobh, east of Cap Nègre (Sidi Mechrig beach), Cap Serrat (lovely deserted beach).
– Near to Bizerte: the Corniche beaches (seaside resort), El Rimel, Rass Jebel, Raf-Raf, Ghar el Melh, ex-Porto Farina (planned seaside resort).
– In the Tunis region: the Raouad, Gammarth, La Marsa, Amilcar, Carthage, La Goulette, Ez Zahra, Hammam-Lif beaches.
– Cap Bon: the Cédria, Sidi Raïs, Sidi Daoud, Rass Mostefa, Menzel Témime, Korba, Tazerka, Nabeul (seaside resort), Hammamet (seaside resort) beaches.
– Gulf of Hammamet: the Bou Ficha, Hergla, Sidi Bou Ali, El Kantaoui (Port El Kantaoui marina), Hammam-Sousse, Sousse, Skanès (seaside resort), Monastir, Khniss beaches.
– Around Mahdia: the Rejiche, Salakta, and Chebba beaches.
– Around Sfax: the Laouza, Sidi Mansour, Kerkennah and Nakta beaches.
– Gabès.
– Isle of Djerba: the Sidi Mahrez (seaside resort), Rass Taguerness (seaside resort), and Séguia (seaside resort) beaches.
– Zarzis (seaside resort).

Water sports

With its gentle climate, warm clear waters and 1,200 km of coastline, Tunisia is a perfect paradise for sea lovers who can enjoy a wide range of water sports here during the spring, summer and part of the autumn.

Tunisia has over 1,640,000 km^2 of territorial waters along its rocky northern coast and sandy eastern coast. *Fishing* and *scuba diving* have been practised here for ages as the two Mediterranean basins have particularly rich underwater flora and fauna. Along with the abundant fish and shell fish, it is also possible to fish for octopus (Kerkennah Islands) and to gather sponges (Gulf of Gabès) and coral (Tabarka coast).

Large diving centres have been set up for amateurs in several places along the coast, in the new Tabarka seaside resorts to the north, and in Port El Kantaoui near to Sousse. They are all affiliated to the *CMAS* (*Confédération mondiale des activités subaquatiques*) and are equipped with boats and their crews, diving monitors and specialised material (isothermal wet suits, face masks, air tanks, compressors, etc.) A diving school has also been set up at Monastir.

Addresses: *Yachting Club de Tabarka*, fishing port, tel. (08) 644 478 (the best season is from April to the end of October). *Centre international de plongée El Kantaoui*, the El Kantaoui yacht basin, Hammam-Sousse, tel. (03) 641 799. *Ecole de plongée de Monastir SHTT*, Ile des Monastères, tel. (03) 661 156.

Along the coast is a string of twenty or so ports and harbours, some of which were already used by the Phoenicians several thousand years ago.

Most have now become very busy fishing and trading ports. To cope with the increasing number of pleasure boats, Tunisia has created yacht berths in its traditional ports (Bizerte, Sidi Daoud, Kélibia, Mahdia, Sfax, Gabès, etc.) and has had several marinas built. All of these developments have been most successful as the country enjoys a longer sailing season than the northern Mediterranean thanks to its gentler climate – with an average annual temperature of 18 °C – and the scarcity of heavy winds.

The recently-built yachting ports include the Tabarka port (50 moorings and all the related services: harbour master, lift, water, quayside electricity, technical assistance), whose marina has hotels, restaurants, banks, shops, pharmacies, etc.; the Sidi Bou Saïd port (360 moorings, water, electricity, telephones, quayside fuel pumps, 26 tonne lift, technical assistance), which has hotels, restaurants, and shops in the immediate vicinity; the cape Monastir port (386 moorings, quayside berths, fresh water, electricity, a quay-side telephone and TV, a careening area, fill up station, conveniences, etc.) near to the shops, hotels and restaurants of Monastir; the Port El Kantaoui marina (300 moorings, water, electricity, quayside fuel pumps, a 40 tonne lift, harbour master, security service, ship repair yards, etc.) with a large nearby seaside resort and its hotels, restaurants, shops, golf course, banks, pharmacies, etc., and the neighbouring major town of Sousse.

Other widely practised water sports include *swimming*, either in the sea or in pools (some of Tunisia's hotels and holiday resorts have up to 4 pools!), water polo, pedalos, water skiing, windsurfing, surfing, and parasailing.

Hiking

Land sports are also very popular. Tennis is played everywhere, golf is becoming more and more widespread, and there are also the more common sports like volley ball, basket ball, boules, etc.

At present, *hiking trips* are organised by specialised travel agents in the deep Tunisian south. Trips set out from the chott el Djérid (Douz) for four to five days' walking across the Grand Erg. Northern Tunisia is also highly conducive to hiking, but hikers have to organise their own trips. From Tabarka, it is possible to climb the cork oak covered Khroumirie mountains, for example (stop off at Aïn Draham where there are hotels with wonderful panoramic views over the region.

The development of golf

Golf is a rapidly developing sport: several major courses have already been created in Tabarka in the northwest of the country, in Hammamet on Cap Bon, and at Port El Kantaoui near to Sousse on the east coast. Donald Fream, one of the top world specialists, was called upon to design the courses.

The Port El Kantaoui golf course, the oldest of the three, has already acquired an international reputation. The golf journalist Nelson Monfort wrote, "For several years now, this course has become one of those one talks about. What golfing! Set by the sea, long and windy, this course reminds you of British links with a touch of oriental charm." Today the Port El Kantaoui golf links has 27 holes with three courses (blue, red and yellow) full of obstacles. Port El Kantaoui naturally has all the relevant installments – a club house with a restaurant, bar, changing rooms, and shop – and it is possible to take lessons with experienced coaches.

In the new, fashionable seaside resort of Tabarka, a golf course has been built on 110 hectares of rolling land by the sea, where pines, cork oaks, and eucalyptus trees have been planted. There is also a school (with a nine hole course), a practice area, and a club house.

The Cytrus in Hammamet, Tunisia's most recent golf course, was inaugurated in 1992. Also designed by Donald Fream, it has 45 holes in all, and is set in a wooded landscape, with olive groves and lakes. It also has a practice area and a large club house.

In the years to come, Tunisia hopes to confirm its "golfing vocation" by creating new golf links, particularly in the south of the country on Djerba and in Tozeur.

El Kantaoui Golf Course, tel. 241 756, fax: 241 756.

Other sporting activities

Tennis courts have been built in practically all the large seaside resort hotels (Tabarka, Nabeul, Hammamet, Skanès, Djerba, etc.).

Squash, table tennis, boules, bowling, billiards, mini golf, archery, darts, swimming, cycling (mountain biking), volley ball and basket ball are also nearly always available.

In response to the demand from guests, the Tunisian hotel owners now also offer gymnasiums and training centres, with aerobics and yoga classes.

Wild boar hunting

For centuries, Tunisians have been great wild boar and game bird hunters. Over recent years, wild boar hunting has attracted more and more Europeans, particularly in the Khroumirie (Tabarka) region in the north-west of Tunisia.

Wild boar hunting, which is allowed from mid-October to the end of January, takes place in battues in the dunes, hills and mountains of the wooded Khroumirie where these animals are particularly abundant. It is not unusual for groups of 6 to 8 hunters to catch 3 or 4 wild boars in a day.

The battues are led by twenty or so Khroumir beaters whose wild boar hunting techniques are passed on from father to son. They take a good twenty dogs with them and firecrackers to scare the boar out of the densest thickets. Generally, 5 to 6 hunts take place during a day's hunting, in superb landscapes: eucalyptus woods, cork oak forests, and in the dunes by the sea. Moreover, hunters will be able to enjoy the gentle Mediterranean climate just as the winter sets in in Europe.

Nighttime leisure

Most of the hotels and holiday resorts have discos. Casinos and gaming rooms are rarer (Tunisia is a Muslim country where, in theory, betting games are forbidden by the religion). There is a casino in the Hana Palace Hotel***** in Sousse-Port El Kantaoui, however, where it is possible to play roulette and blackjack (there are also slot machines).

During the tourist season, innumerable cultural and traditional events are held all over Tunisia: jazz, rock and traditional music (*malouf*) concerts, theatrical and lyrical evenings, and festivals of all kinds.

Antique shops and art galleries

It is always a great pleasure for foreign visitors to go and dig out a splendid work of art in the innumerable antique shops and stalls dotted all over Tunisia. Amongst the "real" antique dealers is *Ayoub*, on avenue Bourguiba in Tunis. The others, especially in the souks, are really second hand dealers. Also worth discovering are the *Soussi brothers'* shops by the El Djem coliseum, which, thanks to the quantity and variety of the objects displayed, resemble true Ali Baba caverns.

As for the art galleries, these are mainly found concentrated in Tunis and its outskirts. In Tunis, visitors should first of all go to the *Musée d'art moderne* in the Belvédère park, then to the following galleries: *Gorji* (31 rue Jugurtha, Mutuelleville), *Yahia* (avenue Mohamed V), *Galerie de l'Information* (avenue Habib Bourguiba), *Galerie de la Médina* (Dar Bouderbala, 11, rue Dar El Jeld), *L'Air Libre* (avenue Ouled Hafouz), and the *Maison de la Culture Ibn Rachiq* (20, avenue de Paris). Other galleries include: the *Chérif Fine Art gallery* in Sidi Bou Saïd, Kalysté (29 bis La Soukra), and *Sophosnibe* in Carthage, and *Mille Feuilles* on La Marsa beach.

Thalassotherapy centres

The Abou Nawas Boujaafar Hotel**** in Sousse, has opened Tunisia's first thalassotherapy centre which has sea water pools and a whole team of therapists and specialised fitness equipment (multi jets,

Tunisian souks are true Ali Baba caverns
where the delighted foreign visitor
can purchase many goods.

underwater massage baths, power and spray showers, bubbling gymnastic pools, massage booths, mud and algae treatment). This centre offers numerous kinds of treatments: thalassotherapy, beauty therapy, algatherapy, fitness and anti-stress treatments, biomarine therapy and relaxation, post-natal therapy and dieting... Other thalassotherapy centres should soon open in Hammamet and Gammarth.

Thermal spas

Tunisia has a lot of thermal springs, especially in the mountainous, humid north of the country. Some have been developed and opened to patients who come to take the waters in their establishments under medical supervision.

Hammam Bourguiba, between Tabarka and Aïn Draham, has three springs – which were already used by the Romans – whose hot (50 °C at the surface), sulphurous, sodic and slightly chloridic are especially recommended for treating inflammatory, infectious or allergic chronic upper respiratory system afflictions and predominantly catarrhal bronchi problems.

In *Korbous* (Cap Bon peninsula), the hot radioactive springs treat afflictions including chronic rheumatism and arthritis, osteo-articulatory traumas, and some nervous system afflictions.

In *Jebel Oust* (Zaghouan), the spa treats afflictions including rheumatism, post osteo-articulatory traumas, and arthritic diatheses.

INNUMERABLE FESTIVALS

■ *Innumerable festivals take place all year round in Tunisia. The International Festival of Hammamet in August and the biannual "Journées Cinématographiques de Carthage" in October are the most famous.*
Here is the programme of other festivals:
– March: the Nabeul orange festival (Cap Bon peninsula). The ksour festival in Tataouine.
– April: the Tamerza festival (mountain oasis west of Gafsa-Metlaoui). The Ulysses (Odysseus) festival in Djerba.
– June: International malouf festival in Testour (between Tunis and Le Kef). Menzel Témime national festival of amateur musicians (Cap Bon). In Dougga, classical theatre in the Roman amphitheatre by the Comédie Française. The sparrowhawk festival in Haouaria (Cap Bon). Thoroughbred Arabian horse festival in Meknassy.
– July: Tabarka Coral festival (music, craft workshops, conférences). Béja summer festival. Regional festival of music and popular arts in Béja. Kef Bou Makhlouf festival. Hammamet festival (in the international cultural centre: modern European theatre). Hammamet festival of the child. Nabeul comic arts

a thousand souvenirs

■ Tunisia is a real Ali Baba's cavern for all those who like browsing. The extremely developed craft work sector has kept the great Arab tradition of what in the past were called the "minor arts" alive: jewellery making and silversmithing, woodwork, brass making, weaving, basketry, pottery, glass making, forging, etc. Although a few large, specialised craft work centres do exist (like the carpet making centre in Kairouan, and the Nabeul ceramics centre), visitors need not necessarily go there to buy their goods as they can be found on sale throughout most of the country in the souks, the big Office national d'artisanat shop-stores, and the hotel and airport boutiques.

It is as enjoyable to bargain for a wonderful item in the souk stalls as to see it being made in the innumerable craft workshops that flourish in nearly all the Tunisian agglomerations.

Buying carpets is always a favorite with foreign tourists as they are a lot cheaper than in Europe. In the large shop-stores there is a choice between the large Kairouan wool and silk carpets (bulky, but the traders can send them by plane), and the *kilims, mergoums,* chales, and Berber dyed cloth which is meant to be hung on walls rather than lain on the floor. This cloth is made notably in the south in Gafsa, the Djérid oases, Matmata and in Djerba.

Be warned! The work is paid for by the number of knot stitches per square metre. Most of the usual carpets have between 10 and 20,000 knots per m^2, and a silk carpet 250,000 per m^2. Every carpet officially sold in the large shop-stores bears the government's stamp which acts as a label guaranteeing its authenticity.

Weaving and embroidery

In Mahdia, a little port on the east coast near to Monastir, silk is still woven, and in Rass Jebel (near to Bizerte), the "petites mains" (little

festival. Menzel Témime national festival of amateur musicians (Cap Bon). The Dar Chaâbane summer festival (Cap Bon). The sea festival of Tazerka (Cap Bon). The Plastic arts days in Kélibia (Cap Bon). Festivals of dance and music in Carthage and El Djem (jazz, opera, popular music). Sidi El Kantaoui festival (Hammam-Sousse). International festival of Sousse. Monastir festival. Kerkennah Islands' festival. Tapaca-Gabès festival (music, folklore and camel races).
—August: Tabarka coral festival. Wheat festival in Béja. Béja summer festival. Nabeul comic arts festival. Menzel Témime national festival of amateur musicians (Cap Bon). Vine festival in Grombalia (Cap Bon). Hammam Ghezaz-Kerkouane cultural festival (Cap Bon). El Mida festival (Cap Bon).
—September: Zerda de Sidi el Bechir in Bizerte (1st Thursday). Bulla Regia festival. Vine festival of Grombalia (Cap Bon).
—December: Douz Sahara festival. Tozeur, Nefta and Degache international oasis festival (chott el Djérid oasis). Mediterranean olive festival in Kalaâ Kébira (near to Sousse). Olive harvest festival in Djerba.

hands) are experts in traditional embroidery. Usually using silver or gold thread, they still embroider the sumptuous wedding dresses. Many of them also embroider tablecloths, napkins, place mats and bedspreads.

In the past, the Maghrebi leather goods makers used to essentially make babouche slippers, leather book covers, boxes, poufs and harness. Nowadays, with the development of transportation, they have partly reconverted to making travel items like bags, purses, and cases which are sold in all the souks.

Leatherwork and basketry

Esparto grass – the long grass found growing in North Africa – is not only used for making paper paste. Artisans in the Djérid region also use it for basketry, weaving mats and baskets. Cane is also used for making baskets, mats, place mats, bread baskets, etc.

Woodwork, cabinet-making

One unusual craft is briar pipe making in Tabarka. In this region of the Khroumirie, olive trees are abundant, and their wood is used for making lots of little wooden bits and bobs.

Traditional cabinet-makers working for rich Tunisian families left a heritage of superb polychrome carved wooden alcove fronts and low tables, not to mention the precious wood furniture, tables, and desks, inlaid with ivory or mother-of-pearl that can now only be found in the antique stores.

Ceramics and pottery

Artisanal and now semi-industrialised ceramic production is simply overflowing in Nabeul, the terracotta capital. Fine quality goods are found alongside with the junk, however, so you will need a keen eye to pick out a traditionally made object with suitably subdued colours and carefully painted designs amidst the mountains of ceramic tiles, crockery, vases and flower pots.

This same attention is necessary in Djerba (Guellala village where there are pots, water jugs, vases, plates, etc), or when choosing Berber pottery in Sejnane in the north between Bizerte and Tabarka (polychrome terracotta statuettes representing figures and camels).

Metalwork and jewellery

Engraved, chased, or embossed, smiths work copper into a wide choice of traditional and modern objects ranging from classic engraved trays to souvenir ashtrays, cauldrons and tea and coffeepots.

It is still possible to find some wonderful old Berber jewellery in the souks and in the antique shops, including necklaces, bracelets, pendants, silver headbands set off with enamel, amber, or coloured glass. Coins and lucky Hands of Fatima are often attached to this jewellery.

Arabic calligraphy

The Arabic calligraphers, who are great masters of arabesque art, transcribe the *sura* from the Koran on paper or ceramic tiles. A few examples of this astonishingly elegant work can be found in antique stalls.

Glass painting

Glass painting, which is very popular throughout the Mediterranean basin, found many practitioners in the Muslim countries. Using bright colours and a naive style, artists generally illustrated scenes of the Prophet's life.

This art developed in Sfax, where studios still perpetrate the technique today. A lot of reproductions of the old small glass mounts can be found in the souks, but unfortunately their mass production does nothing for their charm.

Modern art and antiques

A number of contemporary artists, who mainly paint on easels, live in Tunis and Sidi Bou Saïd. Their works – exhibited in the art galleries in the square – are often highly attractive and are reasonably priced. Do not hesitate to buy them therefore.

In Tunisia, there are both antique and second hand dealers. As visitors push open the doors of their shops and bric-a-brac stores, they will find a large assortment of old goods and curios that will appeal to all tastes: furniture, weapons, jewellery, numerous copies of Roman and Carthaginian coins, terracotta oil lamps and ancient mosaics.

Food products

In the autumn when dates are harvested, visitors can bring back boxes full of the delicious *deglet nour* ("fingers of light") variety produced in the southern oases of Tozeur, Nefta and Douz, and sold in all the grocers' stores in the country. Visitors with a sweet tooth can buy boxes of dates stuffed with almonds all year round (made by the company "La Princess Sarra", Cité de la Gazelle, Tunis).

Delicious, sometimes strange flavoured syrups – rose, grenadine, violet, pistachio, and banana – are artisanally made in Tozeur.

Oil, spices and wine

Given that this is the "land of the olive tree", it would be a shame not to bring back a bottle of good olive oil, having watched olives being harvested and pressed in one of the groves. This is a general science lesson certainly worth seeing, especially as there are presses more or less all over Tunisia.

Another top-quality food product is the wine (see chapter "The food"). In Tunis's supermarkets and grocers stores it is possible to buy a good bottle of *Thibar, Château Feriani* or *Mornag* so that friends at home can savour this tasty nectar (be warned! customs only allow one to two bottles per person).

Spices are also a speciality in all the sunny Mediterranean countries. In the souks one is spoilt for choice: cumin, saffron, nutmeg, cloves, pepper, etc. (be sure to note the name of the spice as you buy it and ask how to use it).

Diverse

The Sidi Bou Saïd wire bird cages shaped like mosque cupolas have become one of the best known items of Tunisian craft work. Also worth bringing back are sponges from the Kerkennah islands or Djerba, bottles of orange flower water or essential perfume oils, stuffed animals (snakes, insects, scorpions, etc.), and minerals (gypsum flowers, etc.).

● **A few addresses :** *Carpets*: souk des Turcs in the Tunis medina: "Palais d'Orient", "Palais Oriental", "Musée des Turcs". Shops in Sidi Bou Saïd. Bizerte old port's craft shops. Hammamet medina. The Kairouan shops: "Tapis des Princes", place de la Grande Mosquée, tel. (07) 20 755, and "Chiraz", "Ben Hassine" workshop, avenue Ibn Jazzar, tel. (07) 220 796. In El Djem: "Soussi Frères", place du Colisée, tel. (03) 690 376. The Midoun and Houmt Souk souks in Djerba. The Tozeur stalls. *Leather goods*: Tunis, Nabeul, Djerba souks. *Wooden furniture (caskets, bed ends)*: "Soussi Frères" in El Djem. *Ceramics and pottery*: the Nabeul shops. In Djerba: "Ben Mahmoud Romdhan", Guellala, tel. (05) 56 021. The Midoun and Houmt Souk souks. *Metalwork*: the Tunis medina souks. *Jewellery* : souks and antique shops. *Calligraphy*: antique shops. *Glass paintings*: antique shops and souks. *Modern art* : Tunis and Sidi Bou Saïd galleries. *Antiques*: "Ayoub", avenue Bourguiba in Tunis, "Soussi Frères" in El Djem. *Fruit and syrups*: "Paradis" in Tozeur. *Olive oil*: in supermarkets, grocers' or at the producers' (Sfax region). *Wine*: in the supermarkets or at the vineyards. *Spices* : in the Tunis medina souks. *Philately*: the kiosques on avenue Bourguiba and in the Tunis central post office. *Bird cages*: the Sidi Bou Saïd shops. *Sponges*: the Djerba souks in Houmt Souk and Midoun. *Perfumes*: souk El Attarine in the Tunis medina. *Stuffed animals and minerals*: little stalls in the Midès, Tamerza, Chebika, Tozeur and Nefta oases.

bibliography

GENERAL WORKS

La Grande Encyclopédie du Monde, volume 10 « Afrique » (éd. Atlas).
Atlas des civilisations africaines (éd. Nathan).
Le Sahara, Jean-Claude Klotzkoff (ACTT/ Livresud/ NEA Togo).
La Tunisie, Michel Camau (Que sais-je ? n° 318, PUF).
Grand livre de la Tunisie (éd. du Jaguar/ JA).

ART, CRAFTS AND TRADITIONS

Islamic Art, DT Rice. 1965.
L'Art islamique, Bassin méditerranéen, Hayat Salam Liebich (La Grammaire des styles/ Flammarion).
Le musée du Bardo, Aïcha Abed Ben Khader (Cérès éditions, Tunis).
Klee en Tunisie, Jean Duvignaud (Cérès productions, Tunis).
Maisons de Sidi Bou Saïd, Ashraf Azzouz and David Massey (Dar Ashrah éditions, Tunis).
The Diaries of Paul Klee, 1898-1918, Paul Klee. 1964.

HISTORY AND POLITICS

A History of the Maghrib, Jamil M. Abun-Nasr. 2nd edition, 1975.
Carthage, BH Warmington. Revised edition 1969.
Daily Life in Carthage at the Time of Hannibal, C. Charles Picard. 1961.
Histoire de l'Afrique, Robert Cornevin (éd. Payot).
La Légende de Carthage (Découvertes/ Gallimard n° 172).
Histoire, Polybius (La Pléiade, Gallimard).
Histoire des Juifs de Tunisie. Des origines à nos jours, Paul Sebag (éd. L'Harmattan).
Histoires, Tacitus (Folio/Gallimard).
Histoire des Berbères et des dynasties musulmanes de l'Afrique septentrionale, Ibn Khaldun (éd. Geunthner, Paris, 1925).
Histoire des Beni Hilal et de ce qui leur advint dans la marche vers l'ouest, Micheline Galley and Abderrahman Ayoub (bilingual French/ Arabic version, Classiques Africains, librairie Armand Colin).
Histoire de l'Afrique du Nord, Charles-André Julien (éd. Payot).
Les Phéniciens, A. Parrot, Chéhab, Moscati (L'Univers des formes/ Gallimard).
North West Africa: A Political and Economic Survey, Wilfred Knapp (ed). 3rd edition 1977
On the Eve of Colonialism: North Africa Before the French Conquest, Lucette Valensi. 1977.
Studies in Islamic History and Institutions, SD Goitein. 1966.
The World of the Phoenicians, Sabatino Moscati. 1968.
Carthage, le rêve en flammes, European writers' most beautiful work dedicated to the Punic town (éd. de l'Omnibus).
Sheïba, l'antique Suffetula, Fathi Béjaoui (éd. de l'Agence nationale du patrimoine).
Les Ruines de Dougga, Claude Poinssot (Ministère des affaires culturelles, Institut national d'archéologie et d'art, Tunis).

EUROPEAN LITERATURE

Odyssey, Homer (Penguin Classics).
Aeneid, Virgil (Penguin Classics).
L'Âne d'or ou les Métamorphoses, Apuleius (Folio/ Gallimard).
Confessions, Saint Augustine (Folio/Gallimard).
Complete Theatrical Works (Andria, Hecyra, Heauton, Timoroumenos, Eunuchus, Phormio and *Adelphoe),* Terence. (Penguin Classics).
Salammbô, Gustave Flaubert (Folio/Gallimard).
Le Prince Jaffar, Georges Duhamel (éd. Mercure de France).
Le Journal des Henderson, Catherine Hermary-Vieille (Folio/Gallimard).
Le Camp Domineau, Pierre Mac Orlan (éd. Gallimard).

TUNISIAN LITERATURE

Anthologie des écrivains maghrébins d'expression française (Présence africaine).
Voix (éd. François Maspéro).
La statue de sel (éd. Gallimard), *Le portrait du colonisateur et du colonisé* (éd. Buchet-Chastel), *Le Portrait d'un Juif* (éd. Gallimard), Albert Memmi.

TRAVEL JOURNALS

– Arab travellers:
Description de l'Afrique septentrionale, El Békri (librairie Adrien Maisonneuve, Paris).
Voyages, Ibn Battuta (éd. Anthropos, Paris).
– European travellers:
Voyages dans les régences de Tunis et d'Alger (au XVIIIᵉ siècle), J.A. Peyssonnel (La Découverte).
De Tunis à Kairouan, Guy de Maupassant (éd. Ibn Charaf, Tunis).
Alexandre Dumas à Tunis (éd. Ibn Charaf, Tunis).
Journal, André Gide (éd. Gallimard).
La Force des choses, Simone de Beauvoir (Livre de Poche).
Notes de route, Maroc, Algérie, Tunisie, Isabelle Eberhardt.

RELIGION

Le Coran (éd. de Jaguar/ JA).
Mahomet, la parole d'Allah (Découvertes/ Gallimard n° 22).
Mahomet et la tradition islamique, Émile Dermenghem (Microcosmes/ Seuil).
What Is Islam?, Chris Horrie and Peter Chippindale. Star Editions, 1990.

ETHNOLOGY

Tribes of the Sahara, Lloyd Cabot Briggs. 1960.
Les Berbères, Jean Servier (Que sais-je ? n° 718, PUF).
Traditions et civilisations berbères, J. Jernier.
Chebika, Jean Duvignaud, sociological survey in one of southern Tunisia's little mountain oases (Terre Humaine/ Plon).
L'Oubli de la Cité, J. Dakhalia (survey in a Djérid oasis).

ECONOMY

Atlaseco, Atlas économique mondial (éd. du Sérail).
Annuaire Jeune Afrique (éd. JA).
Economic Development in Tunisia, Ghazi Duiraji. 1979
Tunisie (collection « Un Marché », CFCE-Centre français du commerce extérieur).

JOURNALS/MAGAZINES

Jeune Afrique.
Afrique Magazine.
Qantara, cultures en mouvement (published by the Institut du Monde Arabe in Paris).

vocabulary

■ Arabic and French are commonly spoken in Tunisia. Below are some Arabic and French phrases.

Time

today: aujourd'hui: *al-youm*
yesterday: hier: *a mess*
the day before yesterday: avant-hier: *wal amess*
tomorrow: demain: *ghodwa*
the day after tomorrow: après-demain: *bâd ghodwa*
evening: soir: *al-achia*
afternoon: après-midi: *bâd edhohr*
soon: bientôt: *karib*
always: toujours: *dima*
never: jamais: *abadann*
quickly: vite: *fissa*
slowly: lentement: *bech-chouia*

Days of the week

Monday: lundi: *al-ithneye-ne*
Tuesday: mardi: *athoulatha*
Wednesday: mercredi: *al-arrbiâ*
Thursday: jeudi: *al-khamiss*
Friday: vendredi: *al-joumoua*
Saturday: samedi: *as-sabtt*
Sunday: dimanche: *al-ahad*

Numbers

zero: zéro: *sifr*
one: un: *wà-had*
two: deux: *itnéyn*
three: trois: *thlàta*
four: quatre: *arbà*
five: cinq: *khamsa*
six: six: *sitta*
seven: sept: *sàbâ*
eight: huit: *thmania*
nine: neuf: *tissâ*
ten: dix: *âchra*
eleven: onze: *ihdàch*
twelve: douze: *ithnàch*
thirteen: treize: *tlàtàch*
fourteen: quatorze: *arbatàch*
fifteen: quinze: *khamstàch*
sixteen: seize: *sittàch*
seventeen: dix-sept: *sabâtàch*
eighteen: dix-huit: *thmanntàch*
nineteen: dix-neuf: *tissâtàch*
twenty: vingt: *ichrrine*
thirty: trente: *thlâtine*
forty: quarante: *arrbà-ine*
fifty: cinquante: *khamsine*
sixty: soixante: *sittine*
seventy: soixante-dix: *sabì-ine*
eighty: quatre-vingts: *thmànine*
ninety: quatre-vingt-dix: *tissi-ine*
one hundred: cent: *mi-a*
two hundred: deux cents: *mitene*
one thousand: mille: *alf*
a million: un million: *melyoun*

Common phrases

yes: oui: *na-ame*
no: non: *laa*
very good: très bien: *taïb*
who is it?: qui est-ce?: *mane?*
what's your name?: comment t'appelles-tu?: *ich ismek?*
please: s'il vous plaît: *min faddhlek*
thank you: merci: *barak alahou fik*
excuse me: pardon: *samâhni*
what time is it?: quelle heure est-il?: *kaddach el-wakt*
I don't understand: je ne comprends pas: *mâ nefhemch*
yesterday: hier: *el-bareh*
Where is...?: Où est...?: *fîn...?*
on the left: à gauche: *allissar*
on the right: à droite: *allimîne*
straight on: tout droit: *imchi toul*
nearby: près: *kerîb*
far: loin: *biîd*

Greetings

hello: bonjour: *sabah el khir*
good evening: bonsoir: *tasbah âla khir*
good bye: au revoir: *beslama*
welcome: bienvenue: *marhaba*
how are you?: comment allez-vous?: *kif halek?*
very well, thank you: très bien, merci: *taïb-alham dou-lillah*
good: bien: *la bess*

Travel

ticket: billet: *tiskra*
exchange: change: *tabdil leflouss*
customs: douane: *diwâna*
train: train: *trîno*
car: voiture: *karhba*
airplane: avion: *tayâra*
airport: aéroport: *matâr*
departure: départ: *mâchye-(khroûj)*
arrival: arrivée: *jey-dkhoul*
delay: retard: *taâkhîr*

Eating

lunch: déjeuner: *leftour*
dinner: dîner: *la'acha*
glass: verre *kass*
knife: couteau: *es-essekkîna*
fork: fourchette: *el-fourchîta*
spoon: cuillère: *el-megharfa*
meat: viande: *elham*
chicken: poulet: *ddjaj*
lamb: mouton: *allouch*
beef: bœuf: *bagri*
tea: thé: *tey*

coffee: café: *qahwa*
fruit: fruit: *ghalla*
ice cream: glace: *jilate*

Emergencies

hospital: hôpital: *sbitar*
doctor: médecin: *tbib*
pharmacy: pharmacie: *sbissiria*
policeman: policier: *boulissi*
police station: commissariat: *merkez chorta*
firemen: pompiers: *asker lahriqua*

Shopping

how much is it?: combien ça coûte?: *keddach?*
it's too expensive: c'est trop cher: *yasser ghali*
tobacconist: tabac: *hanout doukhân*
grocer's: épicerie: *'attâr*
shop: magasin: *maghaza*
gold: or: *dhebab*
silver: argent: *foddha*
terracotta: terre cuite: *tîn*
silk: soie: *h'rir*
cotton: coton: *k'tonn*

carpet: tapis: *zarbia*
pottery: poterie: *fokhkhar*
basket: panier: *qoffa*
jewellery: bijoux: *syagha*
price: prix: *essoum*
bookshop: librairie: *koutbia*
newspaper: journal: *jarida*
book: livre: *ktab*

Terminology

aïn: spring, fountain
bab: gate
chott: a depression filled with salty swamps (*sebkha*)
kasbah: fortified district or town
dar: house
douar: village, nomadic camp
jamaâ: mosque
ksar: (plural: *ksour*): fortified village
medina: old town
oued: river
riad: garden
ribat: fortified monastery
sahel: the shore
sebkha: salty swamp
seguia: canal
souk: open-air market
zawiyya: marabout's headquarters.

Top left: bricks and briouats.
Top right: mechouia salad.
Bottom left: lamb and vegetable couscous.
Bottom right: fish dish.

the food

■ Like all countries in the Mediterranean basin, Tunisia offers a "sun cuisine", based mainly on olive oil, spices, tomatoes, seafood (a wide range of fish) and meat from rearing (lamb).

Breakfast

The foreign visitor's average day begins with breakfast, which will not normally be served in bed. Visitors now tend to go down to the hotel restaurant where a large and particularly copious buffet is set up for part of the morning. Clients will find tea or coffee, baskets full of croissants, pains au chocolate, and cake along with carafes full of home-made fresh lemon and orange juice. Fine slices of ham, galantine and Dutch cheese are arranged on trays, and there are also large baskets of fruit (oranges, bananas, and, when they are in season, dates). Finally, there are delicious Tunisian-made fruit yoghurts, boiled and scrambled eggs. After this good start to the day, visitors will be ready to go to the beach or valiantly begin their visit.

Shortly before lunch, it is common to have an aperitif – alcoholic or non-alcoholic (anisette, beer, fresh fruit juice) – with the "*kemia*" (an assortment of pistachio, peanuts, broad beans, olives and various vegetables either fresh or pickled).

Lunch

Tourists busy visiting may prefer simply to grab a bite to eat at lunchtime. In Tunisia there are innumerable little open-air food stalls, cabins, and caravans selling typically Tunisian fast food: the copious and delicious Tunisian sandwiches filled with tuna, hard-boiled egg, peppers, diced tomatoes and onions, dressed with olive oil and a touch of hot spicy harissa sauce.

If you do not want to stand eating in the sun, you can always buy a drink at a nearby café and ask if you

The highly varied Tunisian dishes are part of the Mediterranean "sun cuisine", which is certainly worth discovering when on holiday in the country. The Dar el Jeld restaurant palace in the Tunis medina (above) is one of the best restaurants for discovering Tunisia's wonderful cuisine.

can eat your sandwich there...

If you have a little more time to spare, it is possible to find good restaurants serving Tunisian food. A typical menu will include the following hors-d'œuvre: *briks* (a kind of thin pancake filled with spinach or mashed potato and soft-boiled egg), *slata mechouia* (tuna and hard-boiled eggs with peppers and diced tomatoes, onion, and grilled garlic), delicious Kerkennah Island octopus salads, Tabarka and Gabès prawn salads, and chick pea soup (*lablabi*), noodle soup (*hlalim*), fresh vegetable soup and Sfax fish soup (*marqa sfaxiya*).

Fish dishes

Thanks to its long coastline and numerous fishing ports, Tunisia can serve a most abundant, varied and exceptionally fresh supply of fish in its restaurants. Before ordering, restaurant owners will usually show you a large plate of fish including red mullet, sole, mackerel, grouper, sea perch, cod, tuna, octopus, etc.

Many fish lovers will be happy to have their fish simply grilled and served filleted or sliced with lemon juice and a little olive oil. Fish can also be baked, fried in olive oil, stuffed, seasoned with cumin (*kamoun*), however. Squid, cuttle fish, and octopus are often served in hot crispy batter with slices of lemon.

The most sought-after speciality is *poisson complet*: the fish you choose is prepared, fried, grilled or sauted (whichever way you choose), accompanied by chips and either normal or spicy *tastira*, depending on the kind of peppers used in the dish. The peppers are grilled with a little tomato, a lot of onion and a little garlic, all of which is finely chopped and served with a poached egg.

Traditional dishes

Like in the rest of North Africa, *couscous* is served on all occasions. It is traditionally eaten with lamb, the semolina must be very fine, and the vegetables (carrots, little white cabbages, turnips, chick peas) only lightly cooked. Depending on the season, the vegetables change: there may also be cardoons, cold broad beans, or pumpkin.

Couscous can also be made with chicken or fish or *osben*, a kind of round sausage made with tripe and various herbs. Different spices are found depending on the region, like cinnamon (*kerfa*) or dried and crushed rose buds (*chouch el ward*).

Sweetened semolina with dried raisins and dates makes a special dessert (*mesfouf*) served with a glass of cold milk.

Tajines are nothing like Moroccan tajines. In Tunisia, they are egg based dishes with chopped meat prepared like a large cake. Cooked in the oven, they can be seasoned with parsley, cheese or grilled peppers (the most common).

Visitors will also be able to try shoulder of lamb with potato (*koucha bil aallouch*), and meat balls (*kaftagi*) with tomato and fried peppers, which are either very spicy or served with mint (*bnadaq*). A great deal of dishes are egg-based: *chakchouka*, a kind of ratatouille provençale made with peppers, tomatoes, and egg; *ojja*, a kind of scrambled egg dish with a little tomato and garlic with chopped up merguez sausage or brains.

Finally, some of the most typical Tunisian dishes will only be found if visitors are lucky enough to have some Tunisian friends who will make them. These include *melthouth*, which is grilled barley served with meat or fish, *mloukhia*, veal stew with powdered *corète* which makes a delicious unusual dark green sauce (*).

Desserts

There are innumerable kinds of desserts ranging from honey cakes stuffed with *makhroud* dates (a Kairouan speciality) to fresh figs, chick pea flour cakes, *brick* layers with almonds and honey (*baklawa*) which are found more or less everywhere, *bouza* (hazelnut or sorghum cream and grilled sesame seeds) served during the Ramadan meals, and *assida*, a thick flour cream and grilled pine seeds, and, depending on the means at hand, pistachio, hazelnuts and pine kernels. These sweets are rarely eaten at the end of the meal, but a little later on in the day with mint tea, or when people visit or meet each other.

Drinks

With the exception of palm wine (*lagmi*), Tunisia's wines come from the northern region's vineyards of Haut Mornag (red, white, rosé), Koudiat (red, white, rosé), Saint-Cyprien (red), Thibar (red, white), Tardi (red) and the Carthage, Hassen Bey and Kélibia muscats.

Numerous springs produce top-quality mineral water, for example Safia, Aïn Garci, Selma, Jetkiss, Zulel. During the summer a lot of fresh fruit drinks are drunk, notably orange and lemon juice. One could not forget to mention the traditional mint tea, sometimes served with pine kernels.

Some good restaurants

In Tunis: *Dar El Jeld*, on the way out of the Medina, near to the Place du Gouvernement. Set in an ancient palace, refined traditional cuisine, business dinners and Ramadan meals (5 rue Dar-El-Djed, La Kasbah, tel.: 260 916). *L'Astragale* at the foot of the Belvédère park, a most beautiful ochre-coloured villa with an unusual garden and delicious French cuisine (17 avenue Charles-Nicolle, tel. 890 455), *Baghdad*, *César*, *Chez Nous*, *La Mamma* (good Italian restaurant/pizzeria). In the cheaper price range are the little restaurants in the Medina (the Central Mosque vaulted passage).

In La Goulette: *Au Vert-Galant* (tel. 735 452), *L'Avenir* (tel. 735 758/154), *Le Café vert* (tel. 736 156), three of the best of the innumerable fish restaurants, with a vast terrace overlooking Avenue Franklin-Roosevelt (tel. 735 452).

In Carthage: *Neptune*. *La Reine Didon* (tel. 733 433).

In Sidi Bou Saïd: *Dar Zarrouk*, tel. 740 591 (set in the bougainvillea with a terrace overlooking the whole Tunis bay).

In Gammarth-La Marsa: *Le Grand Bleu* (fish specialities, a terrace with a magical view over the bay of Tunis), *Le Bon Vieux temps*, *Les Coquillages*, *Les Dunes* (with a terrace overlooking the sea), *Lagon, Vague, Le Golf, Koubet El Hawa, Les Trois Perles* (tel. 271 409).

In Hammamet: *Les trois Moutons, Chez Achour, Pomodoro*. On the medina ramparts: *Barberousse, La Médina*, touristy restaurants (international cuisine), but a splendid view over Hammamet and its bay.

In Sousse: *Le Lido, Le Bonheur, Malouf, Le Gourmet, Restaurant des Sportifs*.

In Sfax: *Le Corail* (three forks), an excellent fish restaurant in the town centre with a pleasant, comfortable decor.

In Djerba: *Haroun*.

In Tozeur: *Le Petit Prince, Restaurant du Dar Chraïet*.

And some remarkable cafés

In Tunis: *Café de Paris* (avenue Bourguiba, the unavoidable rendez-vous spot in Tunis), *la Rotonde* (Galerie du Colisée, for the picturesque). In the Medina: *le Tourbet*, with its mosque decor.

In Nabeul: in the Grand Rue, *l'Errachidia*, an island of beauty in a sea of unsightliness.

In Sidi Bou Saïd: *Café des Nattes*, became famous after being frequented by such celebrities as André Gide and Simone de Beauvoir; *Sidi Chebaane*, bars with terraces overlooking the leisure boat port.

In Sfax: *Diwan*, a café with a terrace set in the medina ramparts near to the Bab Diwan gate.

In Tozeur: *Paradis*, set in the heart of a superb garden.

In La Marsa: *Chez Salem*, with its famous ice creams.

(*)*Les merveilles de la cuisine africaine*, Éditions du Jaguar, Paris.

accommodation

■ Over the last few decades, Tunisia has made extraordinary efforts to develop its hotel network, to such an extent even that Tunisia now offers some 156,000 beds, 12,000 of which were built in 1994 alone.

These somewhat dry statistics do not convey a sense of the variety and quality of the hotels built. A tour around the country will enable visitors to appreciate that the services of talented Tunisian architects and designers have been called upon. In the major holiday resorts of Djerba or Hammamet, for example, developers have not sought to build quickly, constructing great concrete blocks.

Talented architects

On the contrary, the architects have taken inspiration from the great traditions of Islamic art, multiplying the cupolas and interior patios found in the mosques and Tunisian palaces, landscaping gardens and usually using fine traditional materials – marble, ceramic tiles, carved and painted wood –, whilst integrating the most up-to-date equipment (air conditioning, bathroom facilities, electric appliances, pools).

Converted traditional buildings

In addition to this, numerous traditional buildings have been converted and developed into hotels. In the Tunis medina, an ancient palace has been converted into a youth hostel; on Djerba, *fondouks* (caravanserais) and *menzels* (traditional patricians' residences) have been turned into accommodation, as has the old *medersa* near to the beautiful little Sidi Bou Makhlouf mosque in the Kef. As for the deep Tunisian south, there are some even more unusual hotels in the Matmata troglodytic habitations and the *ghorfas* (granaries) and *ksour* (fortified villages) of the Tataouine region.

As a result, Tunisia now offers a

SOME CHARMING OR UNUSUAL HOTELS

■ *Charming hotels:*
– *Tamerza Palace, in the Tamerza mountain oasis (near to Tozeur, in the deep Tunisian south). As the hotel is perched high up on the mountain side, its rooms, terrace (with a pool) and panoramic restaurant enjoy a superb view of the oued and the vestiges of the ancient village set in the palm grove. At night, the view from the restaurant is quite magical as the ancient village below is lit up.*
– *The **Abou Nawas** chain hotels (in Tunis, Sfax, Sousse, Djerba, Gammarth, Tozeur, Hammamet, Port El Kantaoui, Tabarka, Mahdia, Monastir) are all classed in the 3 to 5 star category due to their refined comfort and quality of service.*
– *The **Lac** on Avenue Mohamed-V in Tunis. Hated by some, loved by others, this strange boat or harmonica shaped building is one of the best examples of the Tunisian avant-garde architects' creativity. Very well situated and most comfortable, it is most pleasant to stay in, thanks to the quality of the service and the facilities at the clients' disposal.*
– ***Yati Beach** in Djerba. Modern architecture inspired by the traditions of Islamic art.*
– ***Club Sangho** in Tataouine. Set in the heart of the arid and stony djebels, it is an oasis of calmness and refinement in the*

great deal of new or renovated hotels with a wide range of amenities (bars, restaurants, shops, conference rooms, pools, tennis courts, discos, etc.). These hotels are of all types and categories ranging from five-star palaces in town centres, little family-style boarding houses and modest camps to hotel-clubs, resort villages, apartment hotels, marinas, and even camping and caravaning sites.

Quality for everyone

What is so wonderful is that the majority of these establishments are within the range of most European tourists' budgets, as the value-for-money ratio of this immense hotel network is practically unbeatable.

Which other major tourist destination in the Mediterranean basin can offer a week's holiday in high class hotels (air travel included) during peak periods for under about £350?

The quality of the service

In addition to the price and the beautiful architecture, foreign visitors will appreciate the quality of the service offered in the Tunisian hotels.

Combining their natural kindness with an open-mindedness forged by centuries of exchange with the whole world, the Tunisians provide the hotel network with staff who are particularly qualified and efficient in receiving the public.

These days, in the entrance halls of the Tunisian hotels Germans, Italians, French, Japanese, Arabs, etc. are welcomed in their own language with a traditional fruit juice cocktail. This kind of reception is common whether in the « Abou Nawas » hotels in Sfax or Tunis, the « Iberotel » in Tabarka, the « Assalama » in Tunis (« Grand Hôtel du Lac ») or in the « Club Sangho » in Zarzis or Tataouine, or in the « Continental » in Tozeur.

---

magnificent ksour region (traditional citadels).
*– The **Majestic** in Tunis. A great white Twenties-style sugar loaf dating back to the colonial era, with a restaurant and bar on the terrace overlooking Avenue de Paris.*
*– **Sufetula** in Sbeïtla. Wonderful view over the remains of the Roman town.*
*– **L'Auberge de Jeunesse** in the Tunis Medina, set in the former Dar Saïda Ajoula palace.*
*– **Dar Saïd** in Sidi Bou Saïd, an islet of charm and beauty.*

Unusual addresses:
*– **Ksar Hadada,** set in an authentic ksar (fortress) in the Tataouine-Médenine region. Each "ghorfa" (granary) has been converted into a room. The interior courtyard is a maze of little terraces and steep stairways reminiscent of a modern-day theatre set.*
*– **Sidi Driss** in Matmata. Now abandoned by their former inhabitants, these troglodytic dwellings at the bottom of an man-made crater have been converted into one of the most original hotels.*
*– **Le Fort des Autruches** in Kébili (chott el Djérid), set in an old bordj.*
*– **Au Kef:** the little hotel (currently being converted) in the Sidi Bou Makhlouf mosque's former medersa. For a taste of monk's life!*
*– **Dar Jerba** on the Isle of Djerba, which is both a new town and a "holiday factory": a conglomeration of 4 hotels (1,408 rooms).*

the hotels

TUNIS (dialing code 01)

Abou Nawas Tunis*****, 313 rooms and presidential suites, 2 bars, 4 restaurants, pool, fitness centre, 5 conference rooms (20 to 1,000 places), BP 355, Parc Kennedy, avenue Mohamed-V, 1080 Tunis Cedex, tel. 350 355, fax: 352 882.
Oriental Palace Hotel****, rooms and suites, bar, restaurant, pool, shopping gallery, business centre, conference rooms for up to 1,000 people, 29 avenue Jean-Jaurès, 1001 Tunis, tel. 348 846 or 342 500, telex: 14 122 or 15 210 Orhot TN, fax: 350 327 or 330 471.
Abou Nawas el Mechtel****, 486 rooms, bars, 5 restaurants, shopping gallery, conference rooms (40 to 500 places), business centre, pool, fitness centre, disco, avenue Ouled-Hafouz, 1002 Tunis-Belvédère, tel. 783 200.
International Tunisia****, 406 beds, bar, restaurant, 49 avenue Bourguiba, tel. 254 855.
Belvédère****, 118 beds, avenue des Etats-Unis, tel. 783 133.
Hilton*****, 236 rooms, bar, restaurants, pools, tennis, Belvédère district, tel. 782 800 or 282 000.
Africa*****, 330 beds, bar, restaurant, pool, shop, conference rooms (30 to 450 people), 50 avenue Bourguiba, tel. 347 477.
Grand Hôtel du Lac (*Assalama chain*)***, 400 beds, bar-restaurants, shops, avenue Mohamed-V, 1001 Tunis, tel. 336 100 or 258 322, fax: 342 759.
Ibn Khaldoun***, 252 beds, bar, restaurant, 30 rue du Koweit, tel. 892 211.
Khereddine Pacha***, bars, restaurant, conference rooms, crossroads Mohammed-V and Khéreddine-Pacha, tel. 787 749.
Majestic***, 92 rooms, bar, restaurant, 36 avenue de Paris, tel. 332 666.
Gold Royal***, tel. 344 311.
Le Diplomate***, 42 avenue Hédi-Chaker, tel. 785 233.
Les Ambassadeurs***, 182 beds, 75 avenue Taïeb-Méhiri, tel. 288 011.
Metropole*, 98 rooms, 3 rue de Grèce, tel. 241 377.
Salammbô*, 6 rue de Grèce, tel. 244 252.
Transatlantique*, 50 rooms, 106 rue de Yougoslavie, tel. 240 680.
Youth hostels: in the Tunis Medina (60 to 100 beds, Dar Saïda Ajoula, 23 rue Saïda-Ajoula); in Tunis Radès (56 beds, *Maison des Jeunes,* tel. 483 631); in Tunis-Ez Zahra (72 beds, *Centre d'Hébergement,* Jélili Ez Zahra, Oued Méliane, tel. 481 547).
In Ez Zahra (near to Hammam-Lif): *Ez Zara* hotel****, 120 rooms, bar, restaurant, beach, tel. 450 788.

BEJA (dialing code 08)

Vaga**, 36 beds, tel. 450 818/336
Phénix*, tel. 450 188.
Youth hostel: *Maison des Jeunes* 80 beds, tel. 453 621.

BIZERTE (dialing code 02)

Corniche Palace***, 174 beds, tel. 431 844, telex: 21 004, fax: 431 830.
Nadhor**, 200 beds, tel. 439 309, fax: 433 817.
Petit Mousse**, 24 beds, tel. 432 185.
Youth hostel : route de la Corniche, 100 beds, tel. 431 608.
Also *Jalta*, 200 beds, tel. 431 169, fax: 434 277. *Zitouna*, 28 beds, tel. 431 447. *Africain*, 30 beds, tel. 434 412. *El Khayem*, 24 beds, tel. 432 120. *Le Continental*, 52 beds, tel. 431 437. *Saadi*, 20 beds, tel. 437 528. *Dalia*, 22 beds, tel. 441 669. Residence *Aïn Meriem*, 295 beds, tel. 437 615.
In Menzel Bourguiba:
Ichkeul-Younès*, 30 beds, tel. 461 606.

CAP BON (dialing code 02)

Oktor***, in Korbous, 128 beds, tel. 249 552.
Les Sources***, in Korbous, 103 beds, tel. 294 533.
Medi Sea**, in Bordj Cédria, 220 beds, tel. 430 122.
Solymar**, in Soliman, tel. 290 105.
Témime**, in Menzel Témime, 88 beds, tel. 298 266.
L'Epervier**, in Haouaria, 28 beds, tel. 297 017.
Les Andalous*, in Soliman, 288 beds, tel. 290 280.
Florida*, in Kélibia, 25 beds, tel. 296 248.
Holiday resorts: *El Mansourah* in Kélibia, 232 beds, tel. 296 315. *Mamounia* in Kélibia, 208 beds, tel. 296 088. *Sun Beach Club*, 120 bungalows, bars, restaurants, disco, pool, beach, tennis.
Boarding houses: *Chiraz* in Kor-

bous, 16 beds, tel. 293 230. *Les Amis* in Kélibia, 26 beds, tel. 295 777. *Dar Toubib* in Haouaria, 16 beds, tel. 297 163.
Youth hostels: Maison des Jeunes, Kélibia 80 beds, tel. 296 105, *Maison des Jeunes,* Menzel Témime 80 beds, tel. 298 116.

CARTHAGE (dialing code 01)

*Amilcar****, 250 rooms, 12 of which are suites, bars, restaurant, conference rooms, shops, disco, pool, beach, tel. 740 788.
*Reine Didon****, 48 beds, tel. 275 447, fax: 732 898.
*Résidence Carthage*** 28 beds, tel. 731 072.

DJERBA (dialing code 05)

*César Palace (Prestige Hôtels chain)******, 112 rooms and 2 suites, bars, 2 restaurants, shops, conference rooms, 2 pools, 3 tennis courts, mini-golf, beach, tel. 658 600.
*Djerba Plaza Hôtel******, 300 rooms, bars, restaurants, disco, shops, pool, tel. 658 230.
*Hasdrubal******, 215 rooms, bars, restaurants, disco, pools, beach, tel. 657 650.
*Royal Garden Palace******, bars, restaurants, 3 pools, tennis courts, beach, tel. 658 777.
*Yati Beach*****, 220 rooms, bars, restaurants, pool, shops, tennis, tel. 658 430, fax: 658 659.
*Abou Nawas Djerba*****, 225 rooms and suites, bars, 2 restaurants, shops, disco, conference rooms, 2 pools, beach, Djerba-Midoun, tel. 657 022.
*Dar Djerba*****, (complex of four 4, 3 and 2 star hotels: Yasmine, Zahra, Narjess and Dahlia), 1,408 rooms, bars, restaurants, 4 pools, 12 tennis courts, mini golf, beach, Djerba-Midoun, tel. 657 191/178.
*Dar Midoun*****, 280 rooms and suites, bars, 2 restaurants, conference rooms (250 places), pool, beach, tel. 658 168.
*Djerba Palace*****, 213 rooms, 26 duplexes, 18 suites, bars, restaurants, conference rooms (300 places), 2 pools, volley ball, 3 tennis courts, beach, tel. 658 600.
*El Menzel*****, 240 rooms, bars, restaurants, pools, tennis, volley ball, beach, Djerba-Midoun, tel. 657 070.

*Palm Beach*****, 280 rooms, bars, restaurants, pool, tennis, beach, disco, tel. 657 350.
*Ulysse Palace*****, 219 rooms, bars, restaurants, shop, pools, 4 tennis courts, horse riding, Sidi Mahrez beach, tel. 657 422.
*Yadis*****, 287 rooms, bars, restaurants, pool, tennis, tel. 658 235.
*Djerba Beach****, 183 rooms, bar, restaurant, pool, beach, Djerba-Midoun, tel. 657 200, fax: 657 357, telex: 51 946.
*Haroun****, 80 rooms, restaurant, pool, tel. 658 561/562/563.
*Djerba Orient****, 28 rooms, bar, restaurant, pool, tel. 657 440.
*El Bousten****, 180 apartments, bar, restaurant, pool, tel. 657 200, telex: 40 946.
*Les Sirènes****, 120 rooms, bars, restaurant, pool, beach, disco, tel. 657 266/317.
*Méhari*****, 296 rooms, bars, restaurants, shops, pools, beach, tel. 657 953.
*Néréides****, 70 rooms, bar, restaurants, pool, tennis, tel. 658 551.
*Petit Palais****, 70 rooms, bar, restaurants, pool, tennis, tel. 658 231/234.
*Yasmina****, 186 rooms, bars, restaurants, shops, disco, pool, 4 tennis courts, mini golf, beach, tel. 657 736.
*Hadji***, in Houmt Souk, tel. 650 630.
*El Jazira***, 220 beds, bar, restaurant, tennis, pool, disco, tel. 657 300.
*Médina***, 165 rooms, bars, restaurants, shops, disco, pool, 9 tennis courts, mini golf, volley ball, hand ball, beach, tel. 657 233/387.
*Meninx***, 214 rooms in bungalows, bars, restaurants, shops, disco, pool, 5 tennis courts, volley ball, basket ball, beach, tel. 657 051.
*Sidi Slim***, 351 rooms, bar, restaurant, tennis, pool, disco, tel. 657 021.
*Tanit***, 580 beds, bar, restaurant, pool, tennis, disco, tel. 657 132.
*Dar Faiza et Lotos**, 15 rooms, bar, restaurant, pool, tennis, tel. 650 083.
*Strand**, 120 beds, bar, restaurant, disco, pool, beach, tel. 657 430/014.
Family boarding house: Le Beau Rivage, 20 rooms, tel. 657 130.
Holiday clubs: Club Méditerranée in Djerba-la-Douce and Djerba-la-Fidèle, bungalows, bars, restaurants, pools, shops, crafts centre, meeting rooms, tennis, tel. 657 127 or 657

The hotel and holiday resort styles are
surprisingly varied, beautiful and bold.
Above: the Djerba golf course.
Below left: Club Sangho in Zarzis.
Below right: Abou Nawas hotel in Gammarth.

Above left: Abou Nawas Alhambra hotel in Port El Kantaoui.
Above right: Tunisie Hotel in Sousse.
Middle right: Abou Nawas El Borj hotel in Mahdia.
Bottom left: Menzel hotel in Djerba.
Bottom right: Tamerza Palace in Tamerza.

027. *Eldorador Aladin Jerba*, 144 rooms, bars, restaurants, pool, 5 tennis courts, volley ball, Djerba-Midoun, tel. 658 180. *Oamarit*, 309 rooms, bars, restaurants, pool, tennis, tel. 680 770. *Palma Djerba*, 292 rooms, bars, restaurants, shops, pool, 9 tennis courts, mini golf, beach, tel. 657 830. *Palmariva*, 292 rooms, bars, restaurants, disco, fitness centre, shops, pool, tennis, tel. 657 830. *Pénélope*, 200 rooms, bars, restaurants, shops, pool, beach, tennis, disco, tel. 657 055. *Rym Beach*, 300 rooms, bar, restaurant, conference room (300 places), disco, olympic pool, 6 tennis courts, beach, tel. 657 614. *"Soleil" Aquarius* (near to Cap Tourgueness), 300 rooms, pool, 8 tennis courts, beach, windsurfing, water skiing, tel. 657 792. *Toumana Club*, bar, restaurant, pool, tennis, disco, tel. 657 009.
Youth hostels: avenue Bourguiba in Houmt Souk, 60 beds, tel. 650 619. 11 rue Moncef-Bey in Houmt Souk, 120 beds, tel. 650 619.

DOUZ (dialing code 05)

*Caravansérail***, 85 rooms, restaurant, pool, tel. 495 123.
*Méhari***, 252 rooms, tel. 495 088.
*Sahara***, 154 rooms, bar, restaurant, conference centre, shop, 2 pools, tel. 470 874/864/865.
*Touareg***, 315 beds, tel. 470 245/ 057.
*Le Relais Saharien***, 235 beds, tel. 495 337.
Unclassified hotels: *La Rose des Sables*, 200 beds, bar, restaurant, meeting rooms, pool, tel. 495 366. *El Faouar*, 185 beds, tel. 491 576. *Zaafrane*, 40 beds, tel. 495 074.

GABÈS (dialing code 05)

*Oasis***, 227 beds, bar, restaurant, beach, tel. 270 381/782.
*Chems***, 275 rooms and 7 villas, bar, restaurants, pool, beach, shops, disco, tel. 270 547.
*Nejib***, 142 beds, tel. 271 686.
*Tacapes***, 68 beds, tel. 270 700/ 701.
*Atlantic**, 145 beds, tel. 270 034 or 272 417.
Holiday resorts: *Chela Club*, 122 beds, tel. 224 446.
Unclassified hotels : *Ben Nejima, La Poste, Médina, M'Rabet, Kilani, Régina*.
In Mareth: *Relais du Golfe*.

GAFSA (dialing code 06)

*Maamoun***, 138 beds, tel. 222 432 or 244 441.
*Gafsa Hôtel***, 93 beds, tel. 224 000 or 225 000.
*Une Hôtel**, 18 beds, tel. 222 212.
Unclassified hotels: Khalfallah, El Béchir, La République, Le Tunis, Oasis, Moussa, Alya Bacha, Hédili, Ennour.
In Metlaoui: *Ennecim*, 36 beds, tel. 240 271.

GAMMARTH (dialing code 01)

*Abou Nawas Gammarth****, 117 rooms, 10 suites, 45 studios in bungalows, bars, restaurants, shops, 2 pools, 2 tennis courts, beach, avenue Taïeb-M'Hiri, tel. 741 444, fax: 740 400.
*Club Aqua Viva***, 110 rooms, bar, restaurant, pool, beach, shops, disco, tel. 741 502.
*Cap Carthage***, 350 rooms, bars, restaurants, pool, tennis, shops, disco, tel. 740 064.
*Karim***, 177 rooms, bar, restaurant, pool, tennis, shops, disco, tel. 742 188.
*Molka***, 200 rooms, bar, restaurant, pool, tennis, tel. 740 242.
Near to Carthage:
*Dar Naouar***, 500 rooms in pavilions, bars, restaurants, pool, beach, shops, disco, 9 tennis courts, basket ball, volley ball, mini golf, tel. 741 000.

HAMMAMET (dialing code 02)

*Sindbad*****, 335 beds, tel. 280 122.
*Abou Nawas Hammamet****, 222 rooms, bars, 2 restaurants, 2 pools , beach, shops, disco, conference rooms, BP 7-8050, tel. 281 344, telex: 24 735.
*L'Albatros****, 368 rooms, bar, restaurant, pool, beach, shop, 3 tennis courts, mini golf, volley ball, basket ball, tel. 282 230.
*Aziza****, 218 rooms, bar, restaurant, shop, pools, 3 tennis courts, mini golf, volley ball, basketball, beach, tel. 283 666.
*Hammamet Regency****, 220 beds, 226 776.
*Miramar***, 669 rooms, bar, restaurant, 2 pools, beach, 2 tennis courts, tel. 280 344/019.
*Nahrawess****, 460 beds, tel. 283 077.

Palm Beach****, 408 beds, tel. 280 333.
Phénicia****, 720 beds, bar, restaurant, pool, tel. 226 533, fax: 226 337, telex: 24 659.
Sheraton****, 410 beds, tel. 226 555.
Bel Air***, 140 beds, tel. 226 009.
Bel Azur***, 340 rooms, bars, restaurants, olympic pool, shops, disco, conference room, 4 tennis courts, mini golf, horse riding (riding school), tel. 280 544, fax: 280 275.
Charmes***, 340 beds, tel. 280 492.
Les Colombes***, 243 rooms, bar, restaurants, conference room, 2 pools, 4 tennis courts, volley ball, mini golf, beach, shops, tel. 280 049/247.
Continental***, 180 apartments, bar, restaurant, pool, beach, tennis, disco, tel. 280 456.
Dalia***, 140 beds, tel. 282 188.
Dar Khayem***, 500 beds, tel. 280 439.
Diar Hammamet***, 1,080 beds, tel. 281 400.
El Fell***, 212 rooms and 57 bungalows, bars, restaurant, pool, shops, disco, 4 tennis courts, volley ball, tel. 280 118.
Fourati***, 772 beds, tel. 280 388.
Grand Hôtel***, 250 beds, tel. 280 177.
Hammamet***, 674 beds, tel. 280 160.
Hammamet Beach***, 360 rooms, bar, restaurant, pools, beach, volley ball, shop, disco, tel. 280 400/287.
Hammamet Club***, 450 beds, tel. 281 882.
Kacem Center Le Kalife***, tel. 280 382.
Kilma***, 410 beds, tel. 227 777.
Kerkouane***, 104 beds, tel. 280 291.
Nozha Beach***, 380 rooms, restaurants, pools, tennis, tel. 280 599.
Les Orangers and les Orangers beach***, 766 rooms, bars, restaurants, pools, shops, 2 tennis courts, BP 7-8 050, tel. 280 144, telex: 24 647, fax: 81 077.
Paradis***, 682 beds, tel. 226 338.
Paradise Garden***, 432 beds, tel. 226 666.
Park Place***, 150 bungalows, bar, restaurant, pool, tennis, disco, tel. 280 111, telex: 24 610.
Président***, 616 beds, tel. 280 211.
Saphir***, 674 beds, tel. 224 944.

Sultan***, 788 beds, tel. 280 705.
Vénus***, 544 beds, tel. 226 422.
Yasmina***, 226 beds, tel. 280 222.
Alya**, 70 beds, tel. 280 218.
Bellevue**, 78 beds, tel. 281 121.
El Bousten**, 444 rooms, bar, restaurant, pool, beach, tennis, tel. 280 444, telex: 24 685.
Ceramic**, 50 beds, tel. 281 951.
Les Citronniers**, 114 beds, tel. 281 650.
Emira**, 172 beds, tel. 281 720.
Garsaa**, 60 beds, tel. 226 251.
Kaly**, 34 beds, tel. 283 600.
Khella**, 71 beds, tel. 283 900.
El Pacha**, 150 rooms, bars, restaurants, disco, pool, tennis courts, volley ball, basketball, mini golf, beach, tel. 226 077.
Le Méditerranée**, 336 rooms, bar, restaurants, shops, disco, pools, beach, 4 tennis courts, mini golf, volley ball, basket ball, tel. 280 433.
Nesrines**, 254 beds, tel. 226 531.
Olympia**, 78 beds, tel. 280 622.
Omar Khayam**, 484 beds, tel. 280 355.
Ribat**, 78 beds, tel. 280 806.
Sahbi**, 210 beds, tel. 280 807.
Tanfous**, 734 beds, tel. 226 213.
Tanit**, 608 beds, tel. 226 148.
Small hotels and boarding houses: Bennila, Samaris, Fantasia, Milano. *Holiday resorts*: Baie du Soleil, 480 beds, tel. 280 298. Salammbô, 552 beds, tel. 226 197. Samira Club, 1,088 beds, tel. 226 185. *Apartment-hotels*: Manar*****, 203 rooms, tel. 281 333. Résidences Hammamet***, 360 beds, tel. 280 408. Résidence Mahmoud***, 72 beds, tel. 283 723. Résidence La Paix**, 200 beds, tel. 282 588. Résidence le Jardin, 26 beds, tel. 283 014.

JENDOUBA (dialing code 08)

Atlas**, 32 beds, tel. 630 566.
Simithu**, 54 beds, tel. 631 695, fax: (8) 631 743.

KAIROUAN (dialing code 07)

Continental****, 352 beds, bar, restaurant, pool, tel. 221 135.
Splendid***, 80 beds, tel. 220 522.
Tunisia**, 76 beds, tel. 221 855.
Unclassified hotels: Marhala, 69 beds, tel. 220 736. Sabra, 56 beds, tel. 220 260.

KASSERINE (dialing code 07)

Cillium***, 72 beds, tel. 460 682.

Unclassified hotels: *Pinus*, 26 beds. *La Paix*, 32 beds.
In Fériana (south of Kasserine): *Mabrouk*, 24 beds, tel. 485 202.

KÉBILI (DJÉRID) (dialing code 05)

Les Dunes de Nefzaoua***, 88 rooms, bar, restaurant, shop, disco, pool, meeting room (380 places), tel. 499 211/215.
Oasis***, 128 rooms, bar, restaurants, disco, pool, tel. 491 436/162.
Fort des Autruches**, 200 beds, bar, restaurant, meeting room (100 places), tel. 490 233.
Kitam***, 61 beds, tel. 491 338/465.

KEF (THE) (dialing code 08)

Sicca Veneria***, 64 beds, bar, restaurant, tel. 221 561.
Unclassified hotels: Vénus, 40 beds.

KERKENNAH (Islands) (dialing code 04)

Grand Hôtel**, 225 beds, tel. 281 266.
Farhat**, 154 rooms, bar, restaurant, pool, tennis, disco, beach, tel. 281 236.
Unclassified hotels: *Cercina, El Jazira, Kastil.*

MAHDIA (dialing code 03)

Paradise el Fatimi****, 580 beds, tel. 696 733.
Abou Nawas El Borj***, 228 rooms, bars, restaurants, shops, 2 pools, tennis, disco, beach, tel. 694 602.
El Mehdi***, 213 rooms, bars, restaurants, 2 pools, shops, tennis, disco, tel. 696 300.
Eldorador Cap Mahdia***, route de la Corniche, 263 rooms, bars, restaurants, conference room (120 places), pool, 7 tennis courts, mini golf, volley ball, basket ball, diving, disco, tel. 630 300.
Thapsus***, 710 beds, tel. 694 495.
Sable d'Or*, 202 beds, tel. 681 137.
Unclassified hotels: Corniche, Rand, El Jazira.
In El Djem: *Julius*, 30 beds, tel. 490 044.

MATMATA (dialing code 05)

Matmata**, 67 beds, restaurant, pool, tel. 230 066.

Troglodytic hotels: *Touring Club***, 140 beds, tel. 630 088. *Les Berbères***, 75 beds, tel. 230 024. *Sidi Driss***, 97 beds, tel. 230 005.

MONASTIR (dialing code 03)

Club Méditerranée*****, 175 rooms, bars, restaurants, shops, pool, sailing, tennis, tel. 460 033.
Emir Palace*****, 332 rooms, 17 suites, bars, restaurants, 2 pools, tennis, disco, tel. 457 900.
Festival****, 330 beds, tel. 467 555.
Habib****, 400 beds, tel. 462 944.
Hélia****, 446 beds, tel. 467 713.
Jockey Club****, 200 rooms, restaurants, pool, tennis, tel. 461 833.
Kuriat Palace****, 178 rooms, 44 suites, bars, 4 restaurants, shops, conference rooms, 2 pools, discos, volley ball, beach, tel. 461 200.
Robinson Club****, 628 beds, tel. 431 055.
Skanès El Hana****, 359 rooms, bar, restaurant, disco, 2 pools, tennis, beach, tel. 462 055.
Skanès Palace****, 480 beds, tel. 461 350.
Abou Nawas Sunrise***, 528 beds, tel. 427 146.
Club Palm Inn***, bar, restaurant, shops, pool, tennis, tel. 466 169.
Eden Club***, 370 beds, bars, restaurants, disco, pools, 6 tennis courts, golf tel. 466 610.
Esplanade***, 260 beds, tel. 460 148.
Garden Beach***, 200 beds, tel. 466 190.
Houda***, 274 rooms, bars, restaurants, shops, disco, 2 pools, 4 tennis courts, volley ball, beach, tel. 466 800.
Monastir Centre***, 300 beds, tel. 463 945.
Ribat***, 312 beds, tel. 462 944.
Ruspina***, 170 rooms, bars, restaurants, shop, 2 pools, tennis, beach, tel. 461 360.
Sahara Beach***, 5029 Skanès Monastir, bar, restaurant, pool, tel. 461 088, fax: 460 470, telex: 30 783.
Sidi Mansour***, 254 beds, tel. 461 029.
Tropicana***, bar, restaurant, pool, tennis, disco, tel. 460 554.
Club Sangho Farah**, 488 beds, bars, restaurant, shop, pool, 6 tennis courts, mini golf, beach, tel. 466 190.
Club Calimera**, 410 beds, tel. 430 122.

El Chems**, 1,200 beds, tel. 466 288
Les Palmiers**,126 beds, tel. 461 151.
Tanit**, 550 beds, tel. 464 791.
Yasmine*, 23 beds, tel. 462 511.
Apartment-hotel: Cap Marine, 250 apartments in 26 residences, shopping centre, bars, restaurants, tel. 462 305.
Unclassified hotels: Monastir Beach, Kahla, Mourabou, Pension Ahmed, El Yamama.

NABEUL (dialing code 02)

Khéops****, 274 rooms, 21 suites, bars, 4 restaurants, disco, 2 pools, tel. 286 555.
Aldiana***, 536 beds, tel. 285 400.
Imène***, 156 beds, tel. 222 310.
Lido***, 990 beds, tel. 285 104/491.
Nabeul Beach***, 96 bungalows, 184 rooms, bars, restaurants, shops, pool, tennis, volley ball, beach, tel. 285 008.
Le Prince***, 436 beds, tel. 285 470.
Les Pyramides***, 504 rooms, bars, 3 restaurants, shopping centre, pool, 5 tennis courts, mini golf, tel. 285 775/444/503.
Club Aquarius**, 682 beds, tel. 285 682.
Fakir**, 40 beds, tel. 285 477.
Les Mimosas**, 264 beds, tel. 285 313.
Club Ramsès**, 307 bungalows, bar, restaurants, disco, 2 pools, 2 tennis courts, mini golf, tel. 286 363.
Riadh**, 100 rooms, bar, restaurant, shop, disco, pool, 3 tennis courts, mini golf, volley ball, beach, tel. 285 744.
Saf-Saf**, 40 beds, tel. 286 044.
El Ons*, 58 beds, tel. 286 129.
Les Jasmins*, 106 beds, tel. 285 343.
Boarding houses and unclassified hotels: Ezzouhour, 60 beds, tel. 224 702; *Habib*, 28 beds, tel. 287 190; *Hafsides*, 18 beds, tel. 285 823; *Monia*, 32 beds, tel. 285 713; *Mustapha*, 32 beds, tel. 222 262; *Les Oliviers*, 30 beds, tel. 286 865; *Les Roses*, 18 beds, tel. 286 570; *Les Colombes.*

NEFTA (dialing code 06)

Sahara Palace****, 114 rooms, bar, 2 restaurants, disco, pool, tennis. Currently closed for renovation work, tel. 457 046.

Bel Horizon***, 90 rooms, bar, rest., pool, tennis, tel. 430 088/328.
Caravansérail***, 80 rooms, bar, restaurant, shop, pool, tennis, disco, meeting rooms (300 places), tel. 430 416/355.
Neptus***, 154 beds, bar, restaurant, meeting rooms (220 places), tel. 430 321/378.
La Rose***, 190 beds, bar, restaurant, meeting rooms (200 places), tel. 430 696/697.
Unclassified hotels: El Habib, 32 beds, tel. 457 497; *Le Marhala*, 76 beds, tel. 430 027; *Les Nomades*, 88 beds, tel. 457 052.

SBEÏTLA (dialing code 07)

Suffetula**, 92 beds, bar restaurant, tel. 465 074.
Bakini**, 78 beds, tel. 465 244.
In Sidi Bouzid, east of Sbeïtla:
Horchani*, 52 beds, tel. 630 855.
Chams*, 18 beds, tel. 630 515.

SFAX (dialing code 04)

Abou Nawas Sfax Centre****, 260 beds, bar, restaurant, pool, conference rooms (600 places), avenue Habib-Bourguiba, BP 544, Sfax 3000, tel. 225 701, telex: 40 974 SFACE, fax: 235 960.
Syphax Novotel****, 132 rooms, bars, restaurants, pool, disco, tel. 243 333.
El Andalous***, 184 beds, tel. 299 100.
Les Oliviers***, 112 beds, tel. 225 168.
Donia**, 150 beds, tel. 249 549.
Le Colisée**, 100 beds, tel. 227 801.
Thyna**, 54 beds, tel. 225 317.
Alexandre*, 72 beds, tel. 221 911.
Amin*, 85 beds, tel. 245 600.
Boarding houses and unclassified hotels: Hannibal, Mondial, Essaada, Ennaim, Besbes, Maghreb, Médina, Etoile, Essourour, El Jamiaa, El Jarid, Ennasser.
In Mahrès, south of Sfax: *Marzouk*** 40 beds, tel. 290 261.
Younga (unclassified), 20 beds, tel. 290 098.

SIDI BOU SAÏD (dialing code 01)

Sidi Bou Saïd****, run by the Hotellery School, tel. 740 411.
Dar Saïd**, rue Ettoumi, tel. 740 215.

Unclassified hotel: Bou-Farès, 10 beds.

SOUSSE (dialing code 03)

Orient Palace*****, 244 rooms, 6 restaurants, shopping mall, 3 pools, 3 tennis courts, disco, tel. 242 888.
Abou Nawas Boujaafar****, 234 rooms, 14 of which are suites, bars, restaurants, conference or banquet room (50 to 250 places), 2 pools, beach, thalassotherapy centre, avenue Habib-Bourguiba, 4000 Sousse, tel. 226 030, fax: 226 595.
Chems El Hana****, 243 rooms, bars, restaurants, shops, 3 pools, tel. 228 190.
El Hana****, 258 beds, tel. 225 818.
Marhaba Beach****, 506 beds, tel. 240 688.
Riadh Palms****, 486 rooms, bars, restaurants, pools, tennis, beach, tel. 225 700.
Tej Marhaba****, 700 beds, tel. 229 800.
El Hana Beach***, 1,290 beds, tel. 226 900.
Hill Diar***, 406 beds, tel. 241 811.
Jinene***, 446 beds, tel. 241 800.
Justinia***, 316 beds, tel. 226 381.
Karawan***, 490 beds, tel. 226 139.
Marabout***, 514 beds, tel. 226 245.
Marhaba***, 432 beds, tel. 242 180.
Marhaba-Club***, 918 beds, tel. 242 170.
Nour Justinia***, 172 beds, tel. 226 993.
Rym Résidence***, 72 beds, tel. 229 600.
Said***, 99 beds, tel. 228 900.
Sheherazade***, 416 beds, tel. 241 433.
Tour Khalef***, 1171 beds, tel. 241 844.
Sousse Palace***, bar, restaurant, pool, conference room (500 places), tel. 225 221, telex: 30 793.
Alyssa**, 812 beds, tel. 240 713.
El Kaiser**, 291 beds, tel. 228 030.
El Ksar**, 533 beds, tel. 241 822.
Ennaim**, 80 beds, tel. 227 100.
Essaada**, 105 beds, tel. 220 115.
Jawahra**, 688 beds, tel. 225 611.
Park**, 64 beds, tel. 220 434.
Riadh**, 88 beds, tel. 224 828.
Salem**, 546 beds, tel. 241 966.
Soussana**, 136 beds, tel. 223 287.
Sousse Azur**, 47 beds, tel. 227 760.

Amira*, 30 beds, tel. 226 325.
Claridge*, 60 beds, tel. 224 759.
Médina* 100 beds, tel. 221 722.
Apartment-hotels: Abou Nawas Alhambra, 732 beds, tel. 246 400.
Abou Nawas Nejma, 127 apartments, studios to 2 rooms, restaurants, bar, disco, pool, tel. 226 811.
Africa Beach, 64 beds, tel. 226 763.
Club El Menchia, 132 beds, tel. 242 777. *Farès*, 180 beds, tel. 227 800.
Golf Résidence, 286 beds, tel. 242 633. *Inès,* 120 beds, tel. 243 211.
Les Maisons de la Mer, 1,100 beds, tel. 241 799. *Mariem*, 36 beds, tel. 243 333. *Okba*, 100 beds, tel. 225 522. *Panorama*, 236 beds, tel. 228 155. *Phénix*, 124 beds, tel. 224 288.
Le Printemps, 144 beds, tel. 229 335. *Résidence Boujaafar*, 48 beds, tel. 227 303. *Résidence El Kantaoui*, 242 beds, tel. 242 012. *Résidence La Sofra*, 137 beds, tel. 241 657. *La Roseraie*, 98 beds, tel. 241 533. *Samara*, 808 beds, tel. 226 689. *Sinbad*, 146 beds, tel. 243 655. *Sousse Résidence*, 80 beds, tel. 225 433. *Tej Marhaba*, 5278 beds, tel. 229 800.
Unclassified hotels: Ahla, Corniche, Hadrumète, Mabrouka, Messaouda, Mekki, Royal, Sousse Ribat, Zohra.

In Port El Kantaoui:

Abou Nawas Diar El Andalous*****, 300 rooms, 10 of which suites, bars, restaurants, shops, disco, 2 pools, 6 tennis courts, volley ball, beach, tel. 246 200.
El Hana Palace*****, 96 rooms, bars, restaurants, pools, casino, tel. 243 000.
Hannibal Palace*****, 232 rooms, 7 of which suites, bars, restaurants, disco, conference room, pool, 2 tennis courts, beach, tel. 241 577.
El Kanta****, 255 rooms, bars, restaurants, shops, disco, pool, 5 tennis courts, golf, tel. 240 466.
Green Park****, 462 beds, tel. 243 277.
Hasdrubal****, 235 rooms, bars, restaurants, shops, pools, 6 tennis courts, golf, tel. 241 944.
Marhaba International****, 648 beds, tel. 243 633.
Riviera****, 215 rooms, 38 suites, bars, restaurants, shops, disco, congress room (800 places), 2 pools, 2 tennis courts, beach, tel. 246 180.
Abou Sofiane***, 600 beds, tel. 246 444.
Bulla Regia***, 104 beds, tel. 240 923.
El Mouradi***, 460 beds, tel. 246 355.

Soviva***, 286 beds, tel. 246 143.
Holiday resorts: Résidence-Club El Kantaoui, 650 beds, tel. 246 012.
Sélima-Club, 988 beds, tel. 246 090.
Tergui, 200 rooms and 127 bungalows, bar, restaurants, disco, pool, tennis. *Résidence-Club Alhambra. Les Maisons de la Mer*, tel. 240 500, fax: 240 506. *Green Park.*

TABARKA (dialing code 08)

Méhari Tabarka*** (Iberotel chain), 200 rooms, bar, 3 restaurants, shops, pools, tennis, fitness centre, meeting room (up to 300 people), near to golf course and riding school. Nouvelle route touristique, 8110 Tabarka, tel. 644 088, fax: 644 505.
Abou Nawas Montazah***, 300 rooms, bars, restaurants, shops, pools, tennis, disco, tel. 643 508, telex: 80 044, fax: 643 530.
Paradise***, 364 beds, tel. 643 002, fax: 643 918.
Royal Golf Marhaba***, 316 beds, tel. 643 625, fax: 643 838.
Mimosas***, 80 rooms in pavillons and bungalows, bar, restaurant, seminar rooms, pools, tennis, tel. 643 018, telex: 81 010, fax: 643 276.
El Morjane***, 320 beds, tel. 644 503, telex: 80 001, fax: 644 107.
Novelty**, 52 beds, tel. 643 176, fax: (8) 643 008.
Aiguilles**, 38 beds, tel. 644 250.
De France*, 22 beds, tel. 644 577.
Unclassified hotels: De la Plage, 14 beds, tel. 44 039. *Mamia*, 36 beds, tel. 644 058.
In Hammam Bourguiba: *Hammam Bourguiba****, 116 beds, tel. 632 497, telex: 13 772, fax: 647 106.
In Aïn Draham: *Rihana****, 150 beds, tel. 647 391, telex: 80 025, fax: 647 396. *Col de Ruines****, 122 beds. *La Forêt****, 120 beds. *Les Chênes***, 68 beds, tel. 647 211, telex: 800 25, fax: 647 315. *Beauséjour*, 72 beds, tel. 647 005.

TATAOUINE (dialing code 05)

Club Sangho, 62 bungalows and 4 suites, bars, restaurant, pizzeria, shops, conference room (100 people), pool, 2 tennis courts, volley ball, PO Box 186, route de Chénini, Tataouine 3200, tel. 860 124 or 102, fax: 862 177.

TÉBOURSOUK (dialing code 08)

Thugga**, 66 beds, tel. 465 7113.

TOZEUR (dialing code 06)

Dar Cherait*****, 78 rooms, bars, restaurants, pool, tel. 452 100.
Abou Nawas****, 84 rooms, bar, restaurant, pool, meeting room (150 places), tel. 452 700 or 451 168.
Continental***, bar, restaurant, pool, tel. 450 411.
Basma (Paladien Nouvelles Frontières)***, 176 rooms, bar, restaurant, conference room (120 places), tel. 452 488.
El Hafsi***, 126 beds, tel. 452 558 or 450 966.
Oasis**, 114 rooms, bar, restaurant, 3 pools, shop, conference room (300 places), tel. 450 522/699.
Palmyre***, 106 rooms, bar, restaurant, shop, pools, tennis, conference room (150 places), tel. 452 041/042.
Phedra***, 90 rooms, bar, restaurant, pool, tennis, disco, shops, tel. 452 185/697.
Ras el Aïn (Club Méditerranée)***, 63 rooms, bar, restaurant, pool, tennis, shops, disco, tel. 452 003/444.
Dar Ghaouar**, 102 beds, tel. 452 782/870.
Aïcha**, 100 beds, tel. 452 788 or 450 988.
Unclassified hotels: Essaada, 35 beds, tel. 450 097; *Jérid*, 90 beds, tel. 450 488; *Khalifa*, 24 beds, tel. 450 068; *Splendid*, 52 beds, tel. 450 053; *Warda*, 37 beds, tel. 450 597/744.
In Tamerza:
Tamerza Palace****, 65 rooms and suites, bar, restaurant, shops, conference rooms, pool, tennis, tel. 245 214 or 248 544 / 562.
Les Cascades (unclassified), 150 beds, tel. 248 520.

ZARZIS (dialing code 05)

Holiday clubs:
Club Sangho, bungalows, bars, restaurant, shops, disco, pool, 6 tennis courts, mini golf, volley ball, sailing school, beach, tel. 680 124.
Oamarit, 283 bungalows, bars, restaurant, conference room, pool, 6 tennis courts, beach, tel. 680 770.
Zita, 300 rooms, bar, restaurants, pool, tennis, tel. 680 346.
Zarzis Hôtel, bar, restaurant, shop, conference room, pools, tennis, mini golf, beach, tel. 680 160.
Zéphir Hôtel, 300 rooms, bar, restaurants, disco, 2 pools, mini golf, tel. 681 027/026/028.

business
trip supplement

business trip supplement

Who to contact before leaving

– *The Embassy of Tunisia*, 29 Princess Gate, London SW7 10G, GB. Tel.: (0171) 584 8117;1515 Massachusetts Avenue, Washington D.C. 20005, USA. Tel.: (202) 862 1850; 515 Oscannro Street, Ottawa, 10 KES 3P8, Ontario, Canada. Tel.: (613) 237 0330.
– *Tunisian Investment and Trade Centre*, Sardinia House, 52 Lincolns Inn Fields, London WC2A 3LZ, tel. (0171) 430 1315, fax: 0171-831 8622.
– *International Chamber of Commerce*, British Affiliate ICC, 14 Belgrave Square, London SW1, tel. (0171) 823 2811.
– *The Department of Trade and Industry*, Ashdown House, Victoria Street, London SW1, tel. (0171) 215 5000.
– *Anglo-Arab Trade*, 91 King Street, London W6, tel. (0181) 741 4921.
– *Overseas Business Information*, 70 City Road, London EC14 2BJ, tel. (0171) 490 0690.
– *Le Centre français de promotion industrielle en Afrique* (CEPIA), 11 rue Marbeuf, 75008 Paris, tel. 47 20 22 03.

International air travel

All the major international airline companies flying to Tunisia offer Business or Club Class travel (BA, GB Airways Air France, Tunisair, Lufthansa, Swissair, Sabéna, KLM, Alitalia, etc.) with separate check-in desks, and in-flight service that comes close to that in First Class.

Along with the capital Tunis, the country's other major economic centres also have international airports, for example Sfax and Sousse-Monastir.

Tuninter offers flight services around Tunisia (daily or several weekly flights to Tunis, Djerba, Sfax, Tabarka, Tozeur) in ATR 42 or ATR 72 planes.

Car hire

Hertz, Tunisia's leading car hire company by virtue of the extent of its network and its number of cars, offers businessmen and women a large range of vehicles. At the top of the range, for example, there is a choice between Renault 21s and 25s, Peugeot 405s and 605s or Mercedes 190s, most of which are air-conditioned. Chauffeurs are also available.

Two kinds of prices are offered: the standard day/kilometre price, or an unlimited millage forfeit for a minimum of 3 days' hire. All major credit cards are accepted, as is the Hertz card.

Addresses in Tunis: Direction générale de Hertz, Route no. 8, La Charguia, tel. 790 211, fax: 780 082 or 796 238, telex: Hertz Car Tunis no. 15 002. Tunis-Carthage airport, tel. 236 000, extension 34 96. Town centre: 29 avenue Bourguiba, tel. 248 559.

Travelling by train

Tunisia has a rail network covering the whole country. Trains have air-conditioned first class carriages (it is necessary to reserve in advance).

Accommodation and restaurants

In Tunis:
– *Abou Nawas Tunis******, Heads of States' residence during the last OAU summit, avenue Mohamed-V and by the motorway to the airport and the capital's industrial zone, BP 355, Parc Kennedy, avenue Mohamed-V, 1080 Tunis Cedex, tel. 350 355, fax: 352 882. (NB: the Abou Nawas chain has just opened up an office in Paris: 22 rue Saint-Augustin, 75002, Paris, tel. 47 42 50 50, fax: 47 42 50 60).
– *Le Lac*****, 400 beds, bars, restaurants, shop, business centre, avenue Mohamed-V, tel. 336 100 or 258 322, fax: 342 759.
– *Oriental Palace Hotel****** of Tunis, has a business centre, conference or banquet rooms (up to 1,000 people), 29 avenue Jean-Jaurès, 1001 Tunis, tel. 348 846 or 342 500, fax: 350 327 or 330 471.
– *Hilton******, ND and Belvédère district, has an "executive floor" (with all the services required by business people), seminar rooms,

Preceding pages:
The sober and imposing Porte de France guards the entrance to the Tunis medina and acts as a link between the old and new quarters of the town.

avenue de la Ligue-Arabe, PO Box 345, 1080 Tunis Carthage Cedex, tel. 782 800 or 282 000, fax: 782 208 or 781 713, telex: 15 372 or 18 306.
– *El Mechtel*****, 486 rooms, bar, 5 restaurants, shopping gallery, conference rooms (40 to 500 places), business centre, pool, fitness centre, disco, avenue Ouled-Hafouz, 1002 Tunis-Belvédère, tel. 783 200.
– *Africa******, 330 beds, bar, restaurant, pool, shops, conference rooms (30 to 450 people), 50 avenue Bourguiba, tel. 347 477, fax: 347 432.
– *International Tunisia*****, 406 beds, bar, restaurants, 49 avenue Bourguiba, tel. 254 855, fax: 341 199.
– *Belvédère*****, 118 beds, avenue des Etats-Unis, tel. 783 133, fax: 782 214.
In Sfax:
– *Abou Nawas Sfax Centre*****, rooms and suites, bars, restaurants, pool, disco, congress room (600 places), avenue Habib-Bourguiba, BP 544, Sfax 3000, tel. (04) 225 701, telex 40 974 SFACE, fax (04) 235 960.
In Sousse:
– *Abou Nawas Boujaafar*****, 234 rooms and suites, bars, restaurants, pools, private beach, banquet or conference rooms (20 to 250 people), thalassotherapy centre, avenue Habib-Bourguiba, 4000 Sousse, tel. 226 030, fax: 226 595.

Restaurants

All the large hotels have gastronomic restaurants.
There are also some excellent restaurants for business meals in the main towns, for example the *Dar El Jeld* in Tunis (see earlier section "Some good restaurants").

Seminars and conferences

● Congress centres:
– Tunis Palais des congrès, avenue Mohamed-V. Site of the June 1994 OAU summit (Organisation of African Unity).
– Monastir Palais des congrès, avenue Farhat-Hached.
– Bizerte Palais des congrès (for 1,000 to 2,000 people).
● Conference centres in Tunis:

– *Abou Nawas Tunis******, has 5 conference rooms for 20 to 1,000 people.
– *El Mechtel*****, has 8 meeting rooms for 40 to 500 people, and a business centre.
– *Oriental Palace Hotel******, has conference rooms where seminars, congresses and conferences can be held, takes up to 1,000 people.
– *The Tunis Hilton*****, welcomes groups of 30 to 450 people for congresses or conferences.
● The major economic centres:
In Sfax:
– *Hôtel Abou Nawas Centre******, has a 600 place congress centre.
In Sousse:
– *Hôtel Boujaafar*****, has a 20 to 250 place conference room.
– *Sousse Palace* has a 500 place conference room (equipment: 16 mm film projector, telex, photocopier, paper board, etc.).
● Congresses by the sea:
In Hammamet:
– *Hôtel Parc Plage*****, has a large 350 place conference room (equipment: 16 mm film projector, retroprojector, slide projector, sound system, paper boards, etc.).
– *Royal Azur*****, has an 800 place congress room with simultaneous translation cabins and a business centre.
In Port El Kantaoui:
– *Hôtel Riviera*****, several committee rooms, and a large 800 place congress room.
In Djerba:
– *Dar Midoun*****, an equipped committee room for 250 people.
– *Djerba Palace*****, 300 seat conference room.
– *Abou Nawas Djerba*****, equipped 120 place conference room.
● Other congress centres:
In Tataouine (the deep Tunisian south):
– *Sangho*, polyvalent room that can hold seminars of 100 people.
In Tozeur:
Many 100 to 200 place meeting rooms in the *Oasis*, *Abou Nawas*, *Basma*, *Palmyre*, and *Ras El Aïn* hotels.

Fairs, shows and exhibitions

A great deal of shows and fairs are organized all year round, notably in the Palais de la Foire in Tunis (ave-

*It is a sheer delight to come across
traditional mosques that look like
"cubist" sculptures
when travelling in Tunisia.*

nue Mohamed-V).

The themes of these shows and fairs are: *agriculture* (January), *the hotel and restaurant industry* (January-February), *leather* (February), *craft works* (March-April), *transport* (April), *the electrical and electronics industry* (May), *textiles, cosmetics and jewellery* (May), *youth and employment* (May-June), *packaging* (June), *subcontracting* (September), *medical and hospital equipment* (October), *the environment and safety* (October), *cinema, video and audiovisuals* (October), *computing and office equipment* (November), *telecommunications* (November), *new technology* (December), *buildings, furnishings, hardware and DIY* (December), *toys* (December).

In Gabès: Foire Internationale (end March, beginning of April), crafts, agriculture and industry. Organizers' addresses: *Foire internationale de Tunis,* BP1, 2015 Le Kram, tel. 730 111; *Sogefoires International,* 34 avenue de la Foire. Z.I. La Charguia, 2035 Tunis-Carthage, tel. 787 933 or 789 822; *Exposervices-Promosalons,* 5 bis rue Charles-de-Gaulle, 1001 Tunis, tel. 248 092/349 811 or 340 200; *Tunis Expo,* 11 rue Kemal-Ataturk, 1001 Tunis, tel. 354 835/351 187 or 259 155.

Universities and higher education

In Tunis: *Faculté des sciences économiques et de gestion. Ecole polytechnique.*
In Sfax: *Faculté des sciences économiques et de gestion.*

Stock Exchange and banks

There is a *Stock Exchange* in Tunis where the largest Tunisian and overseas companies are listed.

In addition to the *Banque centrale* (central bank) – the issuing organism that controls the country's entire monetary policy – Tunisia has an increasingly dense banking network. It has ten or so commercial banks or depots, nearly ten development or investment banks, and several "off-shore" banks (subsidiaries of overseas banks that work with non-residents' money and in exports).

These are: the *STB, Société tunisienne de banque* (rue Hédi-Nouira, 1001 Tunis, tel. 258 000 or 340 477, fax: 348 400 or 340 015, telex: 14 135/14 815/15 376); the *BT, Banque de Tunisie* ; the *UIB, Union internationale des banques*; the *BNA, Banque Nationale Agricole* (rue Hedi-Nouira, 1001 Tunis, tel. 791 000, fax: 793 031 or 791 765); the *UBCI, Union bancaire pour le commerce et l'industrie*; the *BS, Banque du Sud*; the *ATB, Arab Tunisian Bank*; the *BH, Banque de l'habitat* (21 avenue Khéreddine-Pacha, 1002 Tunis Belvédère, tel. 785 277, telex: 14 349, fax: (1) 784 417); the *BIAT, Banque internationale Arabe de Tunisie*; *Citybank*; the *CFCT, Crédit foncier et commercial de Tunisie*.

– Development banks: the *BDET* (*Banque de développement économique de Tunisie*), the *BNDT* (*Banque nationale de développement touristique*), the *STUSID* (*Société tuniso-saoudienne d'investissement et de développement*), the *BTKD* (*Banque tuniso-koweitienne de développement*), the *BTEI* (*Banque d'investissement de Tunisie et des Emirats*), the *BTQI* (*Banque tuniso-qatarie d'investissement*), the *BCMA* (*Banque de coopération du Maghreb arabe*), the *BTLDCE* (*Banque tuniso-libyenne de développement et du commerce extérieur*).

– "Off-shore" banks: the *UTB, Union tunisienne de banques* (headquarters in Paris, 13 avenue de l'Opéra, 75001, tel. 49 27 07 23, fax: 49 27 94 95; branch in Tunis: Hôtel Africa, 50 avenue Habib-Bourguiba, tel. 341 211, fax: 340 241, telex: 13 160); the *BEST-Bank* (*Beit Ettamouil Tounsi Saoudi*), 88 avenue Hédi-Chaker, 1002 Tunis, tel. 790 000, fax: 780 235; the *TAAB* (*Tunis Arab African Bank*), the *TIB* (*Tunis International Bank*), the *NAIB* (*North African International Bank*), the *LINC* (*Loan and Investment Company*), the *AIB* (*Alubaf International Bank*).

Foreign trade

– *Cepex* (*Centre des promotions des exportations tunisiennes*), 28 rue Gandhi, 1001 Tunis, tel. 350 344 or 350 698, fax: 353 683.

– SCIT, *Société de commerce international de Tunisie*, export of Tunisian products, international trade, compensation commerce, representation, processing of fresh fruit and vegetables (subsidiaries and representatives throughout the world), 6 rue Ibn-Jazzar, 1001 Tunis-Belvédère, tel. 785 545/483 or 786 901/ 739, fax: 783 287.

Where to set up

– In the industrial zones: in Tunis-Carthage, the Charguia industrial zone.
– In the economic free zones (Bizerte, in the north, will be operational as of 1995, and in Zarzis, right in the south), set up for non-residential export industries which benefit from a particularly encouraging tax regime in Tunisia: exoneration from taxes and custom taxes on imports (raw materials and the equipment necessary for running their business), and on exports. For further information consult law no. 92-81 of 3 August 1992, promulgated in the official journal no. 52 on 7 August 1993.

Sectors open to foreign investors

A certain number of sectors of the Tunisian economy are especially open to foreign investment: tourism; the food and agricultural industries, especially fishing and aquaculture; the mechanical, electrical and electronic industries; the maintenance sector; services and international trade companies.

The economic press

Conjoncture (a monthly journal published by the National Economic Ministry), 37 avenue Khéreddine-Pacha, Tunis, tel. 340 345.
Tunisia News (a weekly), zone industrielle Charguia, 2035 Tunis-Carthage, tel. 786 318.

TUNISIAN FACTS AND FIGURES

■ – GNP: *10.96 billion US dollars in 1991 (72nd position in the world out of 224 countries).*
– GNP per capita: *1.350 US dollars in 1991 (123rd in the world)*
– Growth: *+ 4.1% in 1993.*
– Investment (gross): *2.8 billion US dollars in 1990, 3.2 billion in 1991.*
– State budget: *3.2 billion US dollars revenue in 1989 and 4.3 billion dollars' expenditure (operations: 38%; investment: 18%; price subsidies: 10%; and debt servicing: 22%), that is, a budget deficit of 1.1 billion US dollars in 1989.*
– Foreign trade: *+ 4.03 billion US dollars exports, and – 6.08 billion US dollars imports, i.e. a trade deficit of 2.04 billion US dollars.*
– Balance of payments: *deficit (940 billion dollars).*
– Principal resources in foreign currency: *tourism (655 million US dollars in 1991), textiles and leather (977 million), petrol and petrol products (617 million), phosphates and fertilizers (600 million), transfers by Tunisian emigrants (514 million), olive oil (91 million).*
– Foreign debt: *8.47 billion US dollars at the end of 1992.*
– Debt servicing: *in 1992, 20% of goods and services exports.*

Services for business people

Freight transport:
– by plane: *British Airways Cargo*, Export: (0181) 759 2388. Import: (0181) 897 2066.
– by boat: *SNCM*, 12 rue Godot-de-Mauroy, 75009, Paris, tel. 49 24 24 17 (in Britain, for SNCM contact: Southern Ferries, Ltd, 179 Piccadilly, London W1V 9DB, tel. (0171) 491 4968). *Worms Shipping Ltd*, 4 Red Lion Ct., London EC4A 3EB, tel. (1071) 583 5513.
– by train: *BR* (in Britain, *SNCF* (in France), *SNCFT* (in Tunisia).
Forwarding companies based in Tunisia:
– *Worms*, 4 Red Lion Ct., London EC4A 3EB, tel. (1071) 583 5513.
– *Daher Uk Ltd*, Freight Forwarders, Euro Centre, Waterden Rd., London E15 2EE, tel. (0181) 533 4466.
Insurance companies:
– *AGF Insurance Ltd*, 26 Creechurch Lane, London EC3A 5EH, tel. (0171) 283 2440.
– *Norwich Union Insurance Group*, 51-54 Fenchurch Street, EC3M 3LA, tel. (0171) 867 0131.
Courrier services (in London):
– *DHL International*, (0181) 890 9000
– *TNT* (Super mail), (0171) 637 9898; (Parcel Office), (0181) 959 2222
– *Overseas Courrier Service Ltd*, (0171) 231 7872

"Business centres" and "executive floors"

Temporary secretarial services, photocopying, telex, fax, telephone:
– all the major hotels (the Abou Nawas chain, the Hilton, etc). in Tunis and Tunisia's main towns are now equipped with "business centres" or "executive floors" ("floors reserved for business men and women"), providing them with secretarial services, photocopiers, telexes, faxes, and direct international telephones.

BUSINESS TRIP LEISURE ACTIVITIES

■ *– Beach activities: good hotel-clubs in the 4 and 5 star category: in Hammamet (Sindbad, Abou Nawas), in Djerba (Yati Beach, César Palace, Hasdrubal, Royal Garden Palace, Djerba Plaza), in Port El Kantaoui (Diar El Andalous), in Tabarka (Méhari, Abou Nawas, Paradise, Royal Golf Marhaba), in Gammarth (Abou Nawas).*
– Places to stay and tour around the country: Tamerza Palace**** (in Tamerza, a mountain oasis in the south), Abou Nawas**** (in Tozeur, a Djérid oasis), Club Sangho in Tataouine**** (in the heart of the Ksour region).
– Tennis courts (all the major hotels have at least one tennis court).
– Golf courses (18 hole links in Port El Kantaoui, Tabarka and Hammamet).
– Horse riding: in all the major seaside resorts (Skanès, Port El Kantaoui, Monastir, Djerba, Gammarth).
– Sailing and water skiing (in all the major seaside resorts).
– Sailing (yachting): ports and marinas in Sidi Bou Saïd, Monastir, Port El Kantaoui and Tabarka.
– Hunting (in the north, in the Tabarka region): wild boar hunting in particular (specialised tour operator: Jet Tours Chasse).
– Casinos: Hana Palace hotel**** in Sousse (roulette, blackjack, slot machines).

The fine sand beaches and warm, clear waters of Djerba Island –
the mainstay of Tunisian tourism –
have been welcoming visitors for several decades now.
Most of the hotels and holiday resorts have been built here,
giving Tunisia a good reputation with holiday makers
from all over the world.

index

This index includes the sites, towns and waterways described in this text. Those given particular attention are in bold type.

One of Tunisia's most beautiful natural curiosities:
the Midès gorges in the south of the country
which have been carved away
by the eroding waters of the oueds.

in the same series in french

countries-regions

- l'algérie *(6ᵉ éd.)*
- les antilles *(5ᵉ éd.)*
- l'argentine
- l'australie *(5ᵉ éd.)*
- le brésil *(4ᵉ éd.)*
- le burkina faso
- la californie
- le cameroun *(6ᵉ éd.)*
- le canada *(4ᵉ éd.)*
- la cappadoce, konya et ankara
- capri, naples et pompéi
- le cher en berry *(2ᵉ éd.)*
- la chine *(5ᵉ éd.)*
- les comores *(3ᵉ éd.)*
- le congo *(2ᵉ éd.)*
- la corée du sud
- la corse
- la côte d'ivoire *(6ᵉ éd.)*
- la crète *(3ᵉ éd.)*
- l'écosse
- l'égypte *(8ᵉ éd.)*
- l'espagne, les baléares, les canaries *(4ᵉ éd.)*
- la finlande *(2ᵉ éd.)*
- la floride
- le gabon *(4ᵉ éd.)*
- le ghana *(2ᵉ éd.)*
- les grandes alpes *(2ᵉ éd.)*
- la grande-bretagne *(3ᵉ éd.)*
- la grèce *(6ᵉ éd.)*
- la guinée-bissau
- la guyane *(3ᵉ éd.)*
- la hollande et amsterdam
- l'île de la réunion *(7ᵉ éd.)*
- l'île maurice *(4ᵉ éd.)*
- l'inde *(2ᵉ éd.)*
- l'indonésie *(5ᵉ éd.)*
- l'irlande *(5ᵉ éd.)*
- l'islande, le groenland et les féroé
- le japon *(2ᵉ éd.)*
- le kenya *(4ᵉ éd.)*
- la louisiane *(4ᵉ éd.)*
- madagascar *(5ᵉ éd.)*
- la malaisie
- le mali *(2ᵉ éd.)*
- le maroc *(8ᵉ éd.)*
- la mauritanie
- le mexique *(5ᵉ éd.)*
- le népal
- le niger *(4ᵉ éd.)*
- la nouvelle-calédonie
- le portugal, les açores et madère *(5ᵉ éd.)*
- rhodes
- le rwanda
- la scandinavie *(6ᵉ éd.)*
- le sénégal *(2ᵉ éd.)*
- les seychelles *(4ᵉ éd.)*
- la sicile *(5ᵉ éd.)*
- sri lanka (ceylan) *(3ᵉ éd.)*
- la suisse et le liechtenstein *(2ᵉ éd.)*
- la syrie *(3ᵉ éd.)*
- tahiti et toutes ses îles *(5ᵉ éd.)*
- la thaïlande *(3ᵉ éd.)*
- le togo *(3ᵉ éd.)*
- la tunisie
- la yougoslavie *(4ᵉ éd.)*
- le zaïre *(3ᵉ éd.)*

cities

- barcelone et la catalogne
- bruxelles, flandres et wallonie
- budapest et la hongrie
- chicago
- florence et la toscane *(4ᵉ éd.)*
- hong kong et singapour
- istanbul et la turquie égéenne *(4ᵉ éd.)*
- jérusalem
- la mecque et médine *(3ᵉ éd.)*
- lisbonne
- londres
- madrid et tolède
- moscou et saint-pétersbourg *(4ᵉ éd.)*
- new york *(3ᵉ éd.)*
- prague
- rome et le vatican *(2ᵉ éd.)*
- séville et l'andalousie
- venise *(4ᵉ éd.)*

in preparation

- l'afrique du sud
- le danemark et copenhague
- la guinée équatoriale
- le pakistan
- les philippines
- l'alsace et strasbourg
- tokyo

LES EDITIONS DU JAGUAR

57 bis, rue d'Auteuil - 75016 Paris
honorary series editor : jean hureau
cartography : editerra

© 1995 - 1ˢᵗ edition - all rights reserved
printing completed 4th quarter 1995 by pozzo gros monti (italy)
publisher n° 1466/1 - ISBN-2-86950-268-0 - ISSN 0224-3067
legal copy deposited: november 1995